SECRET COMBINATIONS TODAY

A Voice of Warning

Secret Combinations Today

A Voice of Warning

Robert E. Hales

Copyright © 1996 By
HORIZON PUBLISHERS & DISTRIBUTORS, INC.

All rights reserved.
Reproduction in whole or any parts thereof in any form
or by any media without written permission is prohibited.

Second Printing: July, 1998

International Standard Book Number:
0-88290-569-4

Horizon Publishers' Catalog and Order Number:
1062

Printed and distributed
in the United States of America by

& Distributors, Incorporated

Mailing Address:
P.O. Box 490
Bountiful, Utah 84011-0490

Street Address:
50 South 500 West
Bountiful, Utah 84010

Local Phone: (801) 295-9451
WATS (toll free): 1 (800) 453-0812
FAX: (801) 295-0196

**E-mail: horizonp@burgoyne.com
Internet: http:// www.horizonpublishers.com**

CONTENTS

ABOUT THE AUTHOR 8
1. INTRODUCTION 9
2. SECRET COMBINATIONS OF OLD 14
   Objectives of Secret Combinations 14
   Satan is the Source of Secret Combinations 14
   The First Secret Combinations 15
   What Satan Seeks with Secret Combinations 16
   The Secret Combination Between Satan and Korihor 17
      Korihor Teaches Christ as a Foolish Tradition 18
      Korihor Teaches Against Seers and Prophets 18
      Korihor Teaches Environmental Management 19
      Korihor Teaches about Genius 19
      Korihor Teaches Trust in the Arm of Flesh 21
   Why Do Men Respond to Secret Combinations? 22
      Influence of Satan 23
      Power and Gain 24

3. METHODS AND PRACTICES OF SECRET COMBINATIONS 25
   The Secret Covenants of Secret Combinations 25
   Secret Combinations Can Grow Rapidly 26
   Bound by Secret Covenants 27
   Fair Promises 28
   Flattery 29
   Hate and Anger 31
   Summary of Tactics used by Secret Combinations 34

4. SECRET COMBINATIONS AND THE INDIVIDUAL 35
   Sexual Conspiracies 35
   The Safe Sex Lie 36
   The Homosexuality Misrepresentation 38
   The Abortion Tragedy 41
   Sex Education 48
   Noise, Music, Movies and Pornography 50
   Substance Abuse 53
   Conspiracy to Control Individual Agency 56
   Satan Worship 58
   The Condition of America Question 59

5. SECRET COMBINATIONS AND THE FAMILY 62
Attack on the Family. 62
Attack on Motherhood/Fatherhood 65
Child and Spouse Abuse 69
Education 71

6. SECRET COMBINATIONS AND THE PEOPLE
OF THE UNITED STATES OF AMERICA 74
A Land in Trouble 74
This is a Choice Land 75
A Great and Marvelous Work 79
A Division of the People. 82
Destruction or Protection. 87
Secret Combinations Which Endanger United States Citizens 89
    Terrorism. 89
    Organized crime 94
    Gangs. 95
    Corrupt Politicians 98
    Political Organizations 101

7. SECRET COMBINATIONS AND MONEY IN THE UNITED STATES 103
Money 103
    Types of Money 104
    Money and the Federal Reserve System 106
    The Depression of the 1930s 106
    Recent Developments 107
Banking. 108
Federal Reserve System 109
    Fed History. 110
    Fed Structure. 110
    Monetary Control 111
    Effects of Federal Reserve Policies 111
    Relations with the Government 112
    Is the Fed an Anti-American Secret Combination? 113
Taxes 117
    Principles of Taxation 118
    Taxes Should Be Fair 118
    Tax Collection Should Be Easy 118
    Alternatives to the Current Income Tax 119
Taxes to Control the People 119
Taxes to Control the Pulpit. 122

8. SECRET COMBINATIONS, COMMUNISM, AND
THE CONSTITUTION OF THE UNITED STATES OF AMERICA 125
Perspectives on the Constitution 125
The Constitution as a Changeable and Alterable Document 129
An Opposing View: The Constitution Must Not Change 130
Federalism 135

Communism 140
People vs. the System 143

9. SECRET COMBINATIONS AND ONE-WORLD GOVERNMENT 145
One-World Government 145
   International Finance 147
   Environmental Concerns 149
   Population Control 150
   Youth Education 151
   Control of Civil Unrest 152
   Religion 153
   Summary 155
One-World Banking 155
The Right to Bear Arms 159

10. SECRET COMBINATIONS AND
THE COMMITMENT OF THE LATTER-DAY SAINT 163
Increased Knowledge of God's Plan 164
Increased Knowledge and Understanding of Secret Combinations . . . 165
Informed Family Members 166
Be Involved in the Freedom Process 168
Become a Zion People 169
Follow the Prophet 173
A Word of Caution 174
Summary 175

ABOUT THE AUTHOR

Robert E. Hales is well qualified to write on the significant subjects he discusses in this book. He was raised in Fountain Green, Utah, and served in the Cumorah Mission, in upstate New York, in 1967-69. After graduating from Brigham Young University in 1976, he graduated from Southwestern University School of Law with a Juris Doctor degree in 1979. He practices as an attorney in Estate Planning in Orange County California, with his office also located in the city of Orange. He is a member of the California State Bar Association and the Orange County Bar Association.

He is the advisory chairman of Expansoar, Inc., a non-profit public charity organization which provides scholarships, food, clothing and other services as well as public awareness events for the underprivileged in Southern California.

The author of numerous articles and treatises on legal subjects related to estate planning, he has written three books on estate planning: *The Trustee's Guidebook*, *The Trustee's Handbook*, and *Basic Estate Planning*. He also wrote a continuing-education home study course for professionals in the insurance, real estate and securities industries. He is the president and founder of the College of Estate Planning. He has lectured before tens of thousands concerning the benefits of preparedness and estate planning, and has spoken at BYU Education Week on Estate Planning and on Constitutional issues.

Brother Hales has also written for an LDS audience. He and his wife are the authors of a three-volume individual and family Book of Mormon companion study guide titled *A Standard Unto My People*.

In the Church, he has served as a high councilor, bishop's councilor, High Priest Group Leader, Elder's Quorum President and teacher, Primary teacher and Scout leader. He currently teaches early morning seminary and is the gospel doctrine teacher in his ward.

Brother Hales lives in the city or Orange, in Orange County, California. He and his wife, Sandra, are the parents of seven children.

1
INTRODUCTION

We are deeply involved in a battle for our freedom. Secret combinations, Gadianton Societies of today, are active, powerful, and exercising dominion over many lives. And while the battle rages, many are in their homes, eating, drinking, watching TV, going to church, and believing they are living the Utopian dream. Too many didn't notice! They didn't notice when the right to own and control property became threatened and seriously weakened. They didn't notice when family structure became weakened and threatened by unfavorable legislation. They didn't notice when elected representatives sacrificed future financial stability for temporary special interest groups. They didn't notice when the sovereignty of our nation became threatened by international control and one-world politics and finances. They didn't notice when our political system became corrupted and nearly destroyed the separation of powers established by the founding fathers. And most are not noticing the very real threat to the foundation upon which this nation, and its greatness, rest. Too often, we are passively silent about the threats to those rights and privileges guaranteed by the God-inspired Constitution of this land.

Consider the words of Ezra Taft Benson: "The Devil knows that if the Elders of Israel should ever wake up, they could step forth and help preserve freedom and extend the gospel. Therefore, the Devil has concentrated, and to a large extent successfully, in neutralizing much of the priesthood. He has reduced them to sleeping giants."[1]

The theme of this book is that while we indeed do have secret combinations in our midst—Gadianton societies that are active, powerful and exercising dominion and control over the lives of citizens, yet we can and should have hope. We can perpetuate the purposes of the Father. To do so, we must identify the enemy, the battles we have lost, and those we currently face.

"God will not tolerate a modern Sodom and Gomorrah. This nation is fast approaching the equivalent of that state of affairs." These words of Elder Mark E. Petersen sunk deep into the hearts and souls of those present. I was in a zone conference in the Cumorah Mission, in upstate New York, in the early spring of 1969. Mark E. Petersen, an apostle of the Lord, was speaking to missionaries about the state of affairs in our nation. The Viet Nam War was in full swing, the nation was in turmoil, evil was rampant, and the "God is dead" philosophy was being taught by Marxist advocates. As a missionary those many years ago, I could easily identify with the concepts expressed by Elder Petersen. But as I consider our present status and review the last 25-30 years, I must state my personal belief that compared to 1969, this nation today is much closer to the fullness of iniquity warned of by the Lord.

I love this land. Some of my earliest childhood memories involve my love for and support of the land of America. I remember, for example, from the ages of five to seven using red and blue crayons to make American flags from my mother's old sheets cut up into flag-size banners. That love for this land grew in my later childhood and adolescent years as I studied our U.S. history and the founding fathers. I saw comparisons of the blessings we had in this land and the distinct differences with other places in the world.

I still love this land today, but my heart becomes heavy when I dwell too long on attempting to assimilate, digest, comprehend, and otherwise identify and describe the changes of the last thirty years. When I went to law school in 1977-79, one of my chosen areas of practice was Constitutional Law. But I was totally dismayed by the philosophy of the law school I attended. Both the school and the students embraced the concept that the United States Constitution was out of date and needed to be re-written to meet the modern needs of our nation. Through these and other experiences and exposures, I have found some answers to questions concerning where we came from as a nation, how we got into our current condition, and what we as United States citizens and church members need to do in order to preserve (or re-establish) our personal and national liberties which are guaranteed by the Constitution.

The liberty and freedom upon which this nation was founded have an analogy in the gospel of Jesus Christ. Spiritual liberty comes from Jesus Christ. In the Gospel of John, Jesus told the Jews who believed on him, "If ye continue in my word, then are ye my disciples indeed; And ye shall know the truth, and the truth shall make you *free*." (John 8:31-32) This freedom of which the Savior speaks is distinguished from free agency which we also cherish. Using free agency we decide to accept or reject the truth. But the freedom of which Jesus speaks is obtained after exercising free agency and accepting the truth. So what does Jesus mean? How does the truth make us free? And from what are we made free? The Jews did not understand. They replied to Jesus, "We . . . were never in bondage to any man: how sayest thou, ye shall be made free?" (John 8:33) Thinking that Jesus was speaking to them of the liberty to come and go as they please, to buy and sell, to worship and live as they desired, they missed his meaning. But he made his meaning clear. Jesus answered them, "Verily, verily, I say unto you, Whosoever committeth sin is the servant of sin . . . If the Son therefore shall make you free, ye shall be free indeed." (John 8:34, 36)

Paul understood this freedom and the Saviors meaning and repeated it in his letter to the saints in Rome. "But ye have obeyed from the heart that form of doctrine which was delivered you. Being then made free from sin, ye became the servants of righteousness." (Romans 6:17-18) Here Paul clarifies that this freedom from sin comes from obeying the doctrine of Christ.

Book of Mormon prophets help us even further in grasping the concept taught by the Savior. Moroni describes what actually makes us free as he closes his record: And again, if ye by the grace of God are perfect in Christ, and deny not His power, then are ye sanctified in Christ by the grace of God, through the shedding of the blood of Christ, which is in the Covenant of the Father unto the remission of your sins, that ye become holy, without spot. (Moroni 10:33)

Mankind is indeed made free from sin by the blood of Christ. This freedom or liberty is a direct blessing of the shedding of the blood of the Savior and is and ever was the heart of the everlasting plan of the Eternal God. The Blood of Christ, in some way not yet fully comprehended by us, satisfies the demands of justice and makes possible the forgiveness of sins. We are thus free from sin; free from death and hell and the grave; free from the misery Satan wants to inflict upon us; free to help others; free of the captivity of the Devil and from chains of Hell. We are then spiritually capable of once again entering into the presence of God, there to partake of all that the Father has, becoming joint heirs with Christ.

But what has the shedding of Christ's blood to pay for our sins to do with the freedoms guaranteed by the Constitution of this land? Just as the blood of Christ is the source of freedom from sin, the blood of patriots is the source of political freedom. Many Americans have forgotten, or perhaps never realized, the debt we owe to the founding fathers. These great men, inspired by God and foreordained to their purpose, offered the ultimate sacrifice a mortal can make. They pledged their time, their efforts, their fortunes, and their lives to secure freedom from captivity and oppression. Many shed their blood and ultimately gave their lives that this nation might be born. As two Book of Mormon Scholars, Reid E. Bankhead and Glenn L. Pearson, stated, "The struggle to have the right to own land without being a nobleman or a government bureaucrat was won by the shedding of the blood of Patriots and heroes. The establishment of the United States of America under the Constitution was the ultimate and greatest victory in this struggle."[2]

Consider the tribute of the Lord himself as he acknowledges the sacrifice of the patriots: "For this purpose have I established the Constitution of this land, by the hands of wise men whom I raised up unto this very purpose, and redeemed the land by the shedding of blood." (D & C 101:80)

Just as we do not fully comprehend how the blood of Christ redeems us from sin, we do not fully comprehend how the shedding of patriot's blood redeemed this land. What is evident from the scripture is that God was in control. He inspired and directed these men and their activities, and their blood was shed to redeem the land. This liberty, allowing us to own and control property, pursue worthwhile personal goals, and worship God as we feel appropriate, was purchased with the blood of patriots.

President J. Rueben Clark warned us that, "We stand in danger of losing our liberties, and that once lost, only blood will bring them back; and once lost, we of this church will, in order to keep the church going forward, have more sacrifices to make and more persecutions to endure than we have yet known."[3]

Book of Mormon prophets also taught that bloodshed is indeed sometimes required. Consider the words of Mormon as he records the teachings of the Lord to the Nephites as they prepared for their battles against the Lamanites: "And again, the Lord has said that: Ye shall defend your families even unto bloodshed. Therefore for this cause were the Nephites contending with the Lamanites, to defend themselves, and their families, and their lands, their country, and their rights, and their religion." (Alma 43:47)

And consider the words of Moroni as he states the reasons why the Nephites resisted the aggression of Zerahemnah and the Lamanites:

> 2. Behold, we have not come out to battle against you that we might shed your blood for power; neither do we desire to bring any one to the yoke of bondage. But this is the very cause for which ye have come against us; yea, and ye are angry with us because of our religion . . .
>
> 5. And now, Zerahemnah, I command you, in the name of that all powerful God, who has strengthened our arms that we have gained power over you, by our faith, by our religion, and by our rites of worship, and by our church, and by the sacred support which we owe to our wives, and our children, by that liberty which binds us to our lands and our country; yea, and also by the maintenance of the sacred word of God, to which we owe all our happiness; and by all that is most dear unto us
>
> 6. . . . [and] by all the desires which ye have for life, that ye deliver up your weapons of war unto us . . . (Alma 44:2, 5, 6)

Political Liberty is directly bound to the land. Without ownership and control of property, our liberties can be and often are severely limited. Private ownership and control of property are basic to the fundamental way of life in the United States and to the inalienable God-given rights guaranteed by our Constitution. It is basic to our individual freedoms. It is basic to the independence of the Church. Because the Church owns the property in Provo, Hawaii and Rexburg, it can determine the subjects to be taught at BYU, the Church College of Hawaii, and Ricks College. Because the Church owns the property upon which temples are built, it can determine who, when, and why people enter those temples. Because you have the right to own property, you too can determine how to design your home and how to plant your garden.

Today, this political liberty bound directly to the land and purchased by the blood of patriots is threatened by activities designed to erode rights of ownership and control. While previous world wars were obvious threats to our nation and citizenship, today Satan uses more subtle, dangerous, deadly and subversive methods. Secret combinations of today have attempted to discredit the founding fathers. They have corrupted politicians, severely damaged the financial security of this land, and they currently threaten our sovereignty. This danger today is found in entities, politicians, organizations, societies, philosophies, and special interests which seek power and wealth—men and women, inspired by Satan, who seek destruction of the very liberties the patriots died to establish.

It is now very late in the battle. In fact, the war has been accelerating rapidly over the last thirty years. It is not too late, but we must take action now. We must awake to a sense of our situation and raise a voice of warning to families, fellow saints, and fellow citizens. Fortunately, the voice of warning we must raise need not be one of hopelessness nor of doom. We do have hope and we have great promise.

For Latter-day Saints, this hope is accompanied by a responsibility to which I am convinced we were foreordained. The Book of Mormon will assist us to increase our hope and understand our responsibilities. Consider the words of Moroni as he finishes his record: "And this [The Book of Mormon] cometh unto you, O Ye Gentiles, that ye may know the decrees of God, that ye may repent, and not continue in your iniquities until the fullness come, That ye may not bring down the fullness of the wrath of God upon you as the inhabitants of the land have hitherto done." (Ether 2:11)

May God help us to see and understand what is happening around us, how it endangers us as individuals, our families, our rights, liberties and freedoms, and what we can and must do as members of The Church of Jesus Christ of Latter-day Saints. Let us not be a part of, nor contribute to, a modern-day Sodom and Gomorrah.

2
SECRET COMBINATIONS OF OLD

Objectives of Secret Combinations

Secret Combinations are in our midst today. They take various forms, and engage in different platforms, but they all have the same purposes. As in times past, today's secret combinations seek mankind's misery. They are today's Anti-Christ. They stand against all truth. They promote evil. They seek the elimination and destruction of the children of men both temporally and spiritually. Those who promote them, those who follow them, those who tolerate them, and even those who ignore them are in danger of destruction, both temporally and spiritually. They find success in our world and in our nation by employing ageless principles and concepts of evil.

From ancient times until now, secret combinations have captivated their members. Secret combinations destroy souls, ruin the lives of children and grandchildren, erode traditions, weaken belief in God, and control finances and decisions. They rationalize miracles, lie about divine intervention, and work dark miracles of their own to blind men to truth. They seek to bind all who would listen with a flaxen cord, and then silently, secretly, and unobtrusively weave a web of deceit until the flaxen cord has become a binding string, then a tight-woven rope, and finally the chains of hell. The servants of Satan often obtain this captivity of their members by way of covenants and secret oaths which bind men to their memberships.

Satan is the Source of Secret Combinations

Secret Combinations are founded on principles of evil taught and inspired by Satan. From the very beginning, and before time, Satan exhibited his tendency to lie for his own selfish and evil purposes. After rejecting the Father's plan and having his own plan of restraint and constraint refused, the Father cast him out. He became Satan, the father of lies.

> 3. Wherefore, because that Satan rebelled against me, and sought to destroy the agency of man, which I, the Lord God, had given him, and also, that I should give unto him mine own power; by the power of mine Only Begotten, I caused that he should be cast down;

> 4. And he became Satan, yea, even the devil, the father of all lies, to deceive and to blind men, and to lead them captive at his will, even as many as would not hearken unto my voice. (Moses 4:3-4)

Satan fulfills the role of unrighteousness, evil and opposition in this realm of creation. His quest to destroy man began in the Garden of Eden as he lied to Eve to convince her to partake of the forbidden fruit.

> 7. And he [Satan] said unto the woman [Eve]: Yea, hath God said—Ye shall not eat of every tree of the garden? (And he spake by the mouth of the serpent.)
> 8. And the woman said unto the serpent: We may eat of the fruit of the trees of the garden;
> 9. But of the fruit of the tree which thou beholdest in the midst of the garden, God hath said ye shall not eat of it, neither shall ye touch it, lest ye die.
> 10. And the serpent said unto the woman: Ye shall not surely die;
> 11. For God doth know that in the day ye eat thereof, then your eyes shall be opened, and ye shall be as gods, knowing good and evil. (Moses 4:7-11)

This episode in the Garden established a pattern which Satan has perfected through the ages, and which he continues to follow today. Mixing truth with error, fact with fiction, scriptures with human reasoning, he convinces us that we can obtain our desires by following his lead. He lied when he told Eve that she would not die, and then combined his lie with truth that she would become as God knowing good and evil. From that day to this, Satan has sought his will by lying to the children of men. His followers also lie. They lie about their purposes and intents. They lie to deceive and destroy.

The First Secret Combination

The first secret combination dates back to the beginning of the earth's history. In this mortal world, the pattern began with a conspiracy between Satan and Cain.

> 29. And Satan said unto Cain: Swear unto me by thy throat, and if thou tell it thou shalt die; and swear thy brethren by their heads, and by the living God, that they tell it not; for if they tell it, they shall surely die; and this that thy father may not know it; and this day I will deliver thy brother Abel into thine hands.
> 30. And Satan sware unto Cain that he would do according to his commands. And all these things were done in secret.
> 31. And Cain said: Truly I am Mahan, the master of this great secret, that I may murder and get gain. Wherefore Cain was called Master Mahan, and he gloried in his wickedness. (Moses 5:29-31)

Cain was the first mortal to seek power and gain by secret oaths and combinations. As the first mortal to become bound by the chains of hell, Cain became a co-conspirator with Satan. But Cain was not alone in his conspiracy to kill Abel. He was assisted, at least in covenant, by his brethren who pledged their commitment with their very lives. The scriptures do not record the role of Cain's brethren in the murder of Abel, but they do show that the secret combination they formed was only the first of many such covenants between Satan and the children of men.

Evil covenants, being two-way promises, entail not only mankind promising Satan, but also Satan promising mankind, as in this instance. Accordingly, Satan covenanted that he would obey Cain's command. Satan's desire for Abel's death was so great that he was willing to submit to the desires of Cain and promised to follow Cain's commands.

Satan works the same today, lying through his servants and promising that which men desire as rewards for sin. Temporary but immediate gratification of evil desires, lusts and pleasures are the promises he and his servants make today. And the price we pay to buy those promises is willingly and knowingly transgressing the laws of God.

Unfortunately, the true cost of these purchases is greater than can be comprehended in this lifetime. Those who choose to follow Satan do so in a way and manner similar to that of Cain and his brethren, and successor satanic servants like Lamech.

> 49. For Lamech having entered into a covenant with Satan, after the manner of Cain, wherein he became Master Mahan, master of that great secret which was administered unto Cain by Satan; and Irad, the son of Enoch, having known their secret, began to reveal it unto the sons of Adam;
>
> 50. Wherefore Lamech, being angry, slew him, not like unto Cain, his brother Abel, for the sake of getting gain, but he slew him *for the oath's sake*.
>
> 51. For, from the days of Cain, there was a secret combination, and their works were in the dark, and they knew every man his brother. (Moses 5:49-51)

Secret combinations can exact great commitment from their followers because of the types of secret covenants and oaths made, often carrying the pain of death as the penalty for violation.

What Satan Seeks with Secret Combinations

It is now and always has been the objective of Satan to acquire the power, status and glory of God. To assist him in his objective on earth, he established this pattern. Secret combinations give him power over man and glory among those who follow him on both sides of the veil. The pattern is repeated many times in the Book of Mormon. The evil leaders among the Nephites and Lamanites often required secret commitments from their followers. The participants in these secret societies sometimes swore their allegiance to or by the *living God*. Unfortunately, many participating in these secret societies were unaware of the "god" to whom their allegiance was being pledged. Consider that the god to whom they were pledging their all was really Satan who, "sitteth in the temple of God, shewing himself that he is God." (2 Thessalonians 2:4) In reality, Satan often deceives a receptive and selfish mankind as to his true identity, setting himself up as a god in an attempt to have man obey and worship him. Moses was exposed to this attempt.

> 12. And it came to pass that when Moses had said these words, behold, Satan came tempting him, saying: Moses, son of man, worship me.
> 13. And it came to pass that Moses looked upon Satan and said: Who art thou? For behold, I am a son of God, in the similitude of his Only Begotten; and where is thy glory, that I should worship thee? . . .
> 19. And now, when Moses had said these words, Satan cried with a loud voice, and ranted upon the earth, and commanded, saying: I am the only begotten, worship me. (Moses 1:12-13,19)

Claiming to be the only begotten, Satan clearly shows that his objective in the earth is the same as it was in the pre-mortal life. He wants mankind to worship him. He wants the glory.

The Secret Combination between Satan and Korihor

Not all are as founded as was Moses. And some, when temptation comes, willingly succumb to it, desiring only to accomplish their own selfish desires and plans. One such individual became one of the three anti-Christs of the Book of Mormon. Korihor was educated, taught, and directed by Satan. Shortly after being struck dumb by the Lord, he confessed his guilt.

> 52. And Korihor put forth his hand and wrote, saying: I know that I am dumb, for I cannot speak; and I know that nothing save it were the power of God could bring this upon me; yea, and I always knew that there was a God.
> 53. But behold, the devil hath deceived me; for he appeared unto me in the form of an angel, and said unto me: Go and reclaim this people, for they have all gone astray after an unknown God. And he said unto me: There is no God; yea, and he taught me that which I should say. And I have taught his words; and I taught them because they were pleasing unto the carnal mind; and I taught them, even until I had much success, insomuch that I verily believed that they were true; and for this cause I withstood the truth, even until I have brought this great curse upon me. (Alma 30:52-53)

And so Korihor, knowing there was a God, started teaching otherwise. He started teaching concepts that were pleasing to people in their fallen state. Korihor began to teach things which he at first did not believe. But eventually, he convinced himself that the concepts were true. Korihor entered into a secret combination with Satan to deceive, mislead and captivate the children of men.

Korihor Teaches Christ as a Foolish Tradition

An examination of the teachings of Korihor reveals concepts contrary to the traditions, concepts and gospel of Christ. These concepts are frequently found as objectives of today's secret combinations. The most destructive concept taught by Korihor was the denial of Christ and his divinely appointed mission. Korihor

> 12. . . . began to preach unto the people that there should be no Christ. And after this manner did he preach, saying:
> 13. O ye that are bound down under a foolish and vain hope, why do ye yoke yourselves with such foolish things? Why do ye look for a Christ? For no man can know of anything which is to come.
> 14. Behold, these things which ye call prophesies, which ye say are handed down by holy prophets, behold, they are foolish traditions of your fathers. (Alma 30:12-14)

No one wants to be bound by false hope. No one wants to appear foolish. So when evil-speaking adversaries accuse men of foolishness, they too often back away, shrink, or even totally surrender their position, standards, teachings, and even beliefs. Fallen man yields to the nature of his fallen state. The natural man responds to the mocking of those in the large and spacious building. Desiring to not look foolish to peers, friends, family or others, he walks away from the iron rod, the path of God, and the tree of life.

Self restriction from the ways of the world seems foolish to the natural man. He is capable only of a vision limited to the present. The natural man, without a belief in a God or an eternal plan, views those who would restrict his natural inclinations to be oppressive and bound themselves by foolish traditions. Using this line of logic, Korihor appealed to the natural man to deny the Christ as a foolish tradition.

Korihor Teaches Against Seers and Prophets

Korihor also taught, "Behold, ye cannot know of things which ye cannot see . . . " (Alma 30:15) To the natural man, this is a reasonable concept. The natural man gains human knowledge through his personal experience, the experience of others, and his ability to reason. He then records those experiences and his reasoned conclusions so future generations can benefit from the past.

While human knowledge is expanding every day, it has inherent weaknesses. Human knowledge is limited and is not always truth. Alma, speaking of a different type of knowledge, speaks of an unseen world: " . . . faith is not to have a perfect knowledge of things; therefore, if ye have faith, ye hope for things which are not seen which are true." (Alma 32:21) And Paul indicates that this unseen world cannot be discerned by the natural man. "But the natural man receiveth not the things of the Spirit of God: for they are foolishness unto him: neither can he know them, because they are spiritually discerned." (1 Corinthians 2:14) Human knowledge unenlightened by the Spirit cannot conceive, understand or accept things which are not seen but which are true. Thus, the natural man's knowledge is limited to the things he sees or reasons.

Because the knowledge of the natural man does not encompass spiritual understandings of God, man's knowledge is not always truth. Accordingly, yesterday's facts of science become tomorrow's superstitions. Secret combinations often deal with partial truths, and often deny the existence of an omniscient creator who would speak to man through prophets about things of the future.

Korihor Teaches Environmental Management

Korihor next taught ". . . every man fared in this life according to the *management of the creature* . . ." (Alma 30:17) Elements of truth accompany this statement. A person who puts forth the commitment, time, effort and work to obtain a professional degree, build a business, or enhance a talent, will generally fare better in this life than the person who puts forth no effort. It is indeed good for each of us to manage our time and our talents for our benefit. Proper management of our gifts, time, and talents will result in a more fulfilling life. When man thus uses his free agency to properly manage his abilities, gifts and talents, he uses them to assist and be of service others. He will fare better not only in this life, but also in the life to come.

However, as always, Satan's teaching also includes a lie. The lie begins with the semantic reference to "creatures." Man is not a creature evolved with all other creatures from one source. Man is a created being and a child of God. While creatures may be managed by man for the benefit and well-being of society, the management of men by other men evolves to destroy free agency. Thus, just as Korihor did centuries ago, Satan works today to destroy man's agency by managing the man. Secret combinations manage or control the activities and lives of those who surrender their freedom to the secret covenants. They become prisoners of the organization they support. They thus lose freedom and become managed by their secret oaths.

Korihor Teaches about Genius

Satan also taught Korihor that a man prospers according to his genius. (Alma 30:17) Again the concept has elements of truth. The seal of Brigham Young University declares, "The glory of God is intelligence" (D & C 93:36). As a people, we endorse education. We encourage men and women to make the pursuit of knowledge a lifetime quest. We attempt diligently to employ the admonition of the Father to seek to know of things in heaven and earth, history, wars and perplexities of nations, and the judgments of God (D & C 88:79). We encourage this pursuit of higher education for the glory of God. We seek to find the best employment opportunities our education will afford and our talents will permit. In all these efforts, we are viewed favorably by an all-loving Father provided we follow his admonition to seek first the Kingdom of God.

The lie in Korihor's statement stems from the proposal that our ability to prosper is solely dependent upon our genius or intelligence. Korihor's statement eliminates the factor of an all-powerful God who can intervene in our lives for our benefit. Expecting prosperity solely from our own intellectual undertakings places man's trust in man's wisdom. Trusting solely in man's wisdom and factoring out the element of God opens the door to two potentially destructive concepts: relative reasoning and situational ethics.

Relativism, while initially proposed as a principle of mathematics and physics by Newton and Einstein, has evolved into intellectual and psychological thought. Applied to intellectual reasoning, the theory of relativism states that what is truth to one person is not necessarily truth to another. Accordingly, truth is relative to the person. Truth is perceived differently by different people. The concept further teaches that it is permissible and even desirable for mankind to have this divergence from unity.

But intellectual relativity appears to conflict with truth as defined by the scriptures. As defined in scripture, truth is a knowledge of things as they really were, as they really are and as they really will be. (D & C 93:24; Jacob 4:13)

Intellectual relativity cannot be correct if these scriptures are true. Accordingly, truth is not relative. It is not "A" for one person and "B" for another. In the most simplistic of examples, 13th Century wisdom declared the world to be flat. But no matter how deep the belief nor how strong the conviction of those believers, their relative truth did not alter actual truth. Truth is truth and does not vary dependent upon what mankind wants to believe.

Taken to its inevitable end, intellectual relativity then allows mankind to justify behavior and actions contrary to God's will and commandments. Relative ideology opens the door to situational ethics. A person's ethics are those principles in which a person believes and from whence they establish their moral values which become the basis of behavioral patterns and activities.

Using the relativity theory, situational ethics are devised as a result of human experience and knowledge. Thus, morals and patterns of acceptable behavior evolve and change through time according to man's experience, desires and passions. There is therefore no need for a behavior pattern to be established by a deity. Jacob's warning finds fulfillment in relative truth and situational ethics:

> O the cunning plan of the evil one! O the vainness, and the frailties, and the foolishness of men! When they are learned, they think they are wise, and they hearken not unto the counsel of God, for they set it aside supposing they know of themselves . . . (Jacob 4:28)

Being thus disposed, mankind can therefore rationalize and self-justify behavior abhorrent to the Spirit. Predicted by Nephi and spawned by man's genius, and a desire to prosper, some men dig a pit for their neighbor, take advantage of one because of his weakness and otherwise live by ethics and morals unacceptable to the man or woman of Christ.

Korihor's teaching that man prospers according to his genius allows men in secret combinations to rationalize evil behavior. Activities not acceptable to a civilization with a Christian moral base, can be self-justified in man's minds through use of his ability to reason and mingle that reasoning with scriptural truth.

Korihor Teaches Trust in the Arm of Flesh

Finally, Korihor teaches that "a man conquered according to his strength." (Alma 30:17) This is a direct embodiment of the concept of placing one's trust in the arm of the flesh. Why does mankind persist in placing faith, trust, money and effort in a concept so devoid of God?

In a recent battle identified for history as Desert Storm, United States armed forces completely dominated the opposition forces of Iraq. This nation experienced a short-term burst of internal pride, unity and patriotism. But many fear that this temporary exhilaration of national honor was not the result of this nation giving credit to God, but rather the celebration of the military strength the nation was able to amass to defeat an inferior military power. Placing trust in the arm of flesh will not allow us as a nation to endure. But just as Gideon used the Lord and his small 300-man army to defeat thousands of the enemy, our nation with God, cannot fail.

To be truly strong, this nation must serve the God of this land who is Jesus Christ. There is no alternative secure foundation. Large military and defense budgets will not secure peace. Dominant control by superior military strength of this land, the Western Hemisphere, the world or outer space, will not secure liberty and the principles of the founding fathers. The only source of lasting strength is a repentant people having broken hearts and contrite spirits as a sacrifice and sacrament to the Father.

Why Do Men Respond to Secret Combinations?

The simple and obvious response to this query is that men follow the temptations of Satan. But all those who came to this earth to obtain a body previously rejected Satan. Why would men and women who rejected his temptations and enticements in the prior life suddenly accept his teachings and even promote them in this life?

The review of Satan's secret combinations with Cain, Lamech, Korihor, Sharem and Nehor offer some of the answers to this question. As Adam and Eve taught their sons and daughters about the fall, the redemption and atonement of Christ and the law of sacrifice, Satan came to Cain and said, "Believe it not." (Moses 4:12) And Cain, the scripture records, "loved Satan more than God." (Moses 4:8) Moses records that from Cain, men began to be carnal, sensual and devilish.

> And in those days, Satan had great dominion among men, and raged in their hearts; and from thenceforth came wars and bloodshed; and a man's hand was against his own brother in administering death, because of secret works, seeking for power. (Moses 6:15)

In mortality, lacking a remembrance of his former existence, man seeks for dominion and power. Cain killed Abel for power and gain. (Moses 5:31) Korihor taught false concepts because they were pleasing to the carnal mind. (Alma 30:53) Nehor preached for support and money. (Alma 1:5-6) Sherem used his knowledge of the language and his flattery attempting to overthrow the doctrine of Christ. (Jacob 7:2-4)

Rationalizing with relative intellectualism and situational ethics, Satan's mortal servants teach the carnal, sensual and devilish person that there is no God, no Christ, no plan, no premortal life, and no post-death existence. If there is no life hereafter, then there is no need to fear sin or anticipate reward. If there is no judgment, then men should simply do what they want, satisfying the evils of the flesh and condemning the restraint of physical and emotional tendencies. If there is no heaven hereafter, the only heaven must be satisfaction of the flesh here on the earth. Thus, the blind lead the blind and they shall both fall in the ditch. (Matthew 15:14)

The nature of man has not changed. Men, even today as in times past, are willing to forsake a loving eternal Father in favor of immediate gratification. Too often it is attractive to seek for temporary and momentary, but also immediate, pleasure at the cost of eternal values and rewards. We live in a world where the overriding consideration is the word "I". Will I enjoy it? Will I have fun? Will I be rich? How will I benefit? How can I take advantage of this? What do I get out of the deal?

Simply put, compared to spiritual values, worldly promises are often more easily discerned, recognized and desired by the fallen man. He can more easily identify with flush cash, fashion clothes, fancy cars, flashy jewelry, and a fast lifestyle than he can envision the unexperienced blessings and promises of the future. The flesh yearns for satisfaction today while the spirit teaches patience and forbearance, yielding only to the enticings of God while keeping desires, appetites and passions within the bounds the Lord has set.

Influence of Satan

Because of the flesh, and because of the Great Plan of the Eternal God wherein there must be opposition in all things, people are subject to the influences of Satan. People become lifted up in the pride of their heart and " . . . teach with their learning, and deny the Holy Ghost . . . " (2 Nephi 28:4) As they become subject to Satan, they begin to believe and even to teach vain and foolish doctrines such as,

> 8. Eat, drink, and be merry; nevertheless, fear God—he will justify in committing a little sin; yea, lie a little, take the advantage of one because of his words, dig a pit for thy neighbor; there is no harm in this; and do all these things, for tomorrow we die; and if it so be that we are guilty, God will beat us with a few stripes, and at last we shall be saved in the Kingdom of God.
>
> 12. Because of pride, and because of false teachers, and false doctrine, [they] . . . have become corrupted, and . . . because of pride they are puffed up. (2 Nephi 28:8, 12)

Today's courts are filled with these hypocrites, liars, deceivers and evil doers! Thousands seek to take advantage of their neighbor at the expense of the insurance company or the deep pocket of the innocent. Legal actions based on false claims for personal injury, infringement of rights, or similar groundless claims are served against brother or sister. False accusers and false witnesses seek gain or favor by deceit and conspiracy. The words of Paul to Timothy are magnified daily:

> 1. This know also, that in the last days perilous times shall come.
>
> 2. For men shall be lovers of their own selves, covetous, boasters, proud, blasphemers, disobedient to parents, unthankful, unholy,
>
> 3. Without natural affection, truce breakers, false accusers, incontinent, fierce, despisers of those that are good,
>
> 4. Traitors, heady, high-minded, lovers of pleasures more than lovers of God;

> 5. Having a form of godliness, but denying the power thereof: from such turn away. (2 Timothy 3:1-5)

Power and Gain

Priestcraft also plays a roll in the success of building secret combinations. "... priestcrafts are that men preach and set themselves up for a light unto the world, that they may get gain and praise of the world; but they seek not the welfare of Zion." (2 Nephi 26:29) Truly the lure of gain and power is great. For power, jealousy and gain, Cain killed Abel (Moses 5:31). In Alma 1, we discover that priestcraft was had among the Nephites. Nehor taught "pleasing" things to the Nephites. He preached

> 3. ... that every priest and teacher ought to become popular; and they ought not to labor with their hands, but that they ought to be supported by the people. ...
>
> 5. And it came to pass that he did teach these things so much that many did believe on his words, even so many that they began to support him and give him money. (Alma 1:3, 5)

This concept was appealing before we came to this earth, and it remains appealing now. It is used by some today to first entice, then blind, and finally destroy men. It keeps them from seeking the truth. As children of God, and despite the evil of the flesh, we are endowed with the Spirit of Christ which leads us back to Christ. But if men find a teaching of the adversary which satisfies their internal need and desire for belief in a God, but yet falls short of the full truth, they can become blinded by the craftiness and subtlety of men such that when they are presented with more truth, they receive it not. Thus, priestcraft today keeps many in the world unknowingly fighting against the Lamb of God.

3

THE METHODS AND PRACTICES OF SECRET COMBINATIONS

The Secret Covenants of Secret Combinations

The oaths, covenants and promises of the secret combinations as established by Cain in concert with Satan are not written in the Book of Mormon. As Alma said to his Son, Helaman,

> 27. And now, my son, I command you that ye retain all their oaths, and their covenants, and their agreements in their secret abominations; yea, and all their signs and their wonders ye shall keep from this people, that they know them not, lest peradventure they should fall into darkness also and be destroyed.
> 28. For behold, there is a curse upon all this land, that destruction shall come upon all those workers of darkness, according to the power of God, when they are fully ripe; therefore I desire that this people might not be destroyed.
> 29. Therefore ye shall keep these secret plans of their oaths and their covenants from this people, and only their wickedness and their murders and their abominations shall ye make known unto them; . . . (Alma 37:27-29)

Just as Alma warned his son, Latter-day Saints should not dwell on the negative covenants and secret oaths attendant to the secret combinations of today. Rather, a person should seek to understand their methods of operation. Alma wanted his son to record only the acts of wickedness of these evil combinations and not their secret plans, oaths and covenants. In this way, most of the people were able to be protected from wholesale temptations and captivity attendant to the combinations. Even though a person does not know their oaths and covenants, yet just as a detective seeks to solve a series of crimes by identifying the characteristics attendant to the crimes, one can identify secret combinations and Gadianton societies by their methods of operation. If a person knows how they act and how they teach and how they operate, that person will be better prepared to recognize them, warn others about them, and protect his family against them.

Moroni, when finishing up the book of Ether, followed a similar admonition from the Lord: "And now I, Moroni, do not write the manner of their oaths and combinations, for it hath been made known unto me that they are had among all people, and they are had among the Lamanites." (Ether 8:20)

And they are had in this day and age. Though they are not had in scripture, this author has seen some of the books containing them. Their oaths and covenants are from ancient time, handed down from time to time, family to family, society to society, evil to evil. And they are had in this nation.

As a means of helping others to understand these secret combinations, the prophets were instructed to write down and record the evil actions of the wicked. By understanding how they manipulate men and exercise their control, a person may be better able to understand how to resist his own unintentional involvement with them. By understanding their methods, a person can better avoid being deceived into tolerating, accepting, or worse, supporting secret combinations designed to destroy the freedom and agency of man.

Secret Combinations Can Grow Rapidly

The power of these secret combinations can increase dramatically in very short time periods, as they did in Book of Mormon times. The sixth chapter of Helaman outlines the rapidity with which a secret combination can overcome a government and people not properly prepared or desirous to resist:

> 1. And it came to pass that when the *sixty and second year* of the reign of the judges had ended, all these things had happened and the Lamanites had become, the more part of them, a righteous people, insomuch that their righteousness did exceed that of the Nephites, because of the firmness and their steadiness in the faith. . . .
>
> 7. And behold, there was peace in all the land . . . .
>
> [and the peace continued for some three years through the sixty and sixth year but in the sixty and seventh year,]
>
> 17. . . . they began to set their hearts upon their riches; yea, they began to seek to get gain that they might be lifted up one above another; therefore they began to commit secret murders, and to rob and to plunder, that they might get gain.
>
> 18. And now behold, those murderers and plunderers were a band who had been formed by Kishkumen and Gadianton. And now it had come to pass that there were many, even among the Nephites, of Gadianton's band. But behold, they were more numerous among the more wicked part of the Lamanites. And they were called Gadianton's robbers and murderers. . . .
>
> 20. And now it came to pass that when the Lamanites found that there were robbers among them they were exceedingly sorrowful; and they did use every means in their power to destroy them off the face of the earth.
>
> 21. But behold, Satan did stir up the hearts of the more part of the Nephites, insomuch that they did unite with those bands of robbers, . . .
>
> 22. And it came to pass that they did have their signs, yea, their secret signs, and their secret words; and this that they might distinguish a brother who had

> entered into the covenant, that whatsoever wickedness his brother should do he should not be injured by his brother, nor by those who did belong to his band, who had taken this covenant.
>
> 23. And thus they might murder, and plunder, and steal, and commit whoredoms and all manner of wickedness, contrary to the laws of their country and also the laws of their God. . . .
>
> 26. Now behold, those secret oaths and covenants did not come forth unto Gadianton from the records which were delivered unto Helaman; but behold, they were put into the heart of Gadianton by that same being who did entice our first parents to partake of the forbidden fruit—
>
> 27. Yea, that same being who did plot with Cain, that if he would murder his brother Abel it should not be known unto the world. And he did plot with Cain and his followers from that time forth. . . .
>
> 32. And it came to pass that all these iniquities did come unto them in the space of not many years, [five] insomuch that a more part of them had come unto them in the sixty and seventh year of the reign of the judges over the people of Nephi. (Helaman 6:1, 7, 17, 18, 20-23, 26, 27, 32)

Evil can spread rapidly. In fact, by the end of the sixty-eighth year of the reign of the judges (a period of only six years), ". . . they [the Gadianton Societies] did obtain the sole management of the government." (Helaman 6:39)

Bound by Secret Covenants

Covenants have always been part of Satan's techniques with secret combinations. Sometimes followers enter into the covenants before they know to what they are committing. A classic example is found in the Book of Mormon story of Omer and Jared. Omer was a king. A wicked son of Omer, whose name was Jared, rebelled against his father. He obtained control of the kingdom, but later lost it as his righteous brothers subdued him and returned the throne to their father.

> 7. And now Jared became exceedingly sorrowful because of the loss of the kingdom, for he had set his heart upon the kingdom and upon the glory of the world.
>
> 8. Now the daughter of Jared being exceedingly expert, and seeing the sorrows of her father, thought to devise a plan whereby she could redeem the kingdom unto her father.
>
> 9. Now the daughter of Jared was exceedingly fair. And it came to pass that she did talk with her father, and said unto him: Whereby hath my father so much sorrow? Hath he not read the record which our fathers brought across the great deep? Behold, is there not an account concerning them of old, that they by their secret plans did obtain kingdoms and great glory?

10. And now, therefore, let my father send for Akish, the son of Kimnor; and behold, I am fair, and I will dance before him, and I will please him, that he will desire me to wife; wherefore if he shall desire of thee that ye shall give unto him me to wife, then shall ye say: I will give her if ye will bring unto me the head of my father, the king.

11. And now Omer was a friend to Akish; wherefore, when Jared had sent for Akish, the daughter of Jared danced before him that she pleased him, insomuch that he desired her to wife. And it came to pass that he said unto Jared: Give her unto me to wife.

12. And Jared said unto him: I will give her unto you, if ye will bring unto me the head of my father, the king.

13. And it came to pass that Akish gathered in unto the house of Jared all his kinsfolk, and said unto them: Will ye swear unto me . . . in the thing which I shall desire of you?

14. And it came to pass that they all sware unto him, by the God of heaven, and also by the heavens, and also by the earth, and by their heads, that whoso should vary from the assistance which Akish desired should lose his head; and whoso should divulge whatsoever thing Akish made known unto them, the same should lose his life. (Ether 8:7-14)

Apparently, the Kinsfolk of Akish entered into the covenant of secrecy even before they knew what Akish planned to do or before they knew what Akish might want them to do. The covenant was so strong and binding that violation would result in death.

Fair Promises

The story of Jared and Akish continues.

15. And it came to pass that thus they did agree with Akish. And Akish did administer unto them the oaths which were given by them of old who also sought power, which had been handed down even from Cain, who was a murderer from the beginning.

16. And they were kept up by the power of the devil to administer these oaths unto the people, to keep them in darkness, to help such as sought power to gain power, and to murder, and to plunder, and to lie, and to commit all manner of wickedness and whoredoms.

17. And it was the daughter of Jared who put it into his heart to search up these things of old; and Jared put it into the heart of Akish; wherefore Akish administered it unto his kindred and friends, leading them away by *fair promises* to do whatsoever thing he desired.

18. And it came to pass that they formed a secret combination, even as they of old; which combination is most abominable and wicked above all, in the sight of God. (Ether 8:15-18)

The sons of Adam are enticed to make these types of oaths, and enter into these types of evil combinations because of fair promises made to them. In the story we have been following, the Lord warned Omer in a dream of the evil plan of Akish and Jared, and he thus fled and his life was preserved, but Jared, his wicked son, became temporary king.

> 5. And it came to pass that Akish sought the life of his father-in-law [Jared]; and he applied unto those whom he had sworn by the oath of the ancients, and they obtained the head of his father-in-law, as he sat upon his throne, giving audience to his people.
> 6. For so great had been the spreading of this wicked and secret society that it had corrupted the hearts of all the people; therefore Jared was murdered upon his throne, and Akish reigned in his stead. (Ether 9:5-6)

Thus we see that Satan will not support those who follow him. Those who follow him often fight, struggle and disagree among themselves, always promising that which they cannot completely deliver, offering them fair promises to obtain their own personal gain and power.

These fair promises today are found in money, power and positions of influence. Fair promises can also be used by Satan to blind and deceive those who are seeking to follow God. In the Book of Mormon, Nehor taught that all mankind would be saved at that last day, that people need not fear nor tremble, that whatsoever a man did was no sin, and therefore people should rejoice. (Alma 1:4)

Using the fair promise that all mankind should be saved from whatsoever thing any man did, Nehor taught a doctrine that would be obviously pleasing to men. It is the same story that was preached to the spirits in the pre-mortal existence when Satan promised, "I will redeem all mankind, that one soul shall not be lost." (Moses 4:1) By using that argument, Satan persuaded one-third of the hosts of heaven to rebel against the Father and Christ. And by using that story today and combining it with human reasoning he blinds, deceives and destroys many souls in this life.

Flattery

Besides offering fair promises, Satan also appeals to human pride to persuade the children of men to do evil and combine with secret and evil societies. Among the Nephites, rebellion, sedition and war was the result of the work of another of Satan's servants, Amalickiah.

> 4. And Amalickiah was desirous to be a king; and those people who were wroth were also desirous that he should be their king; and they were the greater part of them the lower judges of the land, and they were seeking for power.

> 5. And they had been led by the *flatteries* of Amalickiah, that if they would support him and establish him to be their king that he would make them rulers over the people. (Alma 46:4-5)

This approach sounds similar to the political parties and participants of today who receive political appointment to rule over our lives by enforcing regulations, and agencies which are often designed and created to limit our liberties and circumvent the balance of power established by the constitution.

> 7. And there were many in the Church who believed in the words of Amalickiah, therefore they dissented even from the church; . . .
>
> 10. [Thus] we see that Amalickiah, because he was a man of cunning device and a man of many *flattering words*, that he led away the hearts of many people to do wickedly; yea, and to seek to destroy the church of God, and to destroy the foundation of liberty which God had granted unto them, or which blessing God had sent upon the face of the land for the righteous' sake. (Alma 46:7, 10)

Latter-day prophets warn us about pride. If someone is telling another how great they are, how talented, how beautiful, how wise and intelligent they are, how righteous, or how much potential they have and how they can accomplish anything they desire, they may be appealing to pride. They may be flattering that person for their own purposes. Caution is required.

Certainly it is not wrong to encourage talents, gifts and abilities of others. It is not wrong to encourage enhancement of these gifts and talents. It is not wrong to compliment others on how well they do. It is proper to encourage them to utilize their gifts and talents for the benefit of others. Indeed, service to others is the very reason the Lord has blessed his children with gifts of the Spirit. It is a fine line which divides righteous compliments and encouragement from evil-intentioned flattery designed to lead, to influence, and to control.

It can be difficult to discern between righteous encouragement and flattery designed to bring about control. Perhaps the distinction can only be made if one is in harmony with the gospel, receptive to the promptings of the Holy Ghost, and capable of recognizing those promptings. Only the Lord knows the heart of another. Only the Lord knows a person's secret intents and purposes. However, we can have made known to us the evil intentions of others. We can know, just as Alma knew when he told Zeezrom, ". . . thou hast not lied unto men only but thou hast lied unto God; for behold, he knows all thy thoughts, and thou seest that thy thoughts are made known unto us by his Spirit." (Alma 12:3) Only if one is accustomed to listening to and feeling the influence of the Holy Spirit can one discern between these two sources.

Hate and Anger

Throughout the history of the Book of Mormon peoples, secret combinations and societies sought to destroy the Nephite nation. Approximately 74 B.C., a Zoramite named Zerahemnah stirred up the Lamanites to war against the Nephites. It is interesting to read how Zerahemnah obtained and maintained power over his soldiers.

> 6. And now, as the Amalekites were of a more wicked and murderous disposition than the Lamanites were, in and of themselves, therefore, Zerahemnah appointed chief captains over the Lamanites, and they were all Amalekites and Zoramites.
>
> 7. Now this he did that he might preserve their *hatred* towards the Nephites, that he might bring them into subjection to the accomplishment of his designs.
>
> 8. For behold, his designs were to stir up the Lamanites to *anger* against the Nephites; this he did that he might usurp *great power over them*, and also that he might gain power over the Nephites by bringing them into bondage. (Alma 43:6-8)

This servant of the adversary maintained power over his armies by keeping them stirred up in *anger*. When anger erupts, a person is not rational and not receptive to the soft voice of the Spirit. Rather than do the acts of a rational person, he loses control and acts pursuant to his evil nature or the suggestions of others. Accordingly, he will respond to suggestions which would not otherwise be considered acceptable.

The Savior warned against anger when he told the Nephites,

> 29. ... he that hath the spirit of contention is not of me, but is of the devil, who is the father of contention, and he stirreth up the hearts of men to contend with anger, one with another.
>
> 30. Behold, this is not my doctrine to stir up the hearts of men with anger ... (3 Nephi 11:29-30)

One of the reasons we have been placed on this earth is to learn self control by harnessing desires, appetites, passions, emotions and reactions. When one gives rise to anger in his heart, he is really reacting to an external stimulus. When in a reactionary mode, he is letting the external stimulus control. Each person must instead, act—and not react. Emotion must be controlled. To allow anger to control is to allow others to control. Unfortunately, the "others" who will control us in this emotional state of anger are Satan and his servants.

In the Book of Mormon, power over men was maintained by preserving the *hatred* of one group of people toward another. Like anger, hate is also an emotion not in conformity with the Spirit of God. Hate drives the Spirit from our soul. If a person hates, he acts in response to evil influences.

The author remembers as a little child, seven years old, a talk he heard in a Sacrament meeting. The words were spoken by the Spirit and the Spirit impressed them upon the soul. Remembrance of the words is as clear today as it was those decades ago. The speaker said, "If a man say, I love God, and hateth his brother, he is a liar." (1 John 4:20)

Hate is an emotion born of Satan. And yet, parents, friends and peers can teach hate. It is taught by prejudice, arguing, talking evil against others, and by exhibiting their own hate and emotions.

Hate is the ripened state of that which is most destructive to the purposes of mortal man. It generates the opposite of that taught by the Savior. While Christ taught unity and prayed that we could become one as he and His Father are one, Satan teaches that man should hate. When man hates, he is in a state of disunity which promotes the purposes of Satan and generates a loss of control for those who allow this emotion to possess them.

> 38. And it came to pass that they who rejected the gospel were called Lamanites, and Lemuelites, and Ishmaelites; and they did not dwindle in unbelief, but they did wilfully rebel against the gospel of Christ; and they did teach their children that they should not believe, even as their fathers, from the beginning, did dwindle.
>
> 39. And it was because of the wickedness and abomination of their fathers, even as it was in the beginning. And they were *taught to hate* the children of God, even as the Lamanites were taught to hate the children of Nephi from the beginning. (4 Nephi 1:38-39)

Hate is the antithesis of love. While the Lord encourages his children to love their enemy and those who do evil, Satan says, "Hate!" Hate enemies, hate competitors, hate those who are different, hate members of the church, hate family members, hate those you do not understand.

This hate coupled with anger, manifests itself in aggressive, offensive, often damaging action against others. Hate is blind, and often those who hate and are stirred up to anger, strike at the innocent. They lose control of their own emotions, objectives, and behaviors.

In another Book of Mormon instance, while Christ was walking the streets of the Old World, the Gadianton robbers in the promised land were being lead by Giddianhi. He wrote a letter to the Nephites and righteous Lamanites and said,

> 3. And it seemeth a pity unto me, most noble Lachoneus, that ye should be so foolish and vain as to suppose that ye can stand against so many brave men who are at my command, who do now at this time stand in their arms, and do await with great anxiety for the word—Go down upon the Nephites and destroy them.

> 4. And I, knowing of their unconquerable spirit, having proved them in the field of battle, and knowing of their *everlasting hatred* towards you because of the *many wrongs* which ye have done unto them, therefore if they should come down against you they would visit you with utter destruction. (3 Nephi 3:3-4)

This recording gives us another insight as to how secret combinations gain control using hate and anger. The *many wrongs* referenced by Giddianhi is a key. The evil minded can inspire anger and hate in the heart of man by claiming that others have wronged them. The degree of the wrong, the nature of the wrong, even the truthfulness of the wrong can be made to be irrelevant. If a person is taught that he has been wronged, and he believes it, he can be stirred up to anger and hate. He then loses his ability to receive the guidance of the Spirit. He has lost the ability to guide his own personal decisions. He has become responsive to flattery and fair promises. And in this state of mind, he reacts to incitements, to aggressive suggestions, and to destructive actions proposed by and from those who would seek to control him and exercise power over him for personal gain and power.

Because of hate and anger today, many fulfill the Lord's prophecy concerning the last days, that ". . . the love of many shall wax cold." (Matthew 24:12) We live in a world where the love of many, perhaps very many, now waxes cold. Freeway shootings, gang murders, racial riots, and sexual assaults evidence this cold love. Our inner cities are in turmoil. Law enforcement officers and politicians are perceived as untrustworthy by many. People would rather sue in court than apply principles of compassion, tolerance, patience or brotherly love. Too many people believe that charitable and reasonable actions are old fashioned, outdated teachings of inferior times and civilizations.

The love of many people has turned from love of their fellow man to love of their possessions. Love of and a quest to acquire those things which moth and rust doth corrupt have become the driving forces of the world. Anything or anyone threatening, or attempting to threaten the advantaged position is the enemy—to be feared, despised, attacked or themselves taken advantage of. Winning by intimidation becomes the accepted standard of business policy, despite the evidence that a win-win policy is superior in every aspect of the business relationship. Exposing the weakness of another and using that weakness to their disadvantage is the accepted way to find the truth in courts, the best deal in business, and the way to get the upper hand or the unfair advantage with our fellow man. And justice, once blind, may now often depend on the depth and contents of one's pocket.

Anger and hate produce the components to destroy charity in men's hearts and peace in the world. Together, hate and anger provide Satan with the fuel he needs to destroy the unity between man and God, between husband and wife, between parent and child, between members of the kingdom, and among members of the human family.

Summary of Tactics Used by Secret Combinations

Methods employed by Satan's servants through secret combinations can be recognized. The scriptures suggest that evil-minded, power-hungry, secret combination and Gadianton society leaders will convince people that they have been *wronged*. Upon convincing them that they have been wronged, the advocates of evil will make *fair promises* unto them promising them power and gain as compensation for the sale of their righteous principles. Additionally, they may use *flattery* to deceive and to build up confidence in the arm of the flesh. The evil ones then, because of the wrong alleged, will stir up the souls to *anger*. Once anger is present, *hatred* follows. And after anger and hatred have root, *agency is lost*, and the infected fall prey to the designs of their captors—being deceived, led by the blind and void of light which could allow them self control. Once a person is driven by hate and motivated by anger, the evil one has control and can subject the talents of the deceived one to his purpose and design. How cunning is the plan of the evil one.

The Book of Mormon is full of these types of scenarios which should be studied. Analyzing the methods of the secret combinations of old will allow a person to recognize, expose and resist today's secret combinations.

The only safe course in this land is to resist these secret combinations. To tolerate them will lead to destruction just as it led to the destruction of previous nations.

As the secret combinations assemble their forces and combine the powers of darkness and hell against the kingdom, we will have the power of the Lamb. We cannot overcome all of the wickedness of the world, but we can overcome the power of the world against us and against our loved ones.

The following scriptural passages reveal the final state of those who love and serve God. They also show the state of the wicked.

> 12. And blessed are the Gentiles, they of whom the prophet has written; for behold, if it so be that they shall repent and fight not against Zion, and do not unite themselves to that great and abominable church, they shall be saved; . . . (2 Nephi 6:12)

> 15. Wherefore, for this cause, that my covenants may be fulfilled which I have made unto the children of men, that I will do unto them while they are in the flesh, I must needs destroy the secret works of darkness, and of murders, and of abominations. (2 Nephi 10:15)

4
SECRET COMBINATIONS AND THE INDIVIDUAL

The apostle Paul wrote, "Know ye not that ye are the temple of God and that the Spirit of God dwelleth in you. If any man defile the temple of God, him shall God destroy for the temple of God is holy, which temple ye are." (1 Corinthians 3:16-17)

Souls are saved one at a time, concept by concept, precept by precept, grace by grace. Souls are also lost one at a time, temptation by temptation, thought by thought, sin by sin. Satan's great conspiracy against God includes his servants and his angels tempting man to act in opposition to that which is best and good for his body and his spirit.

Many times Paul's statement is related to the 89th Section of the Doctrine and Covenants, the Word of Wisdom, and the temporal body. However, the temple of which Paul speaks and of which we are now possessed consists of both the body and the spirit. To limit the counsel to the physical body is to short change Paul's message. Once a person turns the corner in his mind and realizes that the temple consists of both the body and the spirit, he sees numerous additional ways whereby the temple can be defiled. Interestingly, when one defiles the physical portion of the temple, it also affects the spirit. Likewise, defiling the spirit can destroy the physical. The destruction is both temporal and spiritual, and the timing is both during the temporal existence and in the eternal worlds to come.

Seeking to destroy man both temporally and spiritually, Satan continues to tempt him to partake of those things of which God has told him not to partake. Not being satisfied only to keep man from attainment of his full potential in the next life, but also desiring to make him miserable here, Satan deceives mankind with what appears to be fun and good, but is in reality, deadly and destructive, both to the spiritual and to the temporal being.

Sexual Conspiracy

There is in our midst a sexual revolution which rebels against Christian principles of morality. It is a conspiracy between Satan and some of his servants which seeks to degrade the most sacred of acts between a husband and wife. Satan seeks to devalue the worth of virtue and chastity and to entice the sons of Adam and the daughters of Eve to violate covenants relative to the powers of procreation. This danger is not new—it is well known to parents who are concerned about their children, and it is well known to their children. Revolution participants are rebelling against previous standards, rejecting prior generations' teachings of morality, and dismissing the traditions of their fathers. Members of the Church are not immune from the evil of this revolution.

Its symptoms are evident through such practices as sex outside of marriage, homosexuality, abortion and pornography.

Unfortunately, lack of conscience for moral infractions is not limited to youth. People of all ages find it increasingly socially acceptable to live together without the sanctity of the marriage covenant. Some sociological and psychological counselors even advise this relationship as a sort of test to make certain the two parties are compatible. Surely God views the proliferation of sexual sin as a significant step toward the fullness of iniquity warned of by the Book of Mormon prophets.

The Safe Sex Lie

Responding to the concepts taught by evil-inspired individuals, too many have abandoned principles of sexual morality and fidelity in marriage. This nation might well stand before God appropriately and indefensibly accused of worshiping sex. It is everywhere before us. Worse, it is before the youth. It can be seen glorified in the movies, discussed openly on public television talk shows, and taught both objectively and subjectively in schools. It is used in advertising to sell everything from clothes to cars to hardware to household furnishings. It is perhaps the greatest cause of unrighteousness in this nation today.

Modern day prophets are well aware of the problem. Elder Neal A. Maxwell stated,

> When we leave the light of each commandment, our perception of the real problem becomes blurred and our interpretations become bound to be flawed. In no instance is the blurring more evident than with regard to the seventh commandment [Thou shalt not commit adultery].
>
> For instance, there is grave concern, and with justified cause, about the abuse of prostitutes and the terrible problems of child prostitution and child pornography. One scarcely hears, however, any mention of keeping the seventh commandment in order to solve these dreadful problems though it is the ultimate solution. The immediate retort is that since there are so many who do not hold with divine prescriptions or who are too weak to comply, other remedies are needed. Religious restraints are viewed as impractical! The keeping of the seventh commandment, however, would at once erase all the problems associated with prostitution, child prostitution, and pornography. Yet, the more distance societies place

between themselves and the keeping of the seventh commandment, the larger and less manageable these problems become.[1]

Besides the problems referenced by Elder Maxwell, United States citizens face other difficulties. One of them is the problem of AIDS. Consider the story recently printed in a major metropolitan newspaper:

> The nationwide rate of teenagers contracting the deadly AIDS virus has almost doubled in the last two years, and local AIDS workers are taking action . . . . The AIDS Response Program of Orange County has received state money for testing referrals and group discussions . . . "Adult gay men on the whole tend to have safer sex, but we are seeing an increase in unsafe sex among gay youth," says a program spokesman, who believes the discussions could be very beneficial. "If one's friends are practicing safer sex, it's much more likely an individual will follow suit."[2]

The story seems to advocate that "safer sex" is the sole solution.

Evidently some leaders in the U.S. Government have the same corrupt idea. When a basketball superstar was diagnosed with the AIDS virus, he readily admitted, without apparent shame or remorse, that he had been involved in many extramarital affairs. His regret was that he did not practice "safe sex." The President of the United States gave this idol to the young an official appointment on a national council to help teach our teenagers, our children, that they should have safe sex!

What ever happened to chastity? Is abstinence not a better plan? If you want to ignore the moral aspect and teach real safety, it comes from a heterosexual, mutual-fidelity relationship with a spouse and in no other way.

The safe sex promoted by the government sources includes approval in many major metropolitan areas of school boards' distribution of condoms to students to stop the spread of AIDS. The United States Centers for Disease Control is preaching that salvation from AIDS lies in education of the principles of safe sex and not in abstinence. Studies from Planned Parenthood, the National Institute of Health, and many others show clearly and definitely that the condom fail rate is 25% to 35%. While condoms may be somewhat effective as a contraceptive device, it only takes one failure to transmit AIDS.

Youth and children are being lied to. The Department of Health and Human Services has a list for youth of thirteen rules to follow to make sure the condom works. They simply do not understand nor acknowledge that abstinence is the only cure.

Promoting the concept of safe sex has at least four deadly and silent messages: (1) It is appropriate to have safe sex outside of the marriage relationship (this just is not true); (2) that everybody else is doing it so you can too (the people in the large and spacious building); (3) your teachers, national leaders and perhaps even parents expect you to do it; and (4) that since everybody is doing it and everybody expects you to do it, it must be good to do it (just like the Israelites who wanted a king so they could be like other nations).

Columnist Don Feder, after examining government programs which spearhead these false doctrines to our youth, states the following:

> [The advocates of safe sex say]: "If your child were in an airplane that was going down, wouldn't you want him to have a parachute, even if it was only 70 or 85 percent effective?" This is a bad analogy. Teen fornication doesn't have the inevitability of a disaster in process. Here's a better hypothetical. "If your child were about to leap off the World Trade Center, would you : A) hand him a parachute that opened some of the time and wish him bon voyage, or B) attempt to dissuade him? Apparently, the Centers for Disease Control would opt for "A" with best wishes for a safe landing.[3]

Recent estimates indicate that AIDS will affect over twenty million by the turn of the century, that one-fifth of newborn babies in Africa will be born with AIDS, and the disease will have by then escalated to epidemic proportions in the United States.

There is no safe sex for our children, nor for anyone else, outside of the sanctity of the marriage covenant.

Another problem with the sexual revolution is its effect on the innocent. AIDS affects thousands, eventually millions, who had no part, portion or association with evil. Children conceived by parents with aids, blood transfusion recipients, accidental and incidental contact with the blood of one with aids, and even medical personnel treating the victims and patients, run the uncomfortably high risk of contacting the disease. Because of the innocent, this nation must continue to seek ways to fight the disease. But the real answer to stopping the spread of the disease among the inhabitants of the world is to obey the Lord's commandment to honor the relationship between the man and the woman the way God intended. Anything short of this approach will result in failure.

The Homosexuality Misrepresentation

Another destructive element of the moral strength of this nation is found in the fulfillment of a prophesy by Paul. Writing to Timothy, he stated, "This know also, that in the last days perilous times shall come. For men shall be lovers of their own selves, . . . without natural affection, . . . lovers of pleasures more than lovers of God." (2 Timothy 3:1-3)

We have seen an upsurge of gay men and women in this nation. Instead of hiding their sin as they did decades ago, they now emerge seeking social recognition, legal rights, minority status, public support and government grants. What was once deemed indecent, unacceptable, and punishable activity is now flaunted before our youth in news, movies, music, education and in actual life experiences. Our youth become insensitive to the sins of the flesh when compromising activities are constantly portrayed before them.

While previous generations were not exempt from these misdirected spirits, they were at least non-vocal then. Today, special organized groups of homosexuals seek government funding, legal protection, rights of marriage, and recognition of minority status which would qualify them for government grants and similar public funded rights and privileges. That they seek these benefits may not be all that surprising. But that they are obtaining them should be.

Seeking to display the characteristics of the Savior, many look for ways to placate their distaste and attempt to replace it with the concept that all have a right to act under the Constitution of the United States pursuant to the dictates of their own conscience. However, and despite these rights, there are limits to what can be accepted in this society. When the exercise of one's rights begins to infringe upon principles of basic Judeo-Christian morals and practices, they must become subject to a different measurement, a measurement compliant with the laws of God.

All would recognize that the rights to freedom in this land are limited. One does not have the right to burn other people's homes, to take their property, or in any other way infringe upon their God-given rights. From one basic standpoint, one's rights to act freely end where someone else's rights begin. This raises the simple question, "Do I have the right to raise my children in a Christian-moral nation, among a God-fearing people, in an environment free of negative actions of others which would infringe upon my belief of moral elements of righteousness, and which evil actions would jeopardize the cause of the Christians?"

While many would like to respond with a resounding yes to this question, it is apparent from history that such may not be the case. Among the nations of the Book of Mormon, among the kingdoms of the Old Testament, and even in the land of Jerusalem while the Savior was walking the earth, evil governmental powers have often attempted to control and coerce the actions of citizens.

The proposal itself pits the basic concepts of free speech, rights of worship and expression to the test. If one demands that others behave in a way particular to their beliefs, then they have elevated their concepts, beliefs, religion and similar ideas to the point of mandatory compliance, which is what this nation and its founding fathers rebelled against. Indeed, at that point, the nation has adopted the primary teaching of the adversary, that of elimination of free agency. However, in answering the question, one should also remember that the Constitution of this land was prepared under the influence and inspiration of the Almighty.

Accordingly, each person should look to the tenants of the Constitution to determine the appropriateness of their actions in regard to the rights, privileges and freedoms of others. From a scriptural point, this land must remain a nation which has as its God, the Lord, Jesus the Christ. Anything less than this will result in the land being cursed. Where is the balance for the Latter-day Saint? Does one simply sit back and tolerate negative and destructive behavior around him, or does he actively oppose it? Perhaps the answer is that the Latter-day Saint will oppose all that would lead to destruction. But they must do it within the bounds of the law. They do not create their own laws to justify their intents. But they must work in the political arena to assure that the government and its laws are in compliance with the Constitution.

Some may say, "If we really believe that one of the purposes of the Constitution is to allow men to worship how, where, and what they may, we cannot stop man from worshiping sex, money, the same sex, or any other item or concept. Men must be free to choose."

Notwithstanding this line of reasoning, one need not support, be sympathetic to or otherwise express approval of concepts, ideas, or behaviorisms which contain the elements which could bring this nation to its destruction.

While it may be required of citizens to tolerate behaviors and actions which are unacceptable to the conscience, or even abhorrent to the soul, one need not be passive about government policies which financially support and sustain efforts destructive of society's basic fabric. One must therefore use the political process and the methods established by the founding fathers to return to policies, principles and practices which are in harmony with gospel standards.

And, though this conscience-searing activity appears in magazines, on freeway billboards, in homes on the television, in cars while listening to radio DJs , and through explicit lyrics set to soul-destroying rhythms, we need not make it part of our lives. Each must ask if they are able to look on sin without abhorrence. Each should resist the temptation to tolerate the moral decay as an inevitable consequence of the times.

In their quest for government support and acknowledgment as a special interest group (which would qualify for special government treatment or even funding), gays advocate same-sex marriages. In December, 1990, Ninia Baehr and Genora Dancel, two women, applied for a marriage license in Honolulu, Hawaii. As expected, they were denied the licenses, and they and two other same-sex couples then sued the state of Hawaii for denial of rights and discrimination. In May of 1993, the Supreme Court of Hawaii ruled that prohibiting members of the same sex from marrying constitutes sex discrimination and is therefore a violation of the Hawaii state constitution. The case was then sent back down to a lower court to see if the lower court found any justifiable reason(s) to prohibit the marriage.

Other states are now being faced with similar court challenges and legislative actions. If the laws of the various states are found to encompass this homosexual marriage concept, then it would indeed be the political enforcement of that spoken of by Paul, "Lovers of their own selves . . . without natural affection . . . lovers of pleasure more than lovers of God." (2 Timothy 3:1-3)

Those who profess this lifestyle state that there is something different in their makeup, something in their body, something in their genes, which makes them lean to the temptations of unnatural affection. Many in the medical and psychological professions support this frame of mind and concept.

This controversy results in a classic case of man's knowledge versus God's knowledge. We know that man's learning is often constructed from fewer than all the facts in a situation. Accordingly, as newly discovered evidence is presented, what was regarded as fact yesterday is today recognized as a falsehood. But not so with God's revealed wisdom. We know that God is the same yesterday, today and forever. Accordingly, what he revealed as fact yesterday is still fact today. It will be fact tomorrow and will not change. It is truth.

Today's prophets are clear in their position concerning homosexual behavior of this type. It is not acceptable in the sight of God.

The Abortion Tragedy

In 1973, the Supreme Court of the United States made a decision in a case called simply *Roe V. Wade*. Like many decisions in this nation's history, the decision was not decisively persuasive. The court split on its decision. However, and despite the split decision, the result has remained solidly entrenched in our courts and lives. The decision provided the legal basis for women to have abortions.

In the majority decision, Chief Justice Blackmun wrote,

> The Constitution does not explicitly mention any right of privacy. [However], the Court has recognized that a right of personal privacy, or a guarantee of certain areas of zones of privacy, does exist under the Constitution . . . Maternity or additional offspring, may force upon the woman a distressful life and future.

Psychological harm may be imminent. Mental and physical health may be taxed by child care. There is also the distress, for all concerned, associated with the unwanted children, and there is the problem of bringing a child into a family already unable, psychologically and otherwise, to care for it . . . *We therefore conclude that the right of personal privacy includes the abortion decision,* but that this right is not unqualified and must be considered against important state interests in regulation . . .

[If a fetus is a "person"], the appellant's case, of course, collapses, for the fetus' right to life is then guaranteed specifically by the Amendment . . .

[However], the Constitution does not define "person."

The pregnant woman cannot be isolated in her privacy. She carries an embryo and later a fetus . . . It is reasonable and appropriate for a state to decide that at some point in time another interest, that of health of the mother or that of potential human life, becomes significantly involved. The woman's privacy is no longer sole and any right of privacy she possesses must be measured accordingly . . . There has always been strong support for the view that life does not begin until live birth. This was the belief of the Stoics. It appears to be the predominant, though not the unanimous, attitude of the Jewish faith . . . Viability is usually placed at about seven months (28 weeks) but may occur earlier, even at 24 weeks . . . [But] in short, the unborn have never been recognized in the law as persons in the whole sense . . .

[A] woman is free to make the basic decision whether to bear an unwanted child. Elaborate argument is hardly necessary to demonstrate that childbirth may deprive a woman of her preferred life style and force upon her a radically different and undesired future . . . [4]

Since this decision, which elevated personal privacy above the rights of an unborn fetus, there have been between 30 million and 40 million abortions in the United States. The numbers continue to rise as estimates now state that one of four pregnancies will end in abortion (4,400 per day, approximately 1,600,000 per year). From the standpoint of those who advocate choice and therefore abortion, this number is not astounding as they claim that prior to *Roe V. Wade,* there were over 1,200,000 illegal abortions per year in the United States.[5] But to the Latter-day Saint, and surely to the angels of heaven, the number is staggering.

Many use a financial argument to support abortion. They argue that it is far more economical to allow a woman to obtain an abortion, or even to have the government pay for it, than it is to support an unwanted child through the welfare program. The argument makes perfect economic sense. Consider that the cost of an abortion is between $200 and $500 dollars. But the cost of welfare support for the fetus allowed to attain birth is something like $3,000 a year for the primary years, $5,000 per year for the youth years, and up to $10,000 per year for adulthood. The argument continues that if abortion were not allowed, many babies would be born into homes where they were not wanted where they would grow up adverse to society's rules and expectations, and from which they would eventually end up in prisons where taxpayers would dedicate up to $22,000 per year for their support.

Despite the court's decision and the persuasive financial arguments, there continues to be great division in our nation on this issue. Pro-choice advocates claim a court right to have abortion on demand. Pro-life advocates claim the rights of the fetus are being unconstitutionally ignored. Many become involved to the extent of making it their life's mission to protest against the opposition. Both sides are adamant about their beliefs and their purpose. Some become so intent on making their position known and in enforcing their opinion on others that they ignore the principles of law and order. They take the law into their own hands and begin to infringe on the rights of others. These attempts may include actions such as trespass, property damage, assault, battery and even murder.

In recent years, acts of violence by pro-life advocates against abortion clinics and those who work therein have prompted those associated with the pro-choice movement to declare a sort of emergency. They claim (and perhaps correctly) that the advocates against abortion have conspired against them and are in fact terrorists! Could this be possible? Could those who are claiming to do good and acting in behalf of righteousness be actually acting pursuant to principles of evil? In some instances, the evidence is indeed strong that this may be the case. Paul Hill was convicted, in November of 1994, of murdering a doctor and his aid. In fact, anti-abortion acts of violence against clinics include over 153 arsons and bombings in a recent decade.[6] The FBI has been ordered to investigate to determine if these apparently random acts of violence have been in fact the result of a criminal conspiracy to shut down or block access to clinics and doctors who perform abortions.

The actions and investigations are not without apparent justification. From a handbook of a group known as "The Army of God" comes the following statements:[7]

* Never make a bomb threat from anywhere but a pay phone.
* Put holes through clinic windows. The problem with .22 (caliber weapons) is the noise—the Fourth of July and New Year's Eve are great times for gunshots.
* Hot-wire a bulldozer at a construction site, drive it to a clinic, jump off and let the bulldozer crash through a clinic wall.
* Be sure to wrap duct tape around any tools you use; it will not hold fingerprints.

* Extract Freon from the clinic's air conditioning system. This repair is gonna cost major $$$!
* Drop butyric acid into dumpsters or boxes of trash when people are in the building.
* Dump a load of cow manure in front of the clinic.
* Block sewer pipes with concrete.
* Use a high-powered rifle to fire bullets into the engine block of a doctor's car.
* Make friends with the guard dogs at the clinic. They especially like medium-rare spare ribs.
* Don't hesitate to leave a spare hundred gallons of tar at the clinic door.
* Why get out of the way of an abortionist's car? The current lawsuit-crazy attitude can be used against baby-killers, and many awards have been received.
* If terminally ill, use your final months to torch clinics: by the time the authorities identify you . . . you will have gone to your reward.

These statements seem amateurish and simplistic. Surely the grammar and advice of the writer is less than professional. Notwithstanding this, the admonitions can be motivating to some segments of our public. They certainly do not advocate peaceful or legal solutions to this controversy. Pro-choice advocates declare that the fight against their court-declared rights are the result of terrorism.

From *Ms Magazine*, an active pro-choice voice, criticism of the right to life movement includes the following quotes of those who oppose abortion:

> When life hurts we can help . . . the Army of God is the title of a "How to Manual of means to disrupt and ultimately destroy Satan's power to kill our children, God's children.
>
> This underground terrorist publication came to light when a copy was found buried in the backyard of Shelley Shannon after she shot Dr. George R. Tiller, an abortion provider in Wichita, Kansas, in August, 1993. The booklet provides detailed instructions for harassing and destroying abortion clinics, including how to clog front door locks with glue, jam phone systems, trash the premises, set fire to the facility, and build and detonate homemade bombs. The following "declaration" appears at the end.
>
> We, the remnant of God-fearing men and women of the United States of America, do officially declare war on the entire child killing industry. After praying, fasting, and making continual supplication to God for your pagan, heathen, infidel souls—we then peacefully, passively presented our bodies in front of your death camps, begging you to stop the mass murdering of infants.

Yet you hardened your already blackened, jaded hearts. We quietly accepted the resulting imprisonment and suffering of our passive resistance. Yet you mocked God and continued the holocaust.

No longer! All the options have expired. Our most dread sovereign Lord God requires that whosoever sheds a man's blood, by man shall his blood be shed. Not out of hatred of you, but out of love for the persons you exterminate, we are forced to take arms against you. Our life for yours—a simple equation. Dreadful. Sad. Reality, nonetheless. You shall not be tortured at our hands. Vengeance belongs to God only. However, execution is rarely gentle.[8]

Those who adopt these policies and engage in these acts, are professing that they do so in the name of God. One can but conclude that the acts are the result of self- proclaimed saviors, persons who have made their particular point of view their self- appointed life's mission. We must be cautious to not associate with activities, groups nor organizations which in the name of God, violate the most basic of His commandments. Remember the words of the Savior to his apostles, ". . . the time cometh, that whosoever killeth you will think that he doeth God service." (John 16:2) History reveals that throughout time men frequently have unrighteously persecuted others in the name of God.

Notwithstanding the unjustifiable action of the most active of these anti-abortionists, their reasons for such emotion-charged actions and purposes can be rationalized. Understanding of their acts is somewhat increased by events such as what occurred in Los Angeles on February 5, 1982, when the tiny remains of over 17,000 aborted babies were found in a storage bin. We can empathize with the movement when government actions pay tribute to those who defy the law and perform late-term abortions. The Colorado State Senate paid special tribute to Dr. Warren Hern of The Boulder Abortion Clinic, commending his willingness to perform abortions in the eighth and ninth months of pregnancy. Their citation read in part, "One of only three physicians to perform late-term abortions, Dr. Hern has been a target of adversity for more than two decades. We applaud him for his years of personal sacrifice and courage in upholding his beliefs."[9]

We can begin to sympathize with the anti-abortion activists when we read of the events occurring August 6, 1975, when a local hospital's trash was emptied into a trash truck. One of the bags broke and aborted babies were dropped onto the street and scattered over a two-block area.

The prophet in this day and time has not advised the church membership to become involved in the abortion issue with active protests such as those mentioned above. Though the church has made its position clear as to the fact that we do not support abortion, it also is clear that the Church respects the right of others to act under the established legal right invented by the court, even though their act is an abomination in the sight of God. This should not be interpreted by the reader to suggest that the church leadership agrees with the *Roe V. Wade* decision, nor with the resulting activity that has followed, but rather, that the church is willing to abide by the law of the land and lead its members in patience to use the legal processes available to right the wrong.

The movement toward legalized abortion is viewed by many to be a proper and acceptable solution to a controversial legal problem. In determining which set of rights should prevail—the right of the fetus to be born, or the right of privacy and self determination established by the *Roe V. Wade* decision—reasonable minds will definitely disagree. From the Latter-day Saint perspective, the bases for decision when reasonable minds differ should be the scriptures, the prophet, and personal revelation.

The Prophet has revealed that abortion is a grievous sin. Neither the Lord nor the prophet have stated that abortion is murder, but the Lord has let the prophet know it is a sin of grave consequences. It is so grave that missionary service can be denied, temple attendance may be prohibited and other blessings of the restored gospel may be placed in jeopardy.

Thank the Lord for a prophet, for such a complex question and consideration as this will divide a people not led by a prophet. However, even as the world opened its eyes after the Second World War and realized that it had participated in the execution of the Jews by way of refusal to allow them to migrate to Christian nations, even so, we may at some future time open our eyes to the great spiritual darkness which abortion causes. We well may anguish that we did not do more to protect the unborn and to oppose this grievous sin.

Consider the words of the following prophets:

Ezra Taft Benson:

> History reveals why the great Roman Empire fell. These are the major reasons. Note them carefully and try to determine in your mind if there is anything in evidence in our own country today which smacks of these causes, which the historian Will Durant asserts were largely responsible for the fall of the great Roman Empire.
>
> The first group of causes he lists as biological. These he considers the most fundamental. Mr. Durant claims they began with the educated classes, and started with the breakdown of the home and the family- the limitation of children, the refusal to assume the obligations of honorable parenthood, the deferment and avoidance of marriage. Sexual excesses were indulged in outside the marriage covenant. The practices of contraception and abortion became prominent; reduced fertility resulted. Sex ran riot and moral decay resulted.[10]

Spencer W. Kimball:

> Abortion is a serious sin. There is such a close relationship between the taking of a life and the taking of an embryonic child, between murder and abortion, that we would hope that mortal men would not presume to take the frightening responsibility....
>
> Abortion is a calamity, and if the gospel came into play in the lives of men and women, an abortion would be rare indeed, if at all. If men and women are living the gospel of Jesus Christ, which is the cure for all ills, there would be no illegitimate conceptions, and this would erase from the abortion docket the great majority of the abortions. However, weak, selfish women now require abortions, even in many cases where there is not the illegitimate conception.
>
> Abortion calls for Church discipline. Much is being said in the press and in the pulpit concerning abortion. This Church of Jesus Christ opposes abortion and counsels all members not to submit to nor participate in any abortion, in any way, for convenience or to hide sins.
>
> Abortion must be considered one of the most revolting and sinful practices in this day, when we are witnessing a frightening evidence of permissiveness leading to sexual immorality. We take the solemn view that any tampering with the fountains of life is serious, morally, mentally, psychologically, physically.
>
> Members of the Church guilty of being parties to the sin of abortion must be subjected to the disciplinary action of the councils of the Church, as circumstances warrant. We remember the reiteration of the Ten Commandments given by the Lord in our own time, when he said, "Thou shalt not steal; neither commit adultery, nor kill, nor do anything like unto it." (D & C 59:6.) We see some similarities.
>
> Abortion is permissible only in exceptional situations. Abortion, the taking of life, is one of the most grievous of sins. We have repeatedly affirmed the position of the Church in unalterably opposing all abortions, except in . . . rare instances . . . and when competent medical counsel indicates that a mother's health would otherwise be seriously jeopardized.
>
> Those encouraging abortion share guilt. It is almost inconceivable that an abortion would ever be committed to save face or embarrassment, to save trouble or inconvenience, or to escape responsibility. How could one submit to such an operation or be party in any way by financing or encouraging?
>
> Certainly the women who yield to this ugly sin, . . . and those who assist them, should remember that retribution is sure. Easy abortion is related to licentiousness. When abortions are permitted and encouraged even as a means of population limitation, it is the voice of the underworld encouraging sex without license or controls.[11]

Let the court do what it may in its unenlightened and darkened chambers, yet, we may know truth by heeding the prophet's words in these last days. Either he is a voice piece on the Earth for God or he is not. He either speaks the will of the Lord or he does not. He is either a conduit for the Lord's message concerning the action of this church and its members or he is not. When reasonable minds differ, we must look to the prophet and personal revelation to determine the answer. The humble follower of Christ will accept the guidance of the living prophet. The person caught up in his own wisdom and learning will most likely follow the will of his reasoning—even if it is contrary to the teachings of the prophet.

Sex Education

In the United States, we have been involved in another controversy, that of sex education in our schools. The argument for educating our youth states, "We must be enlightened. We must leave the dark ages concerning sex education. We must protect our children from ignorance."

These are indeed clever arguments and appeal to the mind sensitive to the age of enlightenment. However, it is in reality, simply more of Satan's conspiracy and purpose. A thing loses its sacredness when it becomes too common. In the Old Testament, we learn that people did not use the name of Deity often out of respect for our Father. It was doctrine then (and is so today), that out of respect for our Creator, we do not use His name lightly, frequently or without respect. If one hears His name too often, it becomes commonplace. To some, it is now so commonplace in their lives, on TVs, in the movies, the streets and songs that their ears have become numb to the offensiveness of it.

A similar condition exists in the realm of sexual awareness. Those advocating sexual education in schools do so out of a desire to protect innocent children from unintended pregnancy. The erroneous concept is that if the children understand about sex, they will avoid it, or practice it safely. Before deciding, saints should consider the words of prophets on the matter.

Ezra Taft Benson:

> One of the great needs is more parental instruction in life's problems. I know there is a tendency for parents to shrink from this responsibility, the instructing of their own children in the problems of sex, the relationship with other young people, the problem of dating, and all of the many temptations that confront a growing boy and girl. These instructions should not be left to the school or to a class in sociology. The safest place, the best place, to give this vital counsel, these sacred instructions, in matters of moral purity should be in the home on a basis of confidence between parent and child. As parents, we should instruct our children. The sacred books of the ancient Persians say: "If you would be holy, instruct your children, because all the good acts they perform will be imputed unto you."[12]

Spencer W. Kimball:

> Many errors are induced by society's approval. The subject of chastity is hard to preach about. In nearly every group in meetings, firesides, etc., there is a mixed

group, both sexes and youth of different degrees of mentality, training, and experience. To clear the thinking of one youth would put ideas into another mind. I think we should clarify the thinking for the people, but it must be done with great care. If we think and talk sex too much, harm can come from it; and if it is too little, harm may come, so it is hard to know just how far to go. These interviews with singles are most satisfactory. If every youth would voluntarily come to someone in whom he had confidence and discuss boldly and frankly these matters, much good could come. Many missionaries have enthusiastically thanked me after an interview in which I have tried to properly and decently and understandingly discuss with them the dangers and possible damages which can come from masturbation, petting, and especially "heavy petting," and the sin of unchastity. Many young men have seemed a bit surprised that the Church could not wink at the former two. They told me that at the university the doctor and the physical education instructors had spoken of the thing as a necessary thing or as a habit, universal and without harm. Several prospective missionaries have said, after our interview: "Thanks, Brother Kimball. I am so glad you spoke to me of these things. I didn't know. I can wholly give it up and shall do so. I didn't know the Church considered it immoral."[13]

J. Reuben Clark:

Many influences (more than ever before in my lifetime) are seeking to break down chastity with its divinely declared sanctity. . . .

In schoolrooms the children are taught what is popularly called "the facts of life." Instead of bringing about the alleged purpose of the teaching, that is, strengthening of the morals of youth, this teaching seems to have had directly the opposite effect. The teaching seems merely to have whetted curiosity and augmented appetite.[14]

Ezra Taft Benson:

A mind engrossed in sex is not good for much else . . .

Already the schools have taught sex facts ad nauseam. All their teachings have but torn away the modesty that once clothed sex; their discussions tend to make, and sometimes seem to make, sex animals of our boys and girls. The teachings do little but arouse curiosity for experience . . .

A work on chastity can be given in one sentence, two words: Be chaste! That tells everything. You do not need to know all the details of the reproductive process in order to keep clean.[15]

Alvin R. Dyer:

The "new morality" requires that young people solve their own sex problems without the help of teachers or parents. What is moral and what is not moral, or whether morality is involved at all, is to be decided by the student. The most surprising and devastating of all is the effort that is being made to isolate sex education as being completely devoid of moral responsibility, fear, inhibitions, and emotional restraints.

We can measure what will happen in America by the experience and results in other countries that have been saturated with sex education in the school classroom. These statistics apply to one of the countries:

85% of the people believe in sex relations without marriage.

98% have had premarital relations.

50% of the brides who kneel at the altar are pregnant at the time.

The majority of women want free and unrestricted abortions.

Concerning venereal disease, caused no doubt by the impact of sex education in this particular country, one report reveals the fact that "gonorrhea and syphilis are more widespread than in any other civilized country in the world." Another report simply describes it as "catastrophic." Yet the programmers of sex education are trying to tell us that it will curb venereal disease.

Illegitimate births, which, according to SIECUS propaganda, will be reduced by sex education, actually increased by nearly 50% in the country referred to.

To claim any real benefits from such a system would not only need a so-called "brain washing" from the earliest ages up, but would also require individuals to make choices without recognizing moral consequences.[16]

It appears that the warnings of the prophets on this issue may have been largely forgotten. The battle over sex education in the schools was lost. Public Education, the government and the adversary won the battle. The results of the loss of that battle can be seen in the statistics evident in today's world. One need not look now to other countries to see how they did. One need not speculate how sex education in America's public schools will improve public health or decrease moral behavior. The warnings of the prophets from years past which we have just read were not heeded by the American public. One need only look around at the state of the nation to see that of which they warned has come to pass. The statistics shown in the last section of this chapter bear sad testimony of the failed warning.

Noise, Music, Movies and Pornography

The sexual revolution is also manifested in sense-deafening rhythms and lyrics found in modern-day music, movies and printed material. Terms which thirty years ago would have caused a revocation of a station's broadcasting license now appear as Shirley Temples compared to the hard vulgarity expressed by both DJs and artists in many of today's songs.

Many parents would be shocked at the evil apparent in modern music. Many times the lyrics are hidden by the eardrum-breaking percussion rhythms. Dances produce decibels of sound level unsafe for the human ear. Sound blasters (ghetto blasters) and earphones pound the soul-destroying rhymes and rhythms direct to the brain while seemingly blocking out surrounding sensations of reason and sensibility. With the advent of the portable radio, the portable tape player, and the compact disk, the sons of Adam and the daughters of Eve have an almost constant opportunity to replace creative thought, constructive imagination and spiritual pondering with programmed evil and contrived sub-conscious suggestions of impurity, permissiveness and promiscuity.

The Lord stated, "For my soul delighteth in the song of the heart; yea, the song of the righteous is a prayer unto me, and it shall be answered with a blessing upon their heads." (D & C 25:12)

In an interview with one well-known rock star, when asked about the negative effects of his music, he replied that he did not care about the effect of the music on the minds, lives and actions of youth. Rather, he stated that his music is all about money. If mothers hate it, he loves it because he then knows that it will be a money-maker for him.

In a talk recorded by Moroni, Mormon taught, "Every thing which inviteth and enticeth to do good, and to love God, and to serve him, is inspired of God." And he also said, "Whatsoever thing persuadeth men to do evil, and believe not in Christ, and deny him, and serve not God, then ye may know with a perfect knowledge it is of the devil." (Moroni 7:13, 17) We need to use this measurement when we read books, watch movies, and listen to music.

Ezra Taft Benson:

> Inspiring music may fill the soul with heavenly thoughts, move one to righteous action, or speak peace to the soul. When Saul was troubled with an evil spirit, David played for him with his harp and Saul was refreshed and the evil spirit departed (see 1 Samuel 16:23).
>
> Memorize some of the inspiring songs of Zion and then, when the mind is afflicted with temptations, sing aloud, keep before your mind the inspiring words and thus crowd out the evil thoughts. This could also be done to crowd out debilitating, depressive thoughts.[17]

Spencer W. Kimball:

> Lane ends, canyon defiles, desert wastes, and quiet streets at late hours—these are places where people discuss little of art, music, or gospel doctrines, but where they think often of more base things, talk in lower veins. And when talk wears thin there are things to do, the doing of which brings dust and ashes where roses should be blooming. In interviewing repenting young folks, as well as some older ones, I am frequently told that the couple met their defeat in the dark, at late hours, in secluded areas. Troubles, like photographs, are developed in the dark. The car was most often the confessed seat of the difficulty. It became their brothel. At first they intended no evil, but the privacy made easy the passionate intimacies which crept upon them stealthily as a snake slithers through the grass.

Closely allied to the pitfall of immodesty, and partly springing from it, is that of pornography.

Pornography has become a most profitable business in the peddling of ugly, vicious, sexy magazines, books and pictures. There is an immense trade in such things, and very often the boys and girls of our high schools and of younger ages are the victims of this vicious business. Of recent years, this same lewdness has been found in the evil songs and stories put onto phonograph records.

Parents should be warned of these evils, and do all they can to protect their sons and daughters from a corruption which is designed to stimulate sex passions and open the doors to more serious offenses. By a cooperative effort, they can eradicate these things from the newsstands and from the mails, and bring to justice those who would sell the morals of a generation for personal gain.[18]

Bruce R. McConkie:

Not all music is of God. Lucifer has his harpers, pipers and trumpeters. Some singing is sensuous and evil and lust-inciting.[19]

Ezra Taft Benson:

Rock music, with its instant physical appeal, is an ideal door-crasher, for the devil knows that music has the power to ennoble or corrupt, to purify or pollute. He will not forget to use its subtle power against you. His sounds come from the dark world of drugs, immorality, obscenity, and anarchy. His sounds are flooding the earth. It is his day—a day that is to become as the days of Noah before the Second Coming, for the prophets have so predicted. The signs are clear. The signs are here in this blessed land. You cannot escape this mass media environment which is controlled by financial censorship. Records, radio, television, movies, magazines—all are monopolized by the money managers who are guided by one ethic, the words wealth and power.[20]

Spencer W. Kimball:

The devil knows how to destroy them [the youth]. He knows, young men and women, that he cannot tempt you to commit adultery immediately, but he knows too that he can soften you up by lewd associations, vulgar talk, immodest dress, sexy movies, and so on. He knows too that if he can get them to drink or if he can get them into his "necking, petting" program, the best boys and the best girls will finally succumb and will fall.[21]

Gordon B. Hinckley:

Self-discipline was never easy. I do not doubt that it is more difficult today. We live in a sex-saturated world. Notwithstanding the conclusions of a government commission, . . . I am convinced that many of our youth, and many older but no less gullible, are victims of the persuasive elements with which they are surrounded—the pornographic literature, . . . seductive movies that excite and give sanction to promiscuity, dress standards that invite familiarity, judicial decisions that destroy legal restraint, parents who often unwittingly push the children they love toward situations they later regret.[22]

We live in a time and under circumstances which contain the best and the worst. The chosen of God, the Saturday's Warriors, the youth of today, having the greatest potential to do the greatest good for the earth are brought forth at a time when Satan's forces are also greatest, at a time when his evil is rampant, at a time when evil seeks to totally encompass good. But right and good will prevail. The promise is plain and the end is known. Good will triumph over evil and Satan will be bound by the righteousness of the Saints of the Most High. Nonetheless, there will be too many who will be deceived, too many who will become victims, too many who will fall prey to the evil designs and the conspiracies of sexual enticement of this day and age.

Substance Abuse

Another course whereby Satan attempts to destroy mankind physically as well as spiritually is found in the efforts of those who seek to entice others to use substances which are harmful to the body and spirit.

One need not ponder for a long time to realize that it is Satan's desire to destroy us not only spiritually, but also physically. His greatest regret is most probably that he will never receive the opportunity to experience the second estate, mortality, a body of flesh and bones. He knows that because of the resurrection, those who kept their first estate will all receive their bodies back. But he also knows that if he can lessen our receptiveness to spiritual matters, the glory of that body will be lessened.

Thus, as Nephi records the dominion of the Great and Abominable in the 14th chapter of 1st Nephi, he also records that it is Satan's intent to destroy mankind temporally as well as spiritually. (1 Nephi 14:7) He wants to destroy our temporal body here in mortality, he wants us to be miserable and to suffer pain and anguish of body, and then he wants to destroy our physical bodies in the eternities by causing us to receive a less glorified, resurrected body than we might otherwise be capable of attaining.

By enticing the children of men to seek pleasure and yield to the temptations of the flesh, the adversary knows that he can destroy man. The author has several clients working in social services in Los Angeles and Orange counties. Reports from them indicate that the instance of babies being born already addicted to drugs is increasing. One, a doctor, indicates that it is his professional opinion that those born under these circumstances may never fit into society in a normal manner. The problem appears to be that if the parent is taking certain types of drugs during the pregnancy, there are certain neuron connectors in the brain which never become connected, creating insolvable behavior and learning deficiencies. Thus, those under these circumstances may never recover from the injury done to them by their irresponsible parent.

By enticing individuals to utilize substances detrimental to the physical well-being of the children of men, Satan can cause irreparable harm. He can and does inspire evil men to do evil things which appeal to man, but which are in reality destructive to the physical body. The Lord has warned us of these evils. "In consequence of evils and designs which do and will exist in the hearts of conspiring men in the last days, I have warned you, and forewarn you, by giving unto you this word of wisdom by revelation." (D & C 89:4)

Many are the stories about the meetings of those in the tobacco and alcohol industries wherein plans are made to entice mankind to partake of these known-to-be-harmful substances. Hiring the best and most talented advertising agencies money can buy, they produce signs, jingles, slogans, pictures, rhythms and rhymes which appeal to the natural man and his carnal nature and which make that which is evil appear enticing, good and desirable. Special emphasis is placed on youth enticement, the industries knowing that if they can catch them while they are young, they will have the best chance of lifetime use and addiction. They cover their evil by cleverly appealing to the public to not be excessive, don't drink and drive, and other satisfying efforts to imply public interest and good citizenship. But inside they are wolves in sheep's clothing, understanding the injury, the pain and suffering, the anguish, and the misery their products impose upon mankind, yet seeking to have as many as possible succumb to their enticements.

It is most certainly a grave transgression and sin to assist others to defile their body, and one of which it is surely difficult to repent. For how does one restore to a drug addict or an alcoholic his dignity, his control of his body, his mental competence and his injured and damaged mind, self esteem, and physical strength? Though not impossible, it is indeed a great gulf which is created between one injured by evil substance and that safer harbor wherein man stands when he resists the temptation to engage in harmful activities.

The excuse offered by many, "It is a victimless crime because the participant is only damaging him or her self," is indeed a weak and unjustifiable rationalization. The dollars spent on these society problems now number in the billions annually. Each year hundreds of millions more are spent on health care for these who have addicted themselves to these habits, or inflicted the consequences of their actions upon others. Recent realizations are such that in fact millions of others are injured, maimed and killed because of those who so participate.

Recent statistics indicate that over 400,000 will die each year in the United States because of tobacco, and annual costs directly caused by smoking now exceed $50 billion. When a French water company found pollutants in its water, it went to great effort to pull all products from the shelves and protect the public. A legal drug manufacturer spent millions to protect the public when some of its product was poisoned. A food manufacturer exercised great diligence in removing product from the shelves when rumors of lower-than-stated benefits were circulated. But what does the tobacco industry say when its product kills 400,000 in one year? Their reply is that the product has been unfairly attacked and that the product is really not dangerous.

There are some encouraging words for those who earnestly strive to resist those who would assist Satan to destroy this temple. Speaking again of the latter-days, and specifically about the Word of Wisdom, the Lord states:

> 18. And all saints who remember to keep and do these sayings, walking in obedience to the commandments, shall receive health in their navel and marrow to their bones;
> 19. And shall find wisdom and great treasures of knowledge, even hidden treasures;
> 20. And shall run and not be weary, and shall walk and not faint.
> 21. And I, the Lord, give unto them a promise, that the destroying angel shall pass by them, as the children of Israel, and not slay them. Amen. (D & C 89:18-21)

The physical and general well-being of mankind is prophesied to undergo significant burdens beginning even now. In Revelation, we read about the four angels who stand at the four corners waiting the word of the Lord to go forth and "hurt" the earth. In a revelation given to Joseph Smith, he was told that the four angels are crying unto the Lord day and night for the Lord to allow them to accomplish their mission. (D & C 86:4-7) In 1893, Wilford Woodruff stated,

> God has held the angels of destruction for many years, lest they should reap down the wheat with the tares. But I want to tell you now, that those angels have left the portals of heaven, and they stand over this people and this nation now, and are hovering over the earth waiting to pour out the judgments. And from this very day they shall be poured out. Calamities and troubles are increasing in the earth, and there is a meaning to these things. Remember this, and reflect upon these matters. *If you do your duty, and I do my duty, we'll have protection* and shall pass through the afflictions in peace and in safety.[23]

Are these angels yet among the children of men bringing calamities and troubles? Speaking of President Woodruff's statement, Joseph Fielding Smith commented,

> The Lord said that the sending forth of these angels was to be at the end of the harvest, and the harvest is the end of the world. Now, that ought to cause us some very serious reflections. And the angels have been pleading, as I have read it to you, before the Lord to be sent on their mission. Until 1893 the Lord said to them no, and then he set them loose. According to the revelation of President Woodruff, the Lord sent them out on that mission. What do we gather out of that? That we are at the time of the end. This is the time of the harvest. This is the time spoken of which is called the end of the world.[24]

And at the time of the end of the world, Satan will have great power, even dominion over the whole earth. There are yet to be more angels bringing more trials, tribulations and pestilence. Perhaps only those who live strictly by the Word of Wisdom will have the promised blessing of having the destroying angel and the plagues of the latter-days pass them by.

The Conspiracy to Control Individual Agency

Perhaps strangely, the concept of Satan's effort to eliminate mankind's agency is manifested in a belief and attitude that man is not responsible for his individual wrongdoing. Rather, all of society's evils can be traced to a man's environment. A man does wrong to society because of ineffective, defective, or false teaching, lack of proper training or poor example of parents, teachers, friends or other figure authority, or because he has not been properly taught to act otherwise. Accordingly, if the government can control the environment, it will be able to produces a utopia of good behavior. We see this belief evidenced by such acts as urban renewal, public education, welfare grants, and a myriad of public (federal, state, and local) agencies. We see it in our psychology system which teaches that we are not responsible for our own actions. We are a mere product of our environment. Accordingly, if we can improve home environments by providing public housing, increase knowledge through a comprehensive public educational system, and otherwise protect the individual from negative environmental influences, the individual will change. No longer in need of a place to live and possessing the knowledge to be productive in society, the individual will behave as a responsible citizen.

It is this line of reasoning which leads to the current attempt in this nation to control our environment. The effort is everywhere. Pages and pages of new and more restrictive legislation and agency regulations are being added constantly to an already overburdened society. Literally thousands of pages of new laws, rules and regulations are added to our complicated society every year.

And it is not just at the national level—state, county, and city governments are also active in the landslide of regulation and control. One cannot truthfully contemplate this avalanche of control without a stark realization that the individual in this nation is being manipulated and controlled. The objective is simple: produce utopia in this land by controlling the lives, businesses, activities, education and social activities of the citizens.

This idea of management of the creature is one of the foundation pillars of socialism. This socialism is defined by some as governmental regulation, control and administration. Socialism is a soul-destroying philosophy because it removes responsibility from the individual and passes it to the government. With socialism, control is thought best to be positioned in the hands and minds of elected officials who know better than the common man how to operate and administer assets common to a society. In our nation this creeping socialism, which has the ability to destroy the souls of men, evidently has been viewed with favor by the public as we have tolerated immense infringements upon our freedoms. Taxes have become a burden not conceivable by the founding fathers. Through creation of agencies, the government regulates and controls business, education, trade, manufacturing, production, homes, farming, farmland, and every other aspect of the environment. When truly contemplating the massive legislative burden under which this nation labors, one must inevitably be led to the conclusion that the United States is becoming a controlled society.

Men and women, as children of God, must be free to exercise independent activities. Only through a system where people are free to exercise agency and moral judgement can true happiness and peace be found. It will not be the result of more and more legislation, taxation or regulation. Man cannot legislate his conscience to be good.

When man relies on his own fallen nature to determine right and wrong, he relies on man's wisdom and denies the knowledge, wisdom and teachings of Deity. He relies on the values accepted by the society in which he lives. This society has largely accepted the educational philosophy that the government, the courts, and the law, house the cure for all ailments.

Accordingly, behavior can be rationalized to be the result of teachers, or parents, or environment, or someone else, or anything else. This conspiracy results in government and society compensating those perceived to be harmed by society. "It isn't my fault!" becomes the password clause to self justification and eventual society toleration and acceptance. The concept of accountability for one's own actions becomes an antiquated, outdated and old fashioned tradition, inappropriate for today's educated and enlightened society.

The concept of sin becomes a detrimental creation of man designed to restrict and control his activities. It is perceived as a way for religions and leaders of religions to control, captivate and direct other's lives. In this way, Satan and his servants teach that he does not exist. They help mankind to self-justify their actions, and they rob man of the real freedom promised by Christ, as addressed in Chapter One of this book.

Satan Worship

Satan is one who seeks recognition and worship. His comment to Moses reflects this intent when he commanded, "I am the only begotten, worship me." (Moses 1:19) Earlier, Satan had successfully tempted Cain and his brethren, saying about God's plan, "I am also a son of God; . . . believe it [God's plan] not; and they believed it not, and they loved Satan more than God." (Moses 5:13)

Today, there are still those who follow, worship, and love Satan more than God, those who will not believe God's plan.

As Paul wrote to the Thessalonians, he talked about the second coming saying,

> 3. Let no man deceive you by any means: for that day shall not come, except there come a falling away first, and that man of sin be revealed, the son of perdition [Satan];
> 4. Who opposeth and exalteth himself above all that is called God, or that is worshiped; so that he as God, sitteth in the temple of God, shewing himself that he is God. (2 Thessalonians 2:3-4)

Satan, from the pre-mortal existence, has sought to exalt himself to a status above that of God. And he in this day and age continues to do the same. It is one thing to be deceived by Satan and be blinded by his craftiness. It is something quite different to know who he is and then to worship him, denying Christ, the Father, and the plan they created.

While those who actively and knowingly worship Satan are few, the potential danger they can create can be extensive. Satan has levels of power (his priesthood), sacrifices (animal and human), temples (places of worship) and even signs and passwords. He, in fact, has duplicated (in a grotesque way) most of the concepts of the great and eternal plan of God. Some would perhaps question why he has done this. The answer may well be as it appears to have been through the ages. Imitation of the real plan is his attempt to elevate himself to the status of God, that to which he will never attain except temporarily in the eyes of those who here worship him.

The author received a phone call one day from the daughter of a client. The client had disinherited this particular daughter from her estate. The daughter related that the client had recently died and it had just come to her attention that she had been disinherited by her mother. Her discussion transversed to a self analysis of why her mother would so treat her. She was relatively certain that it was because she had forsaken and condemned her mother's religious teachings. She went on to explain that her mother and sister were members of a Satan-worshipping group. She related some of her difficulties and trials as she finally broke away from the group in her early twenties. She related an experience of her younger years where she witnessed the blood sacrifice of a baby.

There are those, sadly, who seek evil. While mostly hidden for centuries, a book titled *Michelle Remembers*, written and published in 1980 by Michelle Smith and her therapist husband, Lawrence Padze, brought forth thousands of participants across the country who have come forward to reveal their own dark horror stories of atrocities incurred in Satanic organizations. The *California Lawyer* reports:

> Cult experts claim 50,000 murders are carried out each year in the name of Satan and that 20 million people world-wide are under the mind control of devil worshippers . . . Reports of babies and children being abused in ritualistic or Satanic acts in San Diego County and elsewhere in the state, are often dismissed by authorities as too heinous to be true, and must be taken seriously say social workers and psychologists.[25]

But many also say that there is just no evidence found to support these numbers. Some believe the experiences and recalled memories are results of overactive imaginations. Others are empathetic. Says Dr. Roland Summat, clinical associate professor of psychiatry at Harbor-UCLA Medical Center,

> I believe that ritualized abuse of children is the most serious threat to children and to society that we must face in our lifetime. This is an assault on the orderly fabric of society and a menace to mental health and physical safety of future generations.[26]

While some may tend to consider this an overstatement of the problem, the family members of those who died in Jonestown or Waco, Texas, would most probably agree. People who come forth claiming falsely to be the Messiah are most certainly being inspired and their activities directed by Satan. And the ends can be tragic.

The Condition of America Question

These efforts of Satan to destroy mankind temporally and spiritually are unfortunately meeting with success too many times. Facts about cultural indicators currently existing in this land can be indeed discouraging. A report, titled "The Index of Leading Cultural Indicators, written by William J. Bennett, analyzes 19 social indicators in an attempt to determine the condition of America question.

The conclusion of the report is that this nation has experienced serious social depression. The report states, "The social regression of the last thirty years is due in part to the enfeebled state of our social institutions and their failure to carry out the time honored task: the *moral education of the young*."[27] To support this statement, the following facts are presented from the report.

> While the population of the United States increased 41 percent in the time period between 1960 and 1990, cultural indicators rose at dramatically higher rates. Violent crime has increased over 500%. The violent crime rate in the United States is higher than any other industrialized nation.[28] Violent crime by Juveniles increased in recent years at a rate far exceeding other age categories, going over 400% since 1960. The FBI reports that the highly increased rate of juvenile crime has involved not only the "disadvantaged minority youth in urban areas, but all races, all social classes and life styles.[29]

Children relying on government welfare through Aid to Families with Dependent Children (AFDC) has increased nearly 400%. In 1991, 8.4 million children were dependent on AFDC. The percent of American children dependent on AFDC welfare has risen from 3.5% of all children in 1960 to 14% of all children in 1994. The report states that "this large increase in welfare dependence among children directly reflects the collapse of the family structure in the United States.[30] Divorce rates have increased over 400%.

Teen pregnancy rates and abortion rates have increased dramatically. The rate of births from unwed teens has nearly doubled in the last two decades. Do not let the lower rate be misleading though, as the slower rate of increase in teen births is a result of the dramatic increase in abortions. Abortions, illegal prior to 1973, have increased dramatically. In 1990, there were approximately 1,600,000 abortions in the United States.[31] Since becoming legal in 1973, over 30,000,000 (some reports claim as many as 40,000,000) abortions have occurred in the United States. Nearly one in four pregnancies now end in abortion. It has been one of Satan's most effective tools against the unborn spirits awaiting their mortal sojourn here upon the earth. It dramatically indicates the nation's moral bankruptcy and again evidences Satan's desire to destroy man both spiritually and temporally.

This effort by Satan, a carefully spun web which entangles all ages, races, cultures and nations, is an expression that today's society seeks and values self-expression over self-control.

All of this social decay, and more which will yet be discussed, has occurred during a time when spending for the purpose of bettering society has increased far faster than inflation or population. Inflation-adjusted Social spending by government increased 500%! Inflation-adjusted welfare spending increased 630%! And inflation-adjusted education spending increased 225%![32] Remember, population went up only 41%.

It seems clear that more government spending is not the answer to the social and cultural ills of society. Nor is the answer to the sexual revolution and decay to be found by promoting such evil and moral degrading concepts as safe sex, sexual education or other evil-inspired programs sold to the United States public as good, but in reality, wolves in sheep's clothing.

Secret Combinations and the Family

Attack on the Family

In that wide-read political platform, the Communist Manifesto, the authors, Karl Marx and Fredrick Engels, talk about the Communist philosophy of eliminating the family.

> Abolition of the family! Even the most radical flare up at this infamous proposal of the Communists . . .
> The bourgeois family will vanish as a matter of course when its complement [ownership of private property] vanishes, and both will vanish with the vanishing of capital . . .
> But, you will say, we destroy the most hallowed of relations, when we replace home education by social [education] . . .
> The bourgeois clap-trap about the family and education, about the hallowed co-relation of parent and child, becomes all the more disgusting, the more, by the action of modern industry, all family ties among the proletarians are torn asunder, and their children transformed into simple articles of commerce and instruments of labor. (*The Communist Manifesto*)[1]

The Manifesto then continues to justify its position of elimination of the family by showing how women and children were subjected to unfavorable treatment by being required to work in factories and being otherwise exploited. True, there have been times in the history of the world when children have been exploited, when women have been treated unfairly. The manifesto uses some partial truths to deceive and mislead mankind.

One of Satan's most hard-fought battle fronts in the war between good and evil can be found in his attack against the family. Satan uses pride, selfishness, and carnal temptations to deceive, misguide, entice and eventually destroy the spirituality of individual family members.

The key to any successful battle against evil is unity. Without unity, mankind is divided, confused, and without power. Satan is therefore capable of conquering bit by bit, piece by piece, person by person, family by family.

By creating disharmony within the ranks of the family, both inside and outside of the Church, Satan is able to use all of his other temptations and influences, his secret combinations and evil purposes to persuade, entice and eventually enchain individual family members. However, where unity of purpose exists in a family, Satan finds his purposes frustrated and his angels powerless to deceive and destroy that family.

In the Savior's great intercessory prayer, he prayed that his disciples might be one as he and his Father are one. He prayed that those who believed on their words might be one with them. From this great unity comes correspondingly great strength. Unity of purpose, vision and action leads to spiritual progress. That unity can be accomplished in our family units and will lead to great spiritual progress and strength.

Latter-day prophets pray that families in the Church will be united and strong. The family is the basic organizational structure of the Church, and as such, it provides the second layer of personal strength in our lives (the first layer being the Rock of Christ and each individual family member's personal relationship with and testimony of Jesus as his Savior). If Satan can bring disharmony within the bounds of the family, if he can destroy that unity and the attendant power it provides, if he can convince us through temptation, pride or priestcraft that something else is more important, he has produced a great crack which can ultimately destroy that family foundation. It is thereafter possible for him to corrupt the very foundational existence of our personal relationship with the Father.

Is it any wonder that the prophets have emphasized so greatly the importance of the family unit? "No success can compensate for failure in the home," and "The greatest work you will ever do will be within the walls of your own home," have become words by which we must live to survive the onslaught of Satan against the family and the consequential destruction of the testimony of Christ.

To generate this unity with his disciples, the Savior spent countless hours teaching, admonishing and counseling them. He invited them to be with him; he showed them how to walk; he found his teaching moments with them as he was being praised or worshiped; but also when he was being accused, challenged, persecuted, mocked, scorned and even crucified. Our scriptural record indicates that the apostles were with the Lord almost constantly. He walked, talked, and prayed with them. He bid them follow him, watch him, and to do the things he did. He was patient with them, understanding of their failings, and encouraging in their weaknesses. His life and his relationship with the apostles can be a likeness of how saints should conduct their family relationships.

Today, people often find themselves too busy to spend the same amount of time with their children that past generations have done. Over the last three decades, society has seen a great burden placed on the family as parents have elected to spend more time out of the home, away from the family, pursuing the good life, the the utopian dream, or just providing for survival.

To cover for their failure to spend time with the family, many use the excuse that they are working, serving, educating, or otherwise engaging in activities which they have rationalized in their mind will bring financial, social or even spiritual blessings to the family. Ironically, the thing they verbally and mentally seek to accomplish—a secure family—is being destroyed by the very act they are performing to prevent the destruction. Clever phrases today are but excuses planted by Satan—phrases such as, "It isn't how much time, but rather the *quality of time* we spend with children which is important." Justifying actions at work, in the community, or in the Church, people rationalize that they will replace quantity of time with quality time by having family home evening, attending Church and a few minutes each day of meaningful communication. They sometimes do not realize that while they are at their jobs, serving in the Church, the community, the schools, or elsewhere doing good for mankind, children are left alone and are subjected to other sources of influence. It seems unreasonable to believe that spending one hour at family home evening and three hours at Church with the family will overcome the potential influences to which the children are subjected during the remaining hours in the week.

One could conclude that quality time is the result of a lot of average time. If one spends a lot of time with his or her spouse and children, then relationships are built, trust is established, friendships are enhanced, communication skills are built and proper teaching and faith-promoting relationships are generated. Only with quantity of time can one be found present at teaching moments. Only if one is present consistently will he find the small quality time elements which unfortunately cannot usually be picked or chosen. Quality teaching moments come about from everyday experiences, questions and involvements. If the parent is not present, believing they can handle it with family home evenings or other chance experiences, they will most likely miss the vast majority of potential teaching moments in their children's lives.

And so Satan continues his deception and lies by seeking to destroy the family organization, in and out of the Church. Critics of the Church sometimes use the Church's emphasis on family to attack the Kingdom, declaring that members place more emphasis on family than they do on Christ. While it is true that family structure and relationships are emphasized, the purpose is to provide the best opportunity for each individual family member to come to know Christ. The great emphasis on family unity is necessary as it provides the training ground for future generations, future local and national leaders, and future Church leaders. If people could truly develop family unity, then they could work on quorum unity, ward unity, stake unity and Church unity. If members were truly united, there is nothing they could not accomplish. And that great unity begins in the family, between the husband and the wife, the father and the daughter, the mother and the son, the brother and the sister. Miracles would increase, communities would change, and the work of Satan would be frustrated.

Attack on Motherhood and Fatherhood

Satan uses secret combinations to directly attack the sacred nature of motherhood. He has instilled a pride and passion among many women which causes them to seek goals and aspire to activities far removed from the divine role of motherhood. Responding to a call from the more affluent side of life, some women become entangled in the ways of sin and rebellion, pride and deception, selfishness and transgression. Seeking happiness and fulfillment, they engage poor and unsatisfactory substitutes for that which brings real joy.

Daughters are taught that they need to go to college, develop their own talents, and develop their own professions. The author does not disagree with the foregoing statement of objectives and encourages his own daughters to discover and develop their talents to as high a degree as possible. But too often, seeking these goals, today's young women postpone their foreordained blessings and objectives of marriage and motherhood in favor of worldly gain, praise and accomplishment. This encouragement comes from parents, peers, and even husbands of these sweet daughters of Christ. It is taught by teachers, books and economics as the only way for a modern couple to survive, progress and find success in today's complicated society.

Much of the burden on today's family is economic. The average family today will spend thirty-seven percent of its income for federal income, social security, state and local taxes. That compares with a family in the 40's and 50's who would spend an average of less than ten percent of its income for the same purposes. Government social programs, plus inefficiencies and waste have placed great burdens on the financial security of every American family. To respond to the increased burden, both parents work. The two-income family provides far less time to spend as husband with wife, mother with son and father with daughter. However, no decrease of time is found for the child who has ample and even excessive time to spend with the negative influences present in his or her surroundings.

Many organizations exist today to promote lesbian and gay activities, encourage abortion, enhance women's rights and in numerous ways to devalue and oppress the ultimate divine purpose of womanhood. Too many times, young women and old become the fulfillment of Paul's prophecy, wherein they become ". . . women laden with sins, led away with divers lusts, Ever learning, and never able to come to the knowledge of the truth." (2 Timothy 3:6-7)

There is an apparent government attitude which seems to downplay the role of the parent and increase the role of the state in the educational processes. The attitude of some in government positions of leadership tends to lean toward the philosophy that we need to be cared for from the cradle to the grave. They propose that only government can make the earthly sojourn tolerable, productive and traversable. Studies by psychologists confirm that the pre-school years are formative and have much to do with behavior patterns of later years. Accordingly, the government is taking steps to assure that children will be ready to enter school when they reach five years of age. This readiness will be the result of increased government involvement in the pre-school-aged lives of our children. By down-playing the role of the parent and increasing the perceived need of the pre-school-aged child to receive proper training, the intent will be to increase the lifetime productivity of the children.

To justify increased government involvement with pre-school children, those professing this action claim that the traditional family no longer exists.

In a Mother's Day talk on May 8, 1994, First Lady Hillary Clinton said,

> If it ever did, [the American family] no longer does consist of two parents, two children, a dog, a house with a white picket fence, and a station wagon in the driveway. Instead of families looking like the Cleavers on "Leave It to Beaver," we have families that include test tube babies and surrogate moms. Instead of Sunday night family dinners, we now have cross-country telephone conference calls. Instead of aunts and uncles and grandmas and grandpas, we have nannies and day care centers.[2]

This pessimistic view of the family, while perhaps generally over-stated for the nation as a whole and definitely incorrect for the LDS community, is nonetheless too often found to be true.

The first lady went on to state that we need to recognize and participate in our "extended family" which could substitute for those traditions, activities and values previously found in the natural family. This extended family, she proposed, would consist of friends, neighbors, fellow citizens, and new government policies created to replace the now-missing foundations no longer found in the family environment.

Little do these advocates and participants understand the sacred nature of the duty of the parent to rear children, teach gospel principles, and prepare their children to better society. Instead, they lean and rely on the government and allow people they do not know to instill values, morals, and principles of life in their children. But the neighbors, the friends, the teachers, cannot do it properly. There is none of these who can adequately replace the love, affection and role of a mother of Zion.

None of this is intended to demean or otherwise degrade working mothers. Some find it absolutely necessary to survive in today's economic climate. To mothers who must work to support or help support the family, the prophets encourage you to do double duty. Do not abandon the responsibility of teaching. The schools, the Primary, and the Sunday School are no substitute for a mother's teachings. By sheer time alone, the odds stand squarely against the children. Spending five to six hours per day in school is not easily counter-balanced with two or three hours of teaching on Sunday. Children should go to seminary. And the gospel should be taught to children by having scripture study, family home evening and other family centered learning and teaching activities.

Having said this, Fathers need not suppose that the responsibility for teaching has escaped them. The responsibility is ultimately theirs. It is unlikely that the Father of us all on judgment day will turn to the mother of the home and ask if the gospel was taught to the children. Rather, the Father will address the patriarch of the family and ask if he taught the gospel principles to his children. It will be well with the father who can answer in the affirmative.

Having stated the importance of mothers being in the home, it is important also for the father to recognize his need to spend time, not just quality time, but time, with his children. Relationships can be built, trust can be fostered, principles can be conveyed, and testimonies can be instilled by spending adequate time with loved ones. When the prophets of the Book of Mormon wanted a relationship with the Father, they had to spend a lot of time seeking answers. Enos prayed all day and into the night before he had his quality time with the Father. Alma prayed and fasted many days and inquired diligently that he might know what happened to the spirit after the death of the body. In these examples is a type which can be applied to modern-day families. Parents who want their children to listen to them, and who want their children to heed counsel and follow the parent's lead and thus live righteous lives, must have a relationship with those children. That relationship must include trust and friendship. That takes time, sacrifice and effort. It takes time, a lot of time. Fathers must sacrifice in today's world to provide that time. The prophets in the Book of Mormon were always teaching their sons and many had tremendous relationships with their sons.

Child and Spouse Abuse

At first, one might question placement of this activity as an activity of secret combinations. But upon reflection, the reader will recognize that abuse is not of the Lord. It is of Satan, it is used by him to control, and it is one of the vilest forms of evil in the world today. We read about it constantly in the newspapers. We see mothers against children, fathers against daughters, brothers against sisters, husbands against wives. President Kimball said,

> We are greatly concerned with the fact that the press continues to report many cases of child abuse. We are much concerned that there would be a single parent that would inflict damages on a child. The Lord loved little children . . .[3]

It is indeed difficult for most to envision a parent abusing a child. Yet, the prophets continue to warn of this danger. Elder John H. Vandenberg said,

> I would like to point to the Savior's warning: "Whoso shall offend one of these little ones which believe in me, it were better for him that a millstone were hanged about his neck, and that he were drowned in the depth of the sea. (Matthew 18:6) This doctrine states it is better to lose your life than wilfully to offend.[4]

And again,

> One of the most moving scenes of sacred writ is the one wherein the Savior said, "Suffer little children, and forbid them not, to come unto me: for of such is the kingdom of heaven. This, coupled with an earlier utterance, suggests the sweetness and cleanness with which children come here from the presence of the Father: "And Jesus called a little child unto him, and set him in the midst of them. And said, Verily I say unto you, except ye be converted, and become as little children, ye shall not enter into the kingdom of heaven."[5]

And as it is with a child, so it is with a spouse. President Benson said, "A priesthood holder who would curse his wife, abuse her with words or actions, or do the same to one of his own children is guilty of grievous sin. Can ye be angry, and not sin?"[6]

Another form of child abuse which appears to be growing at epidemic proportions is that which occurs when parents abandon their children. Frightening statistics are available to support the growing nature of this problem. The greatest problem is found in delinquent fathers who abandon children to live, learn, and grow in a one-parent family, whose only parent is often required to work outside the home to provide the support necessary for day-to-day living expenses.

Statistics now indicate that two of every five children (40%) do not live with their fathers. The term "live with their fathers" in this context means that they see their father at least weekly. A recent report indicates the following;

Dad is destiny. More than virtually any other factor, a biological father's presence in the family will determine a child's success and happiness. Rich or poor, white or black, the children of divorce and those born outside the marriage struggle through life at a measurable disadvantage.[7]

The percentage of children being raised without a father in the home in 1960 was only 17.5 percent. The increase has been devastating to the solidarity of the family image. Sixty-eight percent of black children and thirty percent of all children are now born outside of marriage.[8] A move toward selfishness and pride inspired by seeking after one's own dream, material objective, or personal satisfaction is a major source of this devastating statistic. Song lyrics, social attitudes, philosophers, and others who have in the past proposed such courses of action as "if it feels good—do it" or "do our own thing," have precipitated this great lack of responsibility among our population. Satisfaction of the flesh now, living today without worrying about tomorrow, and being unconcerned about others (love waxed cold) are key selfish attitudes contributing significantly to children being born out of the marriage covenant. They are contributing factors of fathers who simply walk away and abandon their divinely mandated duty and responsibility to care for and teach their offspring.

New theories of thought discount the old theory that external forces such as environment, schools and stress lie behind the increase in crime and family decay. New theories indicate that fatherlessness may be the greatest cause of family and personal decay in our midst. "Growing up with both parents turns out to be a better antidote to teen pregnancy than handing out condoms . . . [and] young women who were reared in disrupted families are twice as likely to become teen mothers."[9]

We are all aware of the government's attempts to bring "dead-beat dads" to justice by requiring them to bear the burden of paying court-ordered child support. But this effort and similar efforts are simply attempts to cure the economic circumstances and crises brought on by the disease. Some use a treatment and not a cure, applying the tourniquet after all the blood has drained out. Following the words of the Savior and his inspired servants is the only way to eliminate this epidemic.

Sadly, research indicates that an abused child has a much higher chance of becoming an abusing parent. Thus, the sins of the parents are sometimes visited upon the heads of their children. Spouses sometimes enter a silent covenant to not report evil and damaging behavior of one or both of them. Using fear, a parent can demand the silence of a child. Using fear, a husband can demand the silence of a wife, or the wife the silence of her husband.

Persons engaging in this type of activity are exercising unrighteousness and are bringing damnation upon their souls. They cannot utilize the power of the priesthood, faith will be inoperative in their homes, and the Spirit of the Lord being grieved, will not dwell with them.

Abuse destroys the ability of a couple to come to a unity. Using abuse, intimidation and threats, an abusive husband can cause his submissive wife to endure unrighteous sexual activities, demeaning verbal accusations, and degrading harassment. Accordingly to many, there comes a point in the life of the abused spouses or children when they must exit from the relationship. There comes a point when patience becomes consent to abuse, when tolerance becomes self destructive, when obedience becomes slavery. There comes a point, when counseling has failed, when the bishop, the stake president and other priesthood counselors have attempted in vain, when professional advise has been extended and ignored. After all that can be done has been done, it is then often best if the abused party is removed from the relationship. These conditions can create real need for action.

> 31. For behold, I, the Lord, have seen the sorrow, and heard the mourning of the daughters of my people . . . because of the wickedness and abominations of their husbands.
>
> 32. And I will not suffer, saith the Lord of Hosts, that the cries of the fair daughters of this people . . . shall come up unto me against the men of my people, saith the Lord of Hosts . . .
>
> 35. Behold, ye have done greater iniquities than the Lamanites, our brethren. Ye have broken the hearts of your tender wives and lost the confidence of your children, because of your bad example before them. (Jacob 2:31, 32, 35)

Spouses finding themselves or their children in this situation may well turn to the New Testament for the solution.

> 14. Be ye not unequally yoked together with unbelievers; for what fellowship hath righteousness with unrighteousness? and what communion hath light with darkness?
>
> 15. And what concord hath Christ with Belial? or what part hath he that believeth with an infidel?
>
> 16. And what agreement hath the temple of God with idols? for ye are the temple of the living God; as God hath said: I will dwell in them, and walk in them; and I will be their God, and they shall be my people.
>
> 17. Wherefore come out from among them, and be ye separate, saith the Lord, and touch not the unclean thing; and I will receive you.
>
> 18. And will be a Father unto you, and ye shall be my sons and daughters, saith the Lord Almighty. (2 Corinthians 6:14-18)

Education

The federal government, in its march to usurp state authority and under the belief that more government can solve the problems of the nation, has entered into and now controls the education of our youth.

It is a worthy and worthwhile goal to have a nation of men and women who can properly fill out a job application, read a novel, and write of their personal experiences. It is a worthy objective to have schools and universities wherein man's wisdom, knowledge and understanding can increase and grow. Yet, that worthy objective was once envisioned to be a local, state responsibility. Through increased taxation and court action, the federal government has obtained control of this once-local concern. By providing a portion of the funds necessary for public education to exist, the federal government has been able to successfully dictate policies, curriculums, and rights within public schools.

Additionally, the Supreme Court has been able to mandate policy extremely detrimental to proper education. For decades, the elimination of prayer in public schools has made the formal place of learning devoid of that which could best help it to progress. The spirit of truth, available to those who seek, is no longer sought by prayer, but is in fact legislated to be banned, condemned and forbidden. It is the absolute folly of man to seek truth from other than the source. The phrase "separation of church and state" has taken on meaning and enforcement in ways never intended nor envisioned by the founding fathers.

We persist as a nation, removing from the schooling of our young those very principles of Christian morals and ethics which could bring them the greatest and most meaningful purposes of life and concepts of education. The lack of teaching of Christian morals and ethics has been a primary source of the dog-eat-dog, take-advantage-of-one's- neighbor, love-waxed-cold attitudes and behaviors so prevalent in today's society.

That evil and wickedness has had undeniable and substantial progress in our education system and in the lives of our youth is evidenced by a statement in the *Leading Cultural Indicators* report referenced earlier. In relevant parts, the report stated,

> Over the years, teachers have been asked to identify the top problems in America's public school. In 1940, teachers identified talking out of turn; chewing gum; making noise; running in halls; cutting in line; dress code infractions; and littering. When asked the same question in 1990, teachers identified drug abuse; alcohol abuse; pregnancy; suicide; rape; robbery; and assault.[10]

> The social regression of the last thirty years is due in large part to the enfeebled state of our social institutions and their failure to carry out a critical and time-honored task: the MORAL education of the young.[11]

Though the decreased teaching of Christian morals constitutes a great education problem, perhaps the greatest concern is the growing acceptance of Humanism in educational circles. Since the early thirties, the influence of the Humanist movement has been increasing in our schools, in our texts, in our teachers, and in our students. What was once thought of as intolerable is now accepted as necessary and even desirable because of the perceived need to separate church and state. And so today, we find that while there is a manipulated feeling among most Americans that religion has truly been separated from the state in the educational arena, some feel that a new religion has been introduced, endorsed and embraced by educational facilities, organizations and educators.

The new religion had its beginnings in the early turn of the century. It was finally stated clearly and succinctly in 1933 when John E. Dewey, and others with similar beliefs and philosophies, determined to establish the Humanist Manifesto. This statement was initially endorsed by many intellectuals in our nation, and since being published, it has been accepted and promoted by educators, politicians, psychologists, sociologists, and psychiatrists from all walks of life. Feeling confident in their gains and objectives, the manifesto was rewritten in 1973.

Briefly summarized, the Manifesto declares, (1) the world is self existing and was not made, (2) man evolved from lower species of animals without the aid of any supernatural force, (3) there is no need of deity, (4) man alone will progress man's life and well being, (5) man is a product of his environment, (6) ethics are situational, (7) no deity will save us—we must save ourselves, and (8) we must work toward a one-world society.

Consider the words of Paul Kurtz and Edwin H. Wilson, in the preface of the Humanist Manifesto II:

> As in 1933, humanists still believe that traditional theism, especially faith in the Prayer-hearing God, assumed to love and care for persons, to hear and understand their prayers, and to be able to do something about them, is an unproved and outmoded faith. Salvationism based on mere affirmation, still appears as harmful, diverting people with false hopes of heaven hereafter. Reasonable minds look to other means for survival.[12]

As a Church, we allow all men to believe in what they will. But if the reader makes the effort to read the Humanist Manifestos, they will be decidedly struck at the similarity found therein with Korihor's teachings.

Unfortunately, the principles espoused by the Humanist Manifestos I and II have been and continue to be incorporated into the education of youth in today's school system through text books, legislation against religious teachings of creationism, elimination of prayer, sex education and advocation of safe sex, by teachers who believe in and support the objectives and ideals of humanism, and by organizations often blinded themselves to problems.

One must be cautious about education. Parents should monitor that which children are taught. They must oppose those concepts which deny God and profess atheism. To fail to do so may result in children being successfully indoctrinated against the principles, ideals and faith of their parents. Parents must monitor school texts, be involved in school activities and in other ways assure that what transpires in the educational system is conducive to and not destructive of those principles and concepts taught at home.

6
SECRET COMBINATIONS AND THE PEOPLE OF THE UNITED STATES OF AMERICA

A Land in Trouble

Consider the following excerpts from news reports:

* Vienna, Virginia recently outlawed the singing of religious songs on public property. Citizens there were held at bay by armed guards behind barricades as they sang Christmas carols.[1]
* A recent Supreme Court decision (*Lee V. Weisman*), held that a Rabbi who gave a to whom it may concern talk (perceived by some to be a prayer) in a school activity, violated the right of a fifteen-year-old to be protected from listening to views with which she did not agree.[2]
* An Illinois city's seal was found to be unconstitutional because it contained a cross.[3]
* Teachers in high schools can freely disseminate condoms, but are forbidden to teach Creationism.[4]
* Drugs, alcohol abuse and crime have risen steadily each year since 1965.[5]
* A recent poll indicated that those who believe the Bible to be true had fallen to 32% in 1993, down from 65% in 1962.[6]
* Consider that in 1960, there were[7]
    * no legalized abortions;
    * no coed dorms on college campuses;
    * no same-sex relationships in public;
    * no AIDS;
    * a radio station could lose its license for using "hell", "damn", or by taking the name of the Lord in vain while on the air.
* Since 1960;[8]
    * the rate of violent crime has increased 422%;
    * the number of violent crimes has increased 525%;
    * property crimes increased 11 times faster than population;

* prosecution of government officials has increased fivefold;
* sexually transmitted disease rates increased 313%;
* per capita alcohol consumption jumped 29%;
* the number of seniors taking marijuana increased 15 times;
* child abuse and neglect cases tripled;
* reported cases of sexual child abuse increased 10 times;
* 70,000 teachers are assaulted each year.

The list could go on for pages. What has caused these changes? According to one analyst, "We are taking away the spiritual element and abandoning morality based on religious trust, counting instead on our heads and our subjective feelings to make us do what is right."[9]

This is a Choice Land

Despite the difficulties referenced above, this is truly a blessed land. We have fertile soil rich for farming; mines full of ores and minerals; seasonal climates producing a varied and abundant harvest. As the Lord told Nephi, "Inasmuch as ye shall keep my commandments, ye shall prosper, and shall be led to a land of promise; yea even a land which I have prepared for you; yea, a land which is choice above all other lands. (1 Nephi 2:20) This is indeed a choice land—a land choice above all other lands in the eyes of God. Approximately twelve hundred years before Nephi, the Lord told the brother of Jared, "I will go before thee into a land which is choice above all the lands of the earth. (Ether 1:42)

This is the land of Joseph—a land promised to his seed forever. When the Savior appeared to the Nephites, he said, "Ye are my disciples; and ye are a light unto this people, who are a remnant of the house of Joseph. And behold, this is the land of your inheritance; and the father hath given it unto you. (3 Nephi 15:12-13)

That Joseph's land would be special was revealed to Moses. As he blessed the different tribes of Israel, Moses said,

> 13. . . . Blessed of the Lord be his [Joseph's] land, for the precious things of heaven, for the dew, and for the deep that coucheth beneath,
> 14. And for the precious fruits brought forth by the sun, and for the precious things put forth by the moon,
> 15. And for the chief things of the ancient mountains, and for the precious things of the lasting hills,
> 16. And for the precious things of the earth and fulness thereof . . . (Deuteronomy 33:13-16)

Joseph was to inherit a land which had the fulness the earth could offer. We know from the Book of Mormon that Lehi was a descendant of Joseph through his son, Manasseh. Those who currently live here and who are descendants from Manasseh through Lehi are partakers of the promise made to Joseph. The American Indians and those people living in Central and South America who are descendants of Joseph, have a God-granted deed to this land of America. Those who were later brought here as descendants of Ephraim (either by birth or adoption) are also partakers of the promise.

> 6. Wherefore, I, Lehi, prophesy according to the workings of the Spirit which is in me, that there shall none come into this land save they shall be brought by the hand of the Lord. . . .
>
> 8. And behold, it is wisdom that this land should be kept as yet from the knowledge of other nations; for behold, many nations would overrun the land, that there would be no place for an inheritance. (2 Nephi 1:6, 8)

And so, the Spirit of God came to rest on the Brother of Jared and brought his people to this promised land. And the Spirit of God rested on Lehi and Nephi and brought their people to this land. And, more recently, the Spirit of God rested on Columbus and the Pilgrims and Puritans and brought them to this land. And all this was according to the foreknowledge of God and pursuant to his plan.

Mark E. Petersen, in *The Great Prologue,* quotes Columbus who wrote;

> Further, [God] gave me joy and cunning in drawing maps . . . , cities, mountains, rivers, islands and harbors, each one in its place. I have seen and truly have studied all books, losmographies, histories, chronicles, and philosophies, and other arts, for which the Lord unlocked my mind, sent me upon the sea, and gave me fire for the deed. Those who heard of my enterprise called it foolish, mocked me, and laughed. But who can doubt but that the Holy Ghost inspired me?[10]

The Gentiles who followed Columbus and went forth out of captivity were the Pilgrims and others who left economic, political and religious captivity to come to a land of freedom; a land of promise; a land choice above all other lands. In Europe, these common people did not own land, they did not elect those who governed them, and most practiced the state religion by mandate. The Spirit of God, resting upon them, gave them hope and promise. He gave them determination and courage. He gave them endurance and strength to overcome tremendous hardships and burdens. He gave them the light of God to help them break the mortal-designed chains with which they were bound. He allowed them to seek a better life where they could worship God as they believed and desired, where they could exercise the free will of their conscience and reap the rewards of their labors.

As we view the history of this nation, and particularly the Revolutionary War, we see the hand of the Lord time after time, bringing blessing upon blessing. The founding fathers recognized the input and effect of Deity.

The Pilgrims who came to this land for freedom and the Puritans who followed seeking to capture the wealth in the New World, had the common goal of living free from oppression and captivity. Through the difficult first three hundred years, the Lord's hand acted to purify and harden the survivors by exposing them to the refiner's fire while still protecting them from destructive external forces and powers.

By the mid 1700's, the people were beginning to exercise their desire for freedom by resisting the oppressive hand of the European Fatherlands. At the time of the Boston Tea Party in 1773, the argument against excessive taxation was wide spread. When open conflict began in April of 1775, the majority of colonists were supportive of an armed resistance to the British presence. As a result of the 2nd Continental Congress, called beginning in May of 1775, King George III declared that England was now at war with the colonies (Aug. 1775). With the writing of Thomas Paine's *Common Sense* in January, 1776, the majority of Americans accepted the inevitability of a revolutionary war. Accordingly, the assembled 2nd Continental Congress produced the Declaration of Independence signed on July 4, 1776. This document, framed by Thomas Jefferson, Benjamin Franklin, John Adams, Roger Livingston and Roger Sherman, became the foundation for the redemption of the Land of Joseph by the shedding of blood. (D & C 101:79-80) Truly, Providence has watched over and blessed this land and the inhabitants of these United States Of America.

Today this land of plenty has become the envy of the world. The standard of living is the best in the world. The United States is the one surviving super power of the cold war. There is truly much for which to be thankful as citizens enhance and enjoy their homes, watch TVs, and eat microwave dinners. This is a land choice above all other lands.

The ability of citizens to partake of the bountiful harvest available in this land does not come without a cost. Indeed, the land itself is bound by a higher law. This land can only be a land of plenty and a blessed land so long as those who inhabit it serve Jesus Christ.

Is it possible that this nation still exists because of the faith and diligence of the members of the church? In probably the most-often-quoted scripture relating to the responsibility of the inhabitants of this land, we read:

> 8. And he [the Lord] had sworn in his wrath unto the Brother of Jared, that whoso should possess this land of promise, from that time henceforth and

forever, should serve him, the true and only God, or they should be swept off when the fulness of his wrath should come upon them.

9. And now, we can behold the decrees of God concerning this land, that it is a land of promise; and whatsoever nation shall possess it shall serve God, or they shall be swept off when the fulness of his wrath shall come upon them. And the fulness of his wrath cometh upon them when they are ripened in iniquity.

10. For behold, this is a land which is choice above all other lands; wherefore he that doth possess it shall serve God or shall be swept off; for it is the everlasting decree of God . . . . (Ether 2:8-10)

The decree of God is plain and simple. There can be no misunderstanding. There can be no substitute, no half-hearted commitment, no compromise. We simply serve God or get swept off. The division is now in process. The marvelous work is here, it will be accepted or rejected. The people who inhabit this land, the sons and daughters of Manasseh and the sons and daughters of Ephraim, must serve Jesus Christ, and anything and everything short of that decree leads toward destruction.

The responsibility to serve Christ is general to the inhabitants, but specific to the Latter-day Saints. Knowing that the latter days would bring tribulation to the earth in general, the Lord stated;

5. Verily I say unto you all: Arise and shine forth, that thy light may be a standard for the nations;

6. And that the gathering together upon the land of Zion, and upon her stakes, may be for a defense, and for a *refuge from the storm*, and from wrath when it shall be poured out without mixture upon the whole earth. (D & C 115:5-6)

While the Western Hemisphere is a promised land, Zion may also be found on other lands. And to Zion (in her stakes) will gather the saints seeking a defense and refuge from the abomination of desolation attendant to the latter days. But this promise is also conditional. Speaking of the law of tithes, offerings, and consecration, the Lord states,

I say unto you, if my people observe not this law, to keep it holy, and by this law sanctify the land of Zion unto me, that my statutes and my judgments may be kept thereon, that it [the land] may be most holy, behold, verily I say unto you, it shall not be a land of Zion unto you. (D & C 119:6)

If the saints live the gospel, the stakes of Zion will be a protection, a defense, a holy ground. But should they fail to live the gospel, individually, and in wards and stakes, then it will *not* be a land of Zion and will *not* be sanctified and its inhabitants will *not* be preserved from the judgments, devastation, plagues and tribulations of the last days. The saints must strengthen faith, improve preparedness and increase testimonies in families, wards and stakes. How great are the burdens and responsibilities of bishops and stake presidents.

Too many times, saints rely unwisely on the promise of the Lord that the gospel will never again be taken from the earth. However, freedoms are not so guaranteed. Many have unwarranted hope or even apathy about individual responsibility to preserve freedom. Some sometimes convince themselves that the people in this nation are too good, too great, too powerful, too righteous for the land to fall. But the prophets of the Book of Mormon do not share that optimism.

> 23. Wherefore, O ye Gentiles, it is wisdom in God that these things [the Book of Mormon] should be shown unto you, that thereby ye may repent of your sins, and suffer not that these murderous combinations shall get above you, which are built up to get power and gain—and the work, yea, even the work of destruction come upon you, yea, even the sword of the justice of the Eternal God shall fall upon you, to your overthrow and destruction if ye shall suffer these things [secret combinations] to be.
> 24. Wherefore, the Lord commandeth you, when ye shall see these things come among you that ye shall awake to a sense of your awful situation, . . . (Ether 8:23-24)

This land of the Americas has seen two prior Christian nations rise to greatness and then sink to utter destruction. This is the third Christian society to dwell on the land. The promises and blessings to this nation have been great. This is the land choice above all other lands. Inhabitants have therefore, a duty higher and greater than the inhabitants of any other land. They must serve Jesus Christ, the King of this land, and protect it against those who would destroy it. They cannot be passive. They cannot stand by idle while the secret combinations work to destroy rights, liberties, freedoms, families, and religion. Each must awake and become aware of his awful situation. Only if a person understands his status can he properly petition Deity for divine intervention, strength and preservation of righteousness.

A Great and Marvelous Work

While visiting his people in the Americas following his resurrection, the Lord Jesus Christ said,

> Thus commandeth the Father that I should say unto you: At that day when the Gentiles shall sin against my gospel, and shall reject the fulness of my gospel, and shall be lifted up in the pride of their hearts above all nations, and above all the people of the whole earth, and shall be filled with all manner of lyings, and of deceits, and of mischiefs, and all manner of hypocrisy, and murders, and priestcrafts, and whoredoms, and of secret abominations; and if they shall do all those

things, and shall reject the fullness of my gospel, behold, saith the Father, I will bring the fullness of my gospel from among them. (3 Nephi. 16:10)

In many ways, the life style of our nation today matches the characteristics spoken of by the Savior. Government officials are often found lying, business is sometimes full of deceit and hypocrisy. Murders continue to rise, as does all violent crime. Priestcraft increases over the many television and radio stations and in churches. Wickedness, violence, unrest and evil are found in all phases, all aspects, all professions of life. And yet many in this nation still believe we are the best, the most powerful, the strongest, and the proudest. Has the nation sinned against the gospel? Are citizens lifted up in the pride of their hearts above all other nations? Has this nation rejected the fullness of the gospel? The answer to these questions can only come from God to his children. What is clear is that when the degree of wickedness in this nation attains the fullness of iniquity, the wicked will be destroyed. (Ether 2:10)

In an attempt to prepare for the future, it is important for us to consider the status of this land before God with regard to our individual lives of service and devotion.

> 31. And the office of their ministry is to call men unto repentance, and to fulfill and to do the work of the covenants of the Father, which he hath made unto the children of men, to prepare the way among the children of men, by declaring the word of Christ unto the chosen vessels of the Lord, that they may bear testimony of him.
>
> 32. And by so doing, the Lord God prepareth the way that the residue of men may have faith in Christ, that the Holy Ghost may have place in their hearts, according to the power thereof; and after this manner bringeth to pass the Father, the covenants which he hath made unto the children of men. (Moroni 7:31-32)

Just as God uses angels to speak to prophets, he uses the seed of Abraham to spread the gospel blessings to all the families of the whole earth. This pattern is evident throughout the Old Testament as God gave his revelations and gospel to the descendants of Abraham. In fact, the pattern continued even during the mortal ministry of Christ. Christ was born to descendants of Abraham, and his mortal mission and teachings were to be accomplished among those inheritors of Abraham's blessing and to no one else:

> 25. For a certain woman, whose young daughter had an unclean spirit, heard of him, and came and fell at his feet:
>
> 26. The woman was a Greek, a Syrophenician by nation; [a non-Israelite, not descended from Jacob] and she besought him that he would cast forth the devil out of her daughter. (Mark 7:25-26)

In the days of Christ, non-Israelite nations (Gentiles) were considered unclean and the Lord had commanded Israel not to commingle with them. Following the non- Israelite mother's plea for a blessing, follows what could be considered some of the most harsh words and actions ever recorded in the life of the Savior during his mortal ministry. "But he answered her not a word. And his disciples came and besought him, saying, Send her away; for she crieth after us. But he answered and said, I am not sent but unto the lost sheep of the house of Israel." (Matthew 15:23-24) Thus the Savior confirmed and verified the role of the Tribes of Israel as the people chosen to receive his direct mortal mission. All other nations and families of the earth would be blessed through Abraham's seed. "Then came she and worshiped him, saying, Lord, help me. But he answered and said, it is not meet to take the children's bread and to cast it to dogs. (Matthew 15:25-26) Truly manifesting the role of the children of Israel as the children of the covenant, the Savior of mankind verified that only they were to receive the blessings of his ministry directly from him. "And she said, Truth, Lord: yet the dogs eat of the crumbs which fall from their masters' table. Then Jesus answered and said unto her, O woman, great is thy faith: be it unto thee even as thou wilt. And her daughter was made whole from that very hour." (Matthew 15:27-28) The woman recognizing her status before the Lord, received the blessing she sought.

But this isolated event did not alter the intent of the Lord to limit his personal ministry to the descendants of Abraham, Isaac and Jacob. Speaking to the Israelites in the New World, the Savior stated:

> 21. . . . ye are they of whom I said: other sheep I have which are not of this fold; them also I must bring, and they shall hear my voice; and there shall be one fold, and one shepherd.
> 22. And they understood me not, for they supposed it had been the Gentiles; for they understood not that the Gentiles should be converted through their preaching.
> 23. And they understood me not that I said they shall hear my voice; and they understood me not that the Gentiles should not at any time hear my voice—that I should not manifest myself unto them save it were by the Holy Ghost. (3 Nephi 15:21-23)

That the Jerusalem disciples eventually understood their role with regard to the Gentiles is clear as a result of Peter's vision in Acts 10. Cornelius, a Gentile, sent to Peter for assistance, and through the revelation given to Peter, he understood that the time had come for the gospel to be preached to the Gentile nations of the earth. In this manner, God used (and continues to use) the seed of Abraham to bless the nations of the earth. As the seed of Abraham, and as members of the Church, we share that responsibility to be a conduit to all who will hear of the saving mission and grace of Christ.

To assist in the fulfillment of that responsibility and blessing, the Lord has established the Marvelous work and Wonder. The title page of the Book of Mormon states clearly its purpose. "Written to the Lamanites, who are a remnant of the house of Israel; and also to the Jew and Gentile . . . to the convincing of the Jew and Gentile that Jesus is the Christ, the Eternal God, manifesting himself unto all nations. (Title Page, Book of Mormon) This book, as part of the Marvelous Work and Wonder, can truly convince the honest in heart that Jesus is the Christ, the Savior and Redeemer of all mankind.

The Book of Mormon, like the Bible, was written by a tribe of Israel, part of the seed of Abraham, Isaac and Jacob, to help fulfill the covenant of the Lord to bless all nations through the seed of Abraham.

> 1. But behold, there shall be many—at that day when I shall proceed to do a marvelous work among them, that I may remember my covenants which I have made unto the children of men, that I may set my hand again the second time to recover my people, which are of the house of Israel;
>
> 2. And also, that I may remember the promises which I have made unto thee, Nephi, and also unto thy father, that I would remember your seed; and that the words of your seed should proceed forth out of my mouth unto your seed; and my words shall hiss forth unto the ends of the earth, for a standard unto my people which are of the house of Israel. (2 Nephi 29:1-2)

The marvelous work spoken of here includes the bringing forth of the Lord's words through the prophet to benefit mankind. The timing to which the Lord has reference is evident. The first time the Lord set forth his hand to recover the children of Israel was with Moses. The second time for the recovery of the house of Israel is now. The Lord continued;

> 7. Know ye not that there are more nations than one? Know ye not that I, the Lord your God, have created all men, and that I remember those who are upon the isles of the sea; and that I rule in the heavens above and in the earth beneath; and I bring forth my word unto the children of men, yea even upon all the nations of the earth?
>
> 8. Wherefore murmur ye, because that ye shall receive more of my word? Know ye not that the testimony of two nations is a witness unto you that I am God, that I remember one nation like unto another? Wherefore, I speak the same words unto one nation like unto another. And when the two nations shall run together the testimony of the two nations shall run together also. (2 Nephi 29:7-8)

A Division of the People

This great blessing, the Marvelous Work and Wonder, the coming forth of additional words of Christ through the Book of Mormon, increases the responsibility of mankind to accept Christ and follow his teachings. Of those who receive much, much is required. Speaking of the latter days, the Lord informs mankind of events which will occur. The prophet Nephi stated, "The time speedily cometh that the Lord God shall cause a *great division* among the people, and the wicked will he destroy; and he will spare his people, yea, even if it so be that he must destroy the wicked by fire. (2 Nephi. 30:10) This division between righteous and evil is taking place right now. It is the Lord's work, separating the wheat from the chaff that the chaff may be burned and the wheat spared. Concerning this division, each man and woman must stand up and be counted on the side of right, the side of the Lord.

The Lord has helped us to understand why the Book of Mormon was needed at this time,

> 25. Forasmuch as this people draw near unto me with their mouth, and with their lips do honor me, but have removed their hearts far from me, and their fear towards me is taught by the precepts of men—
>
> 26. Therefore, I will proceed to do a marvelous work among this people, yea a marvelous work and a wonder, for the wisdom of their wise and learned shall perish, and the understanding of their prudent shall be hid. (2 Nephi 27:25-26)

The objective of the marvelous work and wonder is to bring people back to Christ. It is to help overcome false and insincere tendencies and to replace them with a true faith in Christ. It is to cause hearts to change away from worldly pride and from cares of the world. It is to cause people to have a broken heart and a contrite spirit. It is to confound those who place their own knowledge above that of others and thus begin to practice priestcraft wherein they seek profit and power for themselves but deny the power of God.

The reaction of the world to the coming forth of the Book of Mormon was known to the Lord and revealed to Nephi:

> And because my words shall hiss forth—[the coming forth of the Book of Mormon] many of the Gentiles shall say: A Bible! A Bible! We have got a Bible, and there cannot be any more Bible. (2 Nephi 29:3)

But Nephi continues: "For after the book of which I have spoken shall come forth, and be written unto the Gentiles, and sealed up again unto the Lord, there shall be many which shall believe the words which are written; (2 Nephi 30:3)

And thus, the division begins. The Book of Mormon becomes a sifter, the great dividing tool, the instrument provided by the Lord to separate right from wrong, good from bad, truth from error. The Lord told Nephi,

> 6. Therefore, wo be unto the Gentiles if it so be that they harden their hearts against the Lamb of God.
>
> 7. For the time cometh, saith the Lamb of God, that I will work a great and a marvelous work among the children of men; a work which shall be everlasting, either on the one hand or on the other—either to the convincing of them unto peace and life eternal, or unto the deliverance of them to the hardness of their hearts and the blindness of their minds unto their being brought down unto captivity, and also into destruction, both temporally and spiritually, according to the captivity of the devil, of which I have spoken. (1 Nephi 14:6-7)

Unfortunately, a day of great wickedness was to come in the last days, and this fact was revealed to Nephi:

> But, behold, in the last days, or in the days of the Gentiles—yea, behold all the nations of the Gentiles and also the Jews, both those who shall come upon this land and those who shall be upon other lands, yea, even upon all the lands of the earth, behold, they will be drunken with iniquity and all manner of abominations. (2 Nephi 27:1)

The Lord directed the church with a specific course of action concerning wrong-doing against the church and its members.

> 81. Now, unto what shall I liken the children of Zion? I will liken them unto the parable of the woman and the UNJUST JUDGE, for men ought always to pray and not to faint, which saith—
>
> 82. There was in a city a judge which feared not God, neither regarded man.
>
> 83. And there was a widow in that city, and she came unto him, saying: Avenge me of mine adversary.
>
> 84. And he would not for a while, but afterward he said within himself: Though I fear not God, nor regard man, yet because this widow troubleth me I will avenge her, lest by her continual coming she weary me.
>
> 85. Thus will I liken the children of Zion. (D & C 101:81-85)

The Church is the widow. The point seems to be that even though the judge (in this case the government, both state and federal) was not sympathetic to the cause or purpose of the Church, yet to eliminate the immediate problem, the government will grant the Church its just rights. The Lord, therefore, tells the Church to abide by the law of the land, the Constitution, and be diligent in seeking remedies through legal channels. However, the Lord then continues with a promise and a warning. Speaking of how to obtain redress for wrongs done unto the members individually and the church collectively, the Lord advises:

> 86. Let them importune at the feet of the judge;
>
> 87. And if he heed them not, let them importune at the feet of the governor;

88. And if the governor heed them not, let them importune at the feet of the president;

89. And if the president heed them not, then will the Lord arise and come forth out of his hiding place, and in his fury *vex the nation*. (D & C 101:86-89)

But the governor of Missouri, Governor Lilburn W. Boggs, fearing for his political career and viewing the church as a threat to his status, issued his now infamous extermination order making it legal to kill Mormons and drive them from his state. In the document, dated October 27, 1838, Governor Boggs ordered his militia to war against the Saints, saying in part, "The Mormons must be treated as enemies and must be exterminated or driven from the state, if necessary for the public good."[11]

But, true to the Lord's command, Joseph and the church continued to seek relief from judges, governors and even the president of the United States. In fact, over 600 different documents have been located petitioning different government authorities for redress. And each time and at each level they were denied justice, driven from their homes, and excluded from the very protections and rights for which the Constitution was established. At the highest level of appeal, Joseph reports that the President of the United States, Martin Van Buren, after hearing of the plight of the Church, replied, "Gentlemen, your cause is just, but I can do nothing for you."[12]

It appears certain that the judge, the governor and the President refused to grant redress to the Church. That being the case, one must conclude that the Lord, true to his word, came out of his hiding place and vexed this nation. Webster's definition of vex implies that the nation, the United States of America, is agitated, distressed, and troubled. A critical view of our history could well construe that this vexation has continued to increase since the early history of the church, being at times overshadowed by external conflicts and wars, but nevertheless intensifying internally in degree and scope. This distress and trouble can be found in inner city slums, schools, governments' financial bankruptcy, on streets and most frighteningly, in homes and families.

All of the indicators of trouble, distress, agitation, and vexation, can be and are intensified and proselyted by modern-day secret combinations. That this nation may be under a degree of condemnation (vexed) because of its response to the gospel's restoration is not a pleasant thought.

The Lord further confirmed that all is not well in this land. Speaking of the martyrdom of Joseph and Hyrum Smith, Elder John Taylor stated:

> They were innocent of any crime, as they had often been proved before, and were only confined in jail by the conspiracy of traitors and wicked men; and their innocent blood on the floor of Carthage jail is a broad seal affixed to

"Mormonism" that cannot be rejected by any court on earth, and their innocent blood on the escutcheon of the State of Illinois, with the broken faith of the State as pledged by the governor, is a witness to the truth of the everlasting gospel that all the world cannot impeach; and their innocent blood on the banner of liberty [the American flag], and on the magna charta of the United States [the Constitution], is an ambassador for the religion of Jesus Christ, that will touch the hearts of honest men among all nations; and their innocent blood, . . . will cry unto the Lord of Hosts *till he avenges that blood on the earth*. Amen. (D & C 135:7)

And finally, the Lord himself, through his successor prophet, comments on the deaths of his prophets at Carthage.

32. Let him that is ignorant learn wisdom by humbling himself and calling upon the Lord his God, That his eyes may be opened that he may see, and his ears opened that he may hear;

33. For my Spirit is sent forth into the world to enlighten the humble and contrite, and to the condemnation of the ungodly.

34. Thy brethren have rejected you and your testimony, even the *nation* that has driven you out;

35. And now cometh the day of their calamity, even the days of sorrow, like a woman that is taken in travail; and their sorrow shall be great unless they speedily repent, yea, very speedily.

36. For they killed the prophets, and them that were sent unto them; and they have shed innocent blood, which crieth from the ground against them. (D & C 136:32-36)

The Lord declares that the nation, the United States of America, the people governed by the Constitution which guaranteed the right to worship, this nation rejected the testimony of Jesus Christ and drove the restored Church from its borders. In this, the promised land, kept from the knowledge of other nations and preserved by the hand of the Lord as a land of liberty wherein he could restore the gospel under a heavenly inspired banner of freedom, the gospel was rejected, the church driven out and the prophets, Joseph and Hyrum, were slain. This nation has witnessed some of the calamity promised by the Lord. But before the Lord returns in his glory, it will yet bear more trial, tribulation and calamity as has not yet been seen.

Knowing that the nation would reject Joseph Smith, the restored Church, and Jesus Christ, the Lord made a decree which is binding upon this nation and this earth even today.

32. I, the Lord, am angry with the wicked; I am holding my Spirit from the inhabitants of the earth.

33. I have sworn in my wrath, and DECREED WARS upon the face of the earth, and the wicked shall slay the wicked, and fear shall come upon every man. (D & C 63:32-33)

This status of distress and war decreed upon the face of the earth will not end until the Savior comes again.

> And thus, with the sword and by bloodshed the inhabitants of the earth shall mourn; and with famine, and plague, and earthquake, and the thunder of heaven, and the fierce and vivid lightning also, shall the inhabitants of the earth be made to feel the wrath, and indignation, and chastening hand of an Almighty God, until the consumption decreed hath made a full end of all nations; (D & C 87:6)

Destruction or Protection

While war has been decreed by God, Latter-day Saints are commanded to proclaim peace. "Therefore, renounce war and proclaim peace, and seek diligently to turn the hearts of the children to their fathers, and the hearts of the fathers to the children. (D & C 98:16) The peace we preach comes to the heart by accepting Christ as the Savior and entering into his everlasting covenant, taking upon one his name and promising to keep his commandments. When a person does this, the promise shown to Nephi applies to him.

> 17. Wherefore, he will preserve the righteous by his power, even if it so be that the fullness of his wrath must come, and the righteous be preserved, even unto the destruction of their enemies by fire. Wherefore, the righteous need not fear; for thus saith the prophet, they shall be saved, even if it so be as by fire.
> 18. Behold, my brethren, I say unto you, that these things must shortly come; yea, even blood, and fire, and vapor of smoke must come; and it must needs be upon the face of this earth; and it cometh unto men according to the flesh if it so be that they will harden their hearts against the Holy One of Israel.
> 19. For behold, the righteous shall not perish. (1 Nephi 22:17-19)

The acceptance of Christ and the accompanying protection offered to each of us as one of his children is an individual decision. Each must, for his own salvation, make the election. The people of this nation collectively must also determine to accept or reject Christ.

The Gadianton societies and secret combinations are seeking for allegiance and are in our midst. The Lord said that this nation rejected the Church, the gospel and Christ, when its inhabitants killed the Lord's anointed. It drove the Church from its borders. Never in the history of the world has a nation survived after it has killed the prophets sent to it. The Lord said the nation would be vexed and must speedily repent. Whether or not the nation repented in the eyes of the Lord, and whether or not it is still vexed, is not the purpose of this discourse. Only the Lord and those to whom he may have revealed it know the answer to the status of this nation before God.

But the statistics of crime, evidence of pride, and corruption in government officials and courts all indicate a decline in the moral status of the inhabitants of this land. Latter-day Saints must therefore stand fast, live in righteousness, publish peace, and trust in the Lord that the sacrifice of individually broken hearts and contrite spirits will allow God to fulfill his promise to them that they need not fear and that they will be preserved in the day when those who will not raise up their sword against their neighbor must flee to Zion for protection. (D & C 46:68)

The Lord has given a glimpse of how this unfortunate situation may manifest itself. Speaking to the Nephites, the Lord stated;

> 10. ... when the Gentiles shall sin against my gospel, [which they presumably did when they killed the prophet and drove the church from its boundaries],
> 11. ... then will I remember my covenant which I have made unto my people, O house of Israel, and I will bring my gospel unto them.
> 12. And I will show unto thee, O house of Israel, that the Gentiles shall not have power over you; but I will remember my covenant unto you, O house of Israel, and ye shall come into the knowledge of the fulness of my gospel....
> 15. But if they [the Gentiles] will not turn unto me, and hearken unto my voice, I will suffer them, yea, I will suffer my people, O house of Israel, that they shall go through among them, and shall tread them down, and they shall be as salt that hath lost its savor, which is thenceforth good for nothing but to be cast out, and to be trodden under foot of my people, O house of Israel. (3 Nephi 16:10-12,15)

Later, the Lord continued,

> 15. And I say unto you, that if the Gentiles do not repent after the blessing which they shall receive, after they have scattered my people—
> 16. Then shall ye, who are a remnant of the house of Jacob, go forth among them; and ye shall be in the midst of them who shall be many; and ye shall be among them as a lion among the beasts of the forest, and as a young lion among the flocks of sheep, who, if he goeth through both treadeth down and teareth in pieces, and none can deliver. (3 Nephi 20:15-16)

If the Gentiles attain that status spoken of here by Christ to the Nephites, then they will become subject to the control and whim of the descendants of the prior inhabitants of this land who will be among them as a lion among lambs. In some parts of our country, we perhaps see the foreshadowing of this prophecy. It is suggested that the descendents of the Lamanites may take over political control of some parts of the nation by simple population increases and organization of voting forces. Statistics indicate that in many Southern

California elementary schools, over half of the students attending are of Lamanite ancestry. Additionally, the families from the Lamanite segment of society are not burdened with the zero-growth philosophy of so many others. Accordingly, families among Lamanite Americans tend to be two or three times larger than their Gentile neighbors. This trend will make that segment of society a powerful political voice in the near future.

However, it is also noted that because of the pressure of some segments of society upon the youth, there tends to be more gangs and other unacceptable activity. This is not to suggest that certain segments of society are more inclined by nature to act outside the bounds of the law, but rather to suggest the possibility that political power among the Lamanite descendents may not be the only means whereby they could be among the Gentiles like a lion among lambs.

Although this nation, considered as a whole, may have rejected the fullness of the gospel, yet many have accepted and continue to accept it. Many repent and turn to Christ. If this land is to be a choice land, if the inhabitants are to perpetuate the liberties they have lost, if they are to sanctify this land for the welfare and blessing of those who inhabit it, if there is to be Zion, it will come to pass only through the efforts, prayers and righteousness of his people. To do so, Latter-day Saints must live such that they are worthy of being instruments in his hands. They must recognize that the Lord's blessings and cursings will and do come in his own due time. They must act as responsible children of God and prepare for the future. They must follow the counsel of the living prophets.

Secret Combinations which Endanger United States Citizens

Studying their actions in the Book of Mormon reveals the methods used by secret combinations. They convince others they have been wronged, they make fair promises, they flatter, and finally, they create anger and teach hate. In today's world, there are several classic secret combinations which follow this pattern. We need only look to see them.

Terrorism

One of Satan's great movements in these latter days is terrorism. It is frightening to people, discouraging to government and almost impossible to fight effectively. Strangely, modern-day terrorism finds its beginnings in the Holy Land. The Palestinian Liberation Organization (PLO) has, for many, become synonymous with terrorism. Despite the current attempts between the PLO and the government of Israel to find peace, their attempts will fail, in part because of terrorist actions.

It is not difficult to understand the frame of mind of the PLO terrorist. To set the stage, a brief review of Middle-East history is necessary. Just prior to World War II, and even during the war, Jewish people attempted to leave Germany and flee to other nations. Some even found passage to the United States. But for the most part, the Christian nations of the western alliance (including the United States) refused passage to these refugees. Most often they were sent back on their boats to the port from which they left—often being sent unknowingly to their deaths.

Speaking with hind-sight, it is no wonder that the Lord, speaking of the latter days, said to Nephi,

> 4. . . . And what thank they the Jews for the Bible which they receive from them? Yea, what do the Gentiles mean? Do they remember the travails, and the labors, and the pains of the Jews, and their diligence unto me, in bringing forth salvation unto the Gentiles?
>
> 5. O ye Gentiles, have ye remembered the Jews, mine ancient covenant people? Nay; but ye have cursed them, and have hated them, and have not sought to recover them. But behold, I will return all these things upon your own heads; for I the Lord have not forgotten my people. (2 Nephi 29:4-5)

Truly, the Jewish nation was and is the source of salvation for the Gentiles, having produced the Bible and having been the nation from whence came the Savior and salvation of mankind, even Jesus Christ. Shortly after World War II, and upon realization that much of the pain, anguish and death delivered to the Jewish nation could have been avoided had Christian nations been willing to accept the fleeing refugees, and undoubtedly in an effort to appease and salve the conscience of a shocked Christian world, a decision was made by world powers to establish a homeland for the Jewish nation. Not surprising to those who study scripture, the decision was made to establish this homeland in Jerusalem, the holy city of three major world religions: the Jews, the Moslems, and the Christians. But in order to do this, the world body needed to move people from their homes, jobs and friends. People living in certain areas of the land given to the Jews were removed so the Jewish nation could move in. Put yourself in their shoes. You have a home, a job and a life one day, and the next, you are uprooted, moved and required to live where you do not want to live. If you are a normal person, you would be upset.

Working on this emotion, it becomes simple to gain control of the mind and will of the people. As we have seen in the Book of Mormon, you first *convince the people that they have been wronged.* It was easy to convince the members of the PLO that they had been wronged. They lost their homes, jobs, friends and had their lives turned upside down.

These negative emotions can also affect other individuals and groups in the U.S. today. Some in the United States become convinced that they have been wronged by the IRS. Others become convinced they have been wronged by society, education, family, environment, crime, employers, superiors, etc. Some become convinced of the need to protect the wrong done to others by protecting the rights of unborn children. Others seek to protect what they perceive as their own right of choice to make certain it is not taken from them. Some believe and teach that women are not given the same opportunity in this nation as men and seek ways to stop males from doing wrong to females. Others believe that society needs to accept homosexuality as inevitable or even desirable, while others view it as unconscionable and against the teachings of God or against society. Some become convinced that the government has become too liberal, too socialized, too communistic, too left, too right, too middle of the road—the list can go on.

In a society which teaches a person to look somewhere other than inward to find and place blame, many find it too easy, too convenient, too desirable to join with others with similar disappointments, trials or experiences, they accept the premise that they have been wronged. Once that premise has been taught, recognized, realized, or believed, it matters not the truth of the claim. If a person comes to believe he or she has been wronged, the next step of the organized forces of Satan, whether from another mortal or from a spirit-spoken temptation, becomes certain.

The Book of Mormon terminology for the next step in the corruption of the individual and the enlistment of their dedication to the forces of evil is found in a concept identified as *flattery*. In this step, the person must be convinced that the wrong he received was not deserved. He becomes convinced that he is better than that. It wasn't his fault because he is great. He is good. Groups encountering such individuals reason that they would be beneficial and helpful (needed) in the group. Their story is great. Their position is powerful, their objective is real and attainable. They are unique. By convincing a person that he is of value to the organization, you convince him to join you. Korihor, though he did not at first believe the things he taught, yet began to teach, and continued until he eventually did believe. Tell people they can do it and they will begin to believe that they can do it, and then they will do it. Flattery, as used by secret combinations, is the act of teaching people to trust in the arm of the flesh, to rely on their own abilities, to act independent of God, to be prideful, and to pursue their justification for the wrong they have received outside the bounds of the law.

Once flattery has had its effect, and an alliance or state of trust has been established, the next step found in the Book of Mormon discussions of secret combinations is *fair promises*. Join the PLO, and together we will retake our homeland. Join our tax rebellion and we will destroy the IRS. Join our organization and tell your story to others. You can be a great leader of a great movement to right the wrong. You have talent, you have power, we can do it, we will do it. Fair promises can be found in politics, drugs, gangs, in almost all secret combinations. "If I'm elected, I'll appoint you as an ambassador, an agency administrator, a counselor, etc." If you do this or that, you can join our group, be one of us, use our name, receive our protection, earn money selling drugs, etc. Mixing flattery and fair promises provides the incentive for the frustrated individual to vent his or her emotional dissatisfaction and profit from it too.

And finally, you stir up their *anger* and *hatred* to the point that they are willing to do whatsoever thing you request of them, even to the point of becoming a human bomb. Persuasive arguments include clauses like, "Don't you just hate the IRS, the Israelis, the government, the president, the supreme court, the congress, the gangs, the abortionists, the doctors who perform abortions, the people who have abortions, the people who block access to abortion clinics, the communist form of government, the socialists, OSHA, the post office, your boss, etc." Remove the word hate from your vocabulary. It gives rise to emotion which is not of God. Observe from the foregoing, that secret combinations can arise on the left and the right and from the middle. Satan can work against all angles and all people, all societies, all philosophies and all concepts. He can use strong emotion to persuade, lead and then bind the hearts, thoughts, emotions and actions of the children of men. And secret combinations cannot be limited to the left—or to the right. Secret combinations can be in our midst having the purpose of attacking evil. But by using the tools of Satan, the movement must fail. Evil against itself will fail. And if we are associated, we too will fail.

Terrorism from both the left and the right carries with it the classic secret-combination elements which allow Satan and his servants to exercise control over others. Perhaps the most frightening element of terrorism is its threat and damage to the innocent. There is no way to conduct life without being exposed to the danger of terrorist activities. Terrorists strike out at women and children in pursuit of normal day- to-day activities. In the Holy Land, terrorists continue to bomb busses, buildings, and public places and injure and kill innocent people to extract an eye-for-an-eye philosophy.

In this land, we too appear to be vulnerable to acts of terrorism. And while we are taking action to protect the public against these violent actions of desperate, undisciplined and morals-void misfits, the battle will be difficult. It may cost some of the best and most cherished freedoms we enjoy before it is over.

In response to the terrorist-type bombing of the Federal building in Oklahoma City and the similar but unrelated bombing in New York, the nation forms new agencies designed to identify, resist and frustrate anti-American organizations before other bombings take place. Government begins to examine and hold suspect any organization which holds philosophy different from that of the prevailing parties. Some consider it un- American to own a gun, voice a complaint, organize a political voice or otherwise threaten the status quo. Para-military organizations who teach members to survive against superior forces, shoot a gun or survive in the wilderness are portrayed as threats to the American peace and tranquility we have all come to appreciate.

Perhaps it is possible to over-react to danger by elimination of freedoms. Citizen response is demanded to restrict movement and activity in order to protect the innocent. But citizens and saints must also recognize that once these freedoms become lost, pursuant to J. Rueben Clark's statement, the freedoms cannot be regained without loss of blood. We must act cautiously when rights and privileges guaranteed by the Constitution are threatened.

We protect schools, state and federal buildings, court houses, airports and other public places with metal detectors to deter destructive activities which could kill innocent people. All around us are growing evidences that America may become a nation under siege.

This once-proud nation, thought to be impregnable to terrorism, is now a place feared by many in the world. Tourists fear to come to Florida because of the wanton and senseless murders of innocent people. They fear to come to California because of freeway shootings, riots and gangs. The United States of America, once considered by the rest of the world to be safe, is now perceived by many from the outside to be a land full of problems, lawlessness and disorder—a land where crime reigns. Internally great problems exist. Riots occur all across the nation because of a controversial trial verdict. Bombings by the uni-bomber are threatened and we shut down mail systems, airports and other means of public service. One cannot say that terrorism is not a factor in the life of the average American citizen. Indeed, this nation is perhaps more vulnerable to terrorism than a police state.

But actions to protect citizens, if too overbearing, may also backfire on Constitutionally guaranteed rights. Fear in the heart of man will make him give up rights which he would be unwilling to even consider giving up under normal circumstances. Thus, some seek to limit the possession of arms.

Government force is used to subdue elements of society which the government views as a danger.

In Idaho and Texas, disasters occur as government actions come into question. In these actions, which have as their objective the protection of the innocent, some innocent people are destroyed. In Los Angeles, cultural differences rise to the point of senseless riots. And in Oklahoma and New York, we see havoc wrought as individuals seek and accomplish terrorist actions allegedly against a government viewed by them as overbearing.

But like all terrorist acts, their actions are against innocent victims. Their bombs destroy innocent lives, and they give the government more reason to infringe upon the basic rights of others in an effort to crack down on evil and uncontrollable activities. In reality, terrorism may become a greater and increasing problem in this nation as economic and political conditions continue to deteriorate. If the vexation of the nation declared by the Father continues, as the nation and its people fall victim to temptations, as secret combinations directly attack the Kingdom of God, we will see an increase in those activities thought by many to be inevitable in this land.

Organized Crime

Perhaps the most familiar organized crime syndicate would be the mafia. This criminal organization is designed to produce power and wealth for its members. During Prohibition, the mafia attempted to control boot liquor, prostitution, pornography, and drugs. Today, they have expanded their operations to include legitimate business, banking, and manufacturing industries as well as most other areas of commerce, investment and exchange.

The financial power held by those participating in organized crime can hardly be imagined. After a five-year internal study of the Untied States CIA, FBI and DEA, and their fight against drugs, the following was determined, as reported in a book by James Mills:

> The inhabitants of the earth spend more money on illegal drugs than they spend on food. More than they spend on housing, clothes, education, medical care or any other product or service. The international narcotics industry is the largest growth industry in the world. Its annual revenues exceed half a trillion dollars—three times the value of all United States currency in circulation, more than the gross national product of all but a half dozen of the major industrialized nations. To imagine the immensity of such wealth, consider this: a million dollars in gold would weigh as much as a large man. A half-trillion dollars would weigh more than the entire population of Washington, D.C.
>
> Narcotics industry profits, secretly stockpiled in countries competing for the business, draw interest exceeding $3 million per hour. To what use will this money eventually be put? What will be its ultimate effect?[13]

In the documented work completed by Mr. Mills, he concluded and showed detailed evidence that the existence of the *Underground Empire* involved diplomats, statesmen, global politics and crime, that everything and anything could be bought for cash, including lives, armies and even the governments of nations. Sounds a lot like Satan's comment to Heavenly messengers in another time, doesn't it!

The term "Mafia" originally applied to Sicily, Italy. But it now also equally applies to secret organizations in Asia, North America, South America, Central America and European nations. They do, in fact, cover the whole earth, and are present in every nation, tongue and people.

Organized crime affects local, state and federal governments, politicians, businessmen, policemen, lawyers, judges, diplomats, and normal citizens. In fact, none are exempt from the far-reaching effects of organized crime. Even our monetary system is threatened as recent reports indicate that outside of this nation there exists effective organizations producing literally billions of dollars of counterfeit American dollars.

Truly, organized crime is a vehicle which helps fulfill Satan's intent to control people's lives and to destroy the souls and happiness of men, thus making them miserable like unto himself. By teaching people how to gain power and wealth in this life, he makes them his servants and entices them to place their quest for more wealth and power above all other considerations. He binds them with his chains from whence there may be no delivery without the most difficult repentance steps possible.

Gangs

In previous decades gangs were only a large-city problem, but gangs have now spread to every part of our society and culture. They are growing greatly in power and influence. The southern California city in which the author lives was free from destructive gang infestation for decades. Though there were two local gangs, they were relatively quiet, non-violent and all but unnoticed. That is, they were so until 1992. In that year, the situation rapidly began to change. So fast and dramatic was the change that in mid 1993 at a city council meeting, it was reported that there were then thirteen gangs, an increase of 11 gangs in only one and one-half years. But that was only part of the problem. In the preceding six-month period (the first 6 months of 1993), the local police department had arrested gang members from over 100 different gangs who had come to this town from other towns to either recruit or fight local gang units!

Unfortunately, this gang warfare is not limited to members of the gangs. Innocent bystanders are often injured or killed because they are in the wrong place at the wrong time and become statistics of the uncontrolled violence.

A client told of how he and his wife had fled the state of California to the East Coast. He is not a Church member, but like many in California looked for and found a safer haven. He told of his son who owns and runs a laundromat in a suburb of L.A. One night, this client had a distinct feeling that he should go help his son close up the business. Six weeks earlier, the son had been robbed at gunpoint while closing, and had thereafter purchased his own gun as had his father. The father, upon arriving at the laundromat, found everything in proper order. Upon completion of the closing activities, the father walked out the front to his car while the son went to close up the back. As the son was approaching the front door of the laundromat, a pickup truck sped around the corner. The father was at this time near his own car in the parking lot, but properly perceived the truck's activities to be a danger sign. The truck screeched to a halt in front of the laundromat between the father and the front of the building. A boy in the back opened fire with an automatic weapon, firing into the laundromat and shattering the front windows, glass and doors. The son dropped to the floor as bullets sprayed around him. Seeing this horror, the father pulled out his own gun and began shooting at the person in the back of the truck. Startled, the criminal jumped from the back of the truck, sprayed bullets at the father, and ran down the alley, all the time shooting back at the father, who in turn emptied his own gun at the fleeing figure. The father, not knowing if his son was dead or alive, held the truck driver at gunpoint until the police arrived. Miraculously, the son was uninjured. However, several hours later, the police picked up the criminal who had fled. He was found at a local hospital and had been admitted for treatment of two gunshot wounds, one in his thigh and one in his hand. He was a member of a local gang who, for initiation purposes, had to prove himself by committing a criminal act planned by his superiors. As unnerving and terrible as this experience was, it was what followed which convinced the Father that he had to sell his home, his business, his rental units and move to a rural town in the East. Shortly after the shooting, threats, drive-by shootings, and similar aggressions against the family became a part of his everyday life as the gang evidently swore vengeance and revenge against the man and his family. The police told him they could not protect him 24 hours a day, so he packed up his family and left!

Many gangs require oaths and covenants, have secret passwords and pledges and operate as micro Gadianton Societies. It is probable that they will be as powerful, or perhaps even more powerful, than local resistance factors if government continues to decay and becomes less and less able to stem the tide. The newspapers are full of incidents where innocent people are caught in the violence and carnage. It will surely get worse before it gets better unless this people, this nation, returns to a moral base and insists on upholding and teaching Christian morals and principles. If the Book of Mormon is a foreshadowing of what is yet to be, we can expect a breakdown of civil authority and an increase in the localized power and effect of these gangs.

Some frightening statistics have evolved over the last decade which indicate that youth in our inner-cities are having an increasingly difficult time in just surviving. In past generations, most violent crimes, and especially murders, were traceable to associations or relationships. However, in the last several years that trend has reversed itself. The department of justice states that what it terms *stranger murders* are now four times as common as family killings. The preceding statistic, and those which follow are found in an article by Adam Walinsky printed in the Atlantic Monthly. In this report, the author points out that in the 1960s the United States as a whole had 3.3 police officers for every violent crime reported per year. However by 1993, the trend had almost exactly reversed itself indicating that there were 3.47 violent crimes per officer per year. In essence, today's police officers must deal with ten times more violent crimes than his predecessor. Facts indicate that the person committing the stranger murder has less than a 20% chance of being caught.[14]

The stranger murders referenced above would include random gang murders, murders of strangers committed in robberies, and similar acts of violence. The need for money to pay for drugs, other habits, and initiation rites into some gangs would constitute the reason for a great number of these stranger murders. But the article goes on to indicate some other concerning statistics.

Over the last decade, there have been over 200,000 murders in the United States, and millions have been wounded. By comparison, ten years of Vietnam war killed 58,000 Americans. Accordingly, over the last 10 years, we have had the equivalent of 3 and 1/2 Vietnam war casualties in these United States. But where is the protest? Where is the cry to end the slaughter? Where are the marching crowds and the demand for safety of our children? The author, Adam Walinsky states;

> Several years ago, the Department of Justice estimated that 83% of all Americans would be victims of violent crime at least once in their lives. About a quarter would be victims of three or more violent crimes. Statistics indicate that we are moving steadily toward fulfillment of that prediction."[15]

In seeking for the cause of these unacceptable statistics, the same author declares,

> For more than twenty years, the children of the ghetto have witnessed violent death as an almost routine occurrence. They have seen it on their streets, in their schools, in their families and on TV. They have lived with constant fear, many have come to believe that they will not live to see twenty-five. These are often children whose older brothers, friends, and uncles have taught them that only the strong and the ruthless survive. Prison does not frighten them—it is a rite of passage that a majority of their peers may have experienced. Too many have learned to kill without remorse, for a drug territory or for an insult, because of a look or a bump on the sidewalk, or just to do it: why not?
>
> These young people have been raised in the glare of ceaseless media violence and incitement to every depravity of act and spirit. Movies may feature scores of killings in two hours time, vying to show methods ever more horrific; many are quickly imitated on the street. Television commercials teach that a young man requires a new pair of $120 sneakers each week. Major corporations make and sell records exhorting their listeners to brutalize Koreans, rob store owners, rape women, kill the police. Ashamed and guilt-ridden, elite opinion often encourages even hoodlums to carry a sense of entitlement and grievance against society and its institutions.[16]

Thus, the secret combinations of today attack the people of this nation in an attempt to discredit justice, encourage rebellion, exercise control, justify lawlessness and eventually attack the members of the Kingdom of God on the earth.

Corrupt Politicians

Many today are weary of politicians and their actions and behaviors. It is as though the day when the politician was concerned about his constituents is now long past and we have entered an era when the motivating factors for elected representatives are perks, retirement plans, salaries and similar self-interest concepts.

Many American citizens believe the elected representatives at all levels of government are selling us out to foreign money powers. They feel that elected representatives and appointed officers often work together for the benefit of themselves and to the detriment of the people.

It is indeed frightening to have improper behavior by elected individuals revealed. Some of this behavior would place the normal citizen in jail. This above-the-law attitude of some elected representatives is both shameful and dangerous. It is possible that some elected officials consider themselves an elite class, a ruling sector, benefactors of society rather than our civil servants.

This section will not deeper engage in study of the actions, attributes or intents of politicians. We will simply conclude that there is great danger resulting from apparent behavior indicating a transformation of the politicians from the public servant to the public dictator, a shift from a republic to a democracy.

The founding fathers never intended that we be a democracy. The difference must be examined.

Through the years, debate has been made as to whether the United States is a democracy, a republic, or some hybrid thereof.

The democracy government is a system where man is sovereign, the people elect a governing body, and the power of the government rests in that governing body which then makes laws for the people.

The republic form of government is wherein the power to make and/or change law is vested in the individual people. In a true republic, the voice of each man and woman is registered on an issue. In an expanded republic, an elected representative represents the position of those who elected him or her. Here, the actions of the elected representatives are determined by a Constitution.

At first glance, it may appear that there is no significant difference between the two above defined forms of administration. In each, elected officials govern and make laws. However, in the democracy, once elected, the official has the opportunity to make law without regard to the constituency. The governing body is directly empowered to make laws and enforce them. The danger is that the elected officials adopt the attitude that the general public lacks the sophistication and intelligence to make decisions, and therefore the elected representative will exercise his "significantly better" judgment. In contrast, in the republic, only the people have that right, and the elected representative is only expressing the will of the people.

America is a republic gone bad. We are a republic of the people, by the people, and for the people, who have allowed the Congress and other elected officials to consider themselves in a democracy where their voice becomes sovereign. They therefore determine what is best for us, assuming that we cannot know ourselves.

In a democracy, the voice of the people becomes secondary in importance to that of the elected officials. We, in effect, create a ruling class who make laws which can and will affect us—laws concerning which we have no voice and no active role because they have been made by the Congress in their assumed power as our lawmakers. Many congressmen and congresswomen in our current bodies of congress have assumed this position. The problem is that they have assumed power which was never theirs to assume. They have forgotten that America is a republic and that their role is to represent the citizens within the laws and guidelines of the Constitution. Their's is the obligation to be responsive to the citizens demand and desires. Accordingly citizens must restructure their thought processes and help the politicians realize that they are only to be representative of the voter's view. Though to some, the distinction is small and perhaps even esoteric or argumentative only, to anyone giving this serious thought, the distinction is paramount.

Elected representatives must know that they must not listen to nor heed the voice of the Council on Foreign Relations, the Tri-Lateral Commission, the United Nations, the Federal Reserve Board, the International Monetary Fund, or other foreign or domestic parties and interests when those voices go contrary to the traditional American values and constitutional rights of the people. We, the people, are the ones they must represent and the voice they must follow.

Today the battle continues. It is raging in our midst and sadly, too many are unaware of its existence. It is the eternal battle between good and bad. It is the battle fought by our forefathers as they sought independence and self rule. It is the battle fought by nations, kingdoms, families, and individuals throughout all time. It is the battle to retain and secure those unalienable, God-given rights and privileges embodied in the inspired constitution of these United States of America.

Citizens have within their reach the tools, the power, and the ability to stop the progress of the enemy. The enemy depends upon apathy. It depends upon inactivity. It depends upon the past behavior of Americans to simply take all it has to offer while citizens are striving to make ends meet on a day-to-day basis. It builds and strengthens and binds its web of deceit and misrepresentation until in the end, if Americans do not awake, it will bind them to its philosophies. It will entrench its teachings upon the hearts and minds of youth, and it will bring to an end the great and honorable history of this nation's existence.

To preserve American heritage for future generations, modern-day inspired men have shown us the foundation upon which we must form. For instance, Ezra Taft Benson has taught,

> I have seen this great nation decline spiritually. What happens to a nation collectively is but the result of its citizenry departing from the fundamental spiritual and economic laws of God: making the Sabbath day a day of pleasure; individuals and businesses giving license to immorality; and politicians dignifying the coveting of others' possessions and property by stating, "We will take from the haves and give to the have nots." At first we resisted this philosophy; then

consented; next, demanded; and now have legislated. Politically, we licensed coveting what others had earned![17]

And again,

If Americans should ever come to believe that their rights and freedoms are instituted among men by politicians and bureaucrats, they will no longer carry the proud inheritance of their forefathers, but will grovel before their masters seeking favors and dispensations—a throwback to the feudal system of the Dark Ages.[18]

Political Organizations

Many organizations have been identified by one or more sources as organizations sympathetic with or at least unopposed to the one-world-government concepts. Among those so identified are the Council on Foreign Relations, the Royal Institute of International Affairs, the Trilateral Commission, the Dartmouth Conference, the Aspen Institute, the Humanistic Studies, the Atlantic Institute, the United Nations, the League of Nations, NATO, and the Bilderberg Group.

Admiral Chester Ward stated,

The C.F.R. [Council of Foreign Relations] goal is the submergence of U.S., sovereignty and national independence into an all-powerful one world government . . . The lust to surrender the sovereignty of the United States is pervasive throughout most of the membership.[19]

Senator Jesse Helms commented,

Private organizations, such as the Council on Foreign Relations, the Royal Institute of International Affairs, the Trilateral Commission, the Dartmouth Conference the Aspen Institute, the Humanistic Studies, the Atlantic Institute, and the Bilderberg Group, serve to disseminate and to coordinate the plans for this so-called New World Order in powerful financial academic and official circles.[20]

Author John E. McManus declared,

If we look back at that which the Trilateral Commission seeks, as stated . . . it becomes obvious that the commission's strategy is to create a world monetary system . . . leading to a world government.[21]

Senator Barry Goldwater said,

In my view, the Trilateral Commission represents a skillful, coordinated effort to seize control and consolidate the four centers of power—political, monetary, intellectual and ecclesiastical. What the Trilateralists truly intend is the creation of a worldwide economic power.[22]

And Pat Robertson wrote,

> The American delegation to the U.N. included C.F.R. members . . . In all, the Council sent forty-seven of its members in the U.S. Delegation, in effect controlling the outcome and substance of the [United Nations] charter.[23]

If it is true that these organizations are spearheading, supporting, or even sympathetic to the one-world philosophy, then it follows that they are not supportive of the American Constitution. They cannot support and uphold the Constitution and at the same time support, sustain, participate in or be a member of an organization which has as its objective either the overthrow of the Constitution or the infringement of the sovereignty of this nation by subjecting it to the control of one-world advocates.

The examination of any one of these organizations, its tenants, its purposes, platforms or structure is beyond the scope of this book. However, many studies exist to assist one in this understanding. There are also available to the serious student, sources of information disclosing who in our government structure is associated with one or more of these organizations. This may be helpful in identifying if local representatives are supportive of their oath and of the Constitution.

7
SECRET COMBINATIONS AND MONEY IN THE UNITED STATES

Money

Money is the means whereby the church builds visitor's centers, chapels, and temples. It is the method whereby missionaries are supported throughout the world. It is the means whereby many families form organizations which seek after their departed ancestors so their temple work can be accomplished. Money is the means whereby members invoke the blessings of the Lord by paying tithing, fast offerings and other offerings. Money is the source of homes, food, education and day-to-day living needs of individuals and families. It is the reward for a day's labor. Such a commodity can hardly be evil.

However, "The love of money is the root of all evil." (1 Timothy 6:10) When money becomes the goal, the objective, the love, the religion, the god of people, then they tend to stop at nothing to acquire it. Some people commit crimes, engage in unfair business practices, lie, cheat, and otherwise commit their souls to the attainment of money. When the love of money has consumed one's soul, replaced the true God and interrupted man's desire to do good to all other men, he is captured by the chains of hell from which it becomes difficult indeed to escape.

Many sell their talents for money despite obvious harm to mankind. Consider for example the tobacco and advertising industries. In counsels no longer secret, these industries conspired in times past to entice youth to engage in smoking tobacco. Millions of dollars have been involved. Millions have gone to the advertising agencies. One must ask if there is no ethical responsibility and duty in the advertising industry. Have they "sold their talents" for filthy lucre? With current statistics indicating that in the United States alone, over 400,000 people die each year from tobacco use, is it not probable that the advertising industry and the tobacco industry have conspired together as a secret combination to destroy the children of men? Is not the conspiracy world-wide as tobacco is used even more extensively in Europe and Asia? With world-wide deaths caused by the tobacco grown in the United States well in excess of 1,000,000 per year, how can such actions be justified? In the United States, we are taking significant steps to curtail tobacco use by minors. The justification which Congress and others utilize for continuation of the industry is that of money. It is for money that the tobacco industry conspires to addict men and women. It is for money that the advertising industry agrees to conspire with the tobacco industry to convince youth to become lifetime users of tobacco. And it is for money that the Congress turns it's head and ignores the death, destruction, health crisis and damage done by the tobacco industry.

In the United States today, we are constantly concerned about money. The media has a never-ending stream of news stories about finances. The federal government is voicing increasing desire to stop deficit spending in the United States. Local city, county and state governments struggle to stay out of bankruptcy. Business is constantly concerned about the cost of money for new factories and improved production and distribution of its products and services. Individuals and families strive to have more income than outgo of money. It is indeed a great cause of concern for everyone.

Speaking of just the deficit-spending patterns of our federal government since World War II, one can become equally concerned with government voices about the monetary status of the United States. Our current government debt is approximately five and one-half trillion dollars. Most people have no concept about how much debt this really is. However, the following illustration can perhaps assist to envision the extent of the United States debt. If you had a stack of one million dollars in one thousand dollar bills, your stack would be approximately four *inches* high. A trillion dollars is thousand dollar bills stacked sixty-three *miles* high. Our national debt then would be a stack of thousand dollar bills nearly 346 miles high! The problem with this debt is that each of us must pay interest on this debt. Thus, an increasing percentage of the taxes we pay each year goes to pay the interest on this national debt. Economists warn that in the not-to-distant future, the interest will be so much that the government will be unable to collect enough taxes to pay the interest. So, some congressmen have been seeking to stop the deficit spending patterns of the U.S. Government, attempting to balance the budget. Time will tell if the pressures of society's demands on the government will yield to the pressures of balanced budget spending.

Types of Money

Money today can be identified in several different forms: commodity money, credit money, paper money, coin money and fiat money.

The most secure of these measures of money is *commodity money*. In this form of money, the instrument of exchange is valued according to its intrinsic worth. Thus, gold, silver, copper, and other precious metals are considered commodity money. Additionally, diamonds, gemstones and similar stones of beauty and rarity can be used as money, though there is often more difficulty in determining the actual value of these types of money. The gold and silver coins that circulated in the U.S. before 1933 were examples of commodity money. The founding fathers specified in the Constitution that only the Congress could determine the weights and values for the commodity money.[1]

Credit money is essentially a promise by the person or government or bank issuing the credit, to pay to the holder of the credit money an amount of commodity money in exchange for the credit money. Credit money in the United States became popular as a medium of exchange when we developed the silver certificates. The credit paper money was backed by the gold (and silver) in Fort Knox and other private or government institutions, and by a promise of the government that it could and would, upon demand, redeem all outstanding credit money for real gold or silver from its vaults. Thus, the credit or paper money became a step to an even easier way to transport funds, engage in commerce, pay for goods and otherwise function in our society. It proved to be much lighter than commodity money, could be transported more easily, and could be issued in various denominations to facilitate small, medium and very large transactions.

Credit money eventually evolved into *fiat money*. Fiat money is money issued by a government which is not redeemable for commodity money. Rather, the value of fiat money is that value established by the issuing government. Thus, without having the necessity to have real commodity money to back the value of the fiat money, a government can issue fiat money to pay for expenses like war, social problems, government officers and employees, and other purposes. This fiat money concept first appeared in our nation during the Civil War. The federal reserve note we use today is fiat money. Additionally, most coins being used for exchange purposes today would be considered fiat money as the intrinsic value of the coin is substantially less than the face value of the coin.

As a general rule, fiat money becomes a medium of exchange when a government decrees that the fiat money is to be accepted and used by its constituents. Thus, the dollar bill issued by the Federal Reserve carries the words "This note is legal tender for all debts, public and private." Generally speaking, if the money is issued in amounts corresponding with the intake of the government, then it holds its value. But when the government issues amounts in excess of what it collects, it incurs deficit spending and the fiat money declines in value. It is this action by government which causes inflation and instability. Somewhat ironically, it is this axiom which allows the government (or the entity controlling the fiat money) to control, manipulate and otherwise interfere with the economy of a free nation.

The United States government used commodity money (gold) to measure the value of its currency until the early 20th century. In 1933, the United States abandoned the use of the gold standard as the basis of its currency. Great Britain abandoned the gold-bullion standard for its pound in 1931.

To some, it is of great importance that most monetary systems used throughout the world today are fiat money systems established by various governments. It was initially thought by economists that fiat money could remain stable over long periods of time. However, as we have witnessed in the United States, fiat money becomes unstable when the government engages in deficit spending. Without intrinsic value, money becomes worth whatever the market perceives its interest-earning power will bring. Today, fiat money is all debt. The reason the dollar bill is considered a "note," as it states on its face, is because somebody borrowed the money from a bank. The borrower may have been the government, a business, or an individual seeking to buy a home, car, or other commodity. But all fiat money can be traced back to someone or some entity borrowing money. The money is loaned by the federal banking system, today identified in the United States as the Federal Reserve System.

Money and the Federal Reserve System

Money changed dramatically with the introduction of the Federal Reserve Act of 1913. Challenged by many today as a calculated and deceptive act of international monetary forces, the Federal Reserve Act became the basis for money in the United States. The Federal Reserve Act established twelve regional banks. Member banks are able to receive money from the Federal Reserve Bank in two basic ways: They may draw on their deposits with the FED, or they may borrow money (Federal Reserve Notes). These notes are not redeemable for commodity (gold or silver).

The Depression of the 1930s

With the coming of the depression in the 1930s, hundreds of banks failed. This bank failure opened the way for the political powers at that time to eventually eliminate the gold standard. Accordingly, in 1933, gold imports and exports by government entities became illegal. In 1934, the country adopted a significantly different gold standard wherein the devalued dollar made gold worth only 50-60 percent of its value under the 1900 act. Also in

1934, all silver, with the exception of certain coins, fabricated silver and silver owned by foreign governments, was ordered to be delivered to the government for coinage. Much silver was purchased from foreign governments and silver producers. This action raised the price of silver abroad.

Recent Developments

The next most significant development was probably the conference held in New Hampshire near the end of World War II. At this meeting, the International Monetary Fund (IMF) was established. The intent was to stabilize world money markets. The U.S. dollar played a key roll in that it became, in effect, the world's currency, with all other currencies being measured in their relation to the dollar. The U.S. agreed to convert all dollars held by foreign governments into gold on demand and at the exchange rate agreed on at the time of the establishment of the IMF.

Officially, this meant that the world was on a gold exchange standard since governments could change their currencies into gold via the U.S. dollar.

This program worked well while the majority of the world's gold was housed in the United States. However, eventually foreign governments gained in their possession of gold and the system began to fail. By the early 1970s, foreign interests held over five times more gold than the U.S. Finally, in 1971, the U.S. stated that we would no more exchange gold for U.S. currency. With this move, the U.S. dollar was officially removed from any support of gold or silver. We now have a financially managed system with no metallic base. As citizens, therefore, we can hold, sell and otherwise participate in gold and silver to the same extent we can with other commodities.

In 1980, the Federal Reserve elected to restructure its measurement of the money supply. It set up five categories of money measurement identified as M-1A, M-1B, M-2, M-3 and L. These measure and reflect the extent money instruments work for different purposes. M-1A is the best known and measures the currency in existence and demand deposits.

Deregulation of interest rates also was instituted in 1990, and allowed banks and others to eliminate interest ceilings. It also made all banks subject to the minimum reserve requirements as established from time to time by the Federal Reserve Board.

The following statement summarizes the current status of money in the United States:

> Recent experience with policy and legislation shows that the U.S. monetary system is still evolving. Historically, the nation has gone from a wholly metallic system, when coins were the primary money in circulation, to a managed system, in which, aside from the currency in people's pockets, most of the money consists

of entries in the books of banks. At the close of 1990 only about 30 percent of the primary money supply consisted of currency; the remaining 70 percent of total M-1 consisted of demand and other deposits, much of which came into existence through borrowing. In the continuing evolution, as more money is exchanged and transferred electronically, the U.S. money supply will increasingly be represented by entries in computer data banks.[2]

Thus, given the wide definition of money by the world today, the Federal Reserve Notes we all carry in our pockets are money. However, the real commodity money, gold or silver is not recognized by our government as money. One might well wonder what has happened to the world's supply of silver and gold. Interestingly, there have been some economic trends which show where most of the gold has gone.

The gold standard, once established by the IMF, allowed foreign countries to exchange their U.S. federal reserve notes for gold. A United States citizen could not exchange his notes for gold, but a foreign government could. As a result, the gold flowed from this nation to foreign nations. Indications are that the majority of the gold has flowed to nations like Israel and Germany. Perhaps there will be a resurgence of the value of gold as we move closer and closer to a world currency. If so, the United States will be found virtually bankrupt, having almost no gold or silver while some other governments will fare quite well under such a move. Should we move to an international monetary standard other than the Federal Reserve Note produced by this country, the United States would suffer greatly.

If the United States dollar can be brought to a lowered status on the world market, this collapse could occur. It could occur as the result of our inability to bring government spending under control. If we cannot control our spending, and all our income is spent on interest, inflation and devaluation of the dollar's value is inevitable. Accordingly, some other medium will need to be adopted by the world (IMF) to stand as the basis for world-wide exchange. Secret combinations at work today could well have as one of their objectives the destruction of the United States economy and the strength of the dollar.

Banking

The banking concept is ages old. It began in medieval times when a group of religious soldiers identified as Knights templars guarded riches, loaned money and protected transfers of money between countries. The first modern-concept bank originated in 1694 with the Bank of England. The Bank of England became the financial engine which allowed the King to wage war with gold he did not own. The king gave a charter to the bank allowing it to collect gold and issue paper certificates evidencing the citizen's deposit. The bank promised to return the depositor's gold upon demand with interest. Depositing gold with the bank in exchange for redeemable certificates allowed the English citizens to increase the value of their earthly treasures by earning interest on their funds. The bank then loaned the gold to the crown at an interest rate higher than it paid to its depositors. Eventually, people wanted their gold back only to find that the gold had been loaned to the crown and that there was inadequate gold left in the Bank of England. The king then simply revoked the rule requiring the bank to redeem the certificates. Thus, the gold was transferred from the citizens to the crown. This worked so well for England that the other countries in Europe quickly followed the example.

Today, just as with the Bank of England, there is far more held in deposit than there exists currency to redeem the deposits. And additionally, as stated before, there exists no commodity support for the certificates. This over-extension of cash allows the bank to make loans with money it does not have. It allows the government to spend money it cannot repay. It allows the FED to control the money policies and, to some extent, the economy of the United States. Through this mechanism, inflation is established. The ability of the FED to create money allows business to borrow, consumers to purchase and government to spend more than they could otherwise justify based on income. Thus, credit becomes the financing tool which allows the economy to progress.

Today, U.S. Banks have become pawns of a much-larger organization, the Federal Reserve System. Having lost their independence, they have become subject to the terms, policies, rates, and discretions of the larger power which governs their existence. They could play an important role in any effort to undermine U.S. financial policies and to move the United States toward a one-world financial system.

Federal Reserve System

The Federal Reserve System is comprised of twelve banks and a central controlling committee known as the Federal Reserve Board. The Federal Reserve System is responsible for issuing our national currency, regulating our monetary policy and in many ways supervising the banks of this nation. This nation refers to the Federal Reserve System as simply the FED.

The operation of the FED is complex and mostly unknown to the general public, but its power is not questioned. For example, in the very important area of regulation of money in the United States, the FED is independent of government interference and operates at its own direction to control the availability of credit and money.

The income and expenses of the FED and its twelve banks are not subject to review by Congress. In fact, in the history of the FED, they have never been audited. The FED receives no money from the United States. It is self-financing. It makes literally billions of dollars each year from income-earning securities and from the U.S. government.

FED History

The argument allowing for implementation of the Federal Reserve System originates from the standpoint that prior to the system, the monetary policies of the United States were unable to cope with or otherwise adopt to the changing economies and trends of this nation and the world. Accordingly, while the nation was on the gold or silver standards, recurring economic collapses occurred followed by economic growth and then recurring cycles. The argument was that the U.S. banking system was unable to cope with these inflation/deflation cycles. There needed to be a more stable source and system which could adopt to economic cycles without collapse and without international robbing of the support base of our nation through exchange of our certificates for gold by foreign nations. The Federal Reserve Act of 1913 established the Federal Reserve System which began operation in 1914. The concept sold to the citizens, then and now, is that the FED is necessary to bring financial stability to this nation. History indicates strongly that the FED's action in this area has been disappointing at best.

FED Structure

The 12 district Reserve banks are located in Boston, New York, Philadelphia, Cleveland, Richmond, Atlanta, Chicago, St. Louis, Minneapolis, Kansas City, Dallas, and San Francisco. Each bank is administered by a board of directors. Each board of directors consists of nine members, six of whom are elected by member banks (and are known as class A and B), and three which are appointed by the Federal Reserve Board. These directors approve banking discount rates (the rate the district bank will charge member banks for funds loaned to the member banks). This discount rate is allegedly set at the local level, but the Board of Governors (Federal Reserve Board) in Washington, D.C. is the real source of the discount rate and can override all district bank decisions.

The Federal Reserve Board is the head of the Federal Reserve System. The Board consists of a total of seven members, five of whom are appointed by the Office of the President of the United States. No two can be from the same banking district. The additional two members are the Secretary of the Treasury and the Comptroller of the Currency. The term of office for the five appointed members, while initially set at ten years, was later changed to fourteen years. The long terms were designed to be a safeguard against political influence, thus allowing the FED to be independent. Consider that this independence also allows them to be independent of the American voter, the ultimate voice of authority in this nation. This raises the questions, "What control does the FED have over us?", and "If the government does not control the FED, and the American Voter does not control the FED, who does?"

Monetary Control

The answer to the first question is that the FED controls the money supply. This control is administered through the twelve district banks and the member banks in the system. The FED exercises the following controls which affect the economy:

(1) The FED controls the actual amount of money in circulation. If the money supply is growing too rapidly, creating pressure for inflation, the FED can tighten money availability by increasing the discount rate (the amount they charge member banks for borrowing money). As the rate goes up, so does the interest rate the bank must charge. This reduces the ability of the customer to borrow money because the interest rate is higher. On the other hand, if the money supply is growing too slowly, creating the need to spur the economy and eliminate stagnation or recession, the FED can increase the money supply by lowering the discount rate and by purchasing U.S. government securities. This allows creditors to obtain more favorable loan rates and thus expand business with less risk and cost.

(2) The FED can attain similar results by changing the required reserve ratio for its banks. The reserve ratio is the percentage of deposits which the bank must retain in reserve. By increasing the ratio, the bank must retain more funds on deposit, and this allows fewer funds to be available for loans to the public. Likewise, if the ratio is lowered, there are more funds available to loan.

Effects of Federal Reserve Policies

History records that the FED and its policies have increased, not decreased, economic instability. Additionally, small adjustments made by the FED are not productive. Most economists blame the FED for the depression of the 1930s, and almost all agree that while the FED attempts to provide assistance, they have no ability to control or manipulate other economy problems. While the FED attempts to legislate economic well-being, their policies exert control over what the founding fathers felt should be a free economy. Their independence lends credence to challenges and attacks by groups who believe that manipulation of the economy and our money supply are beyond the authorized acts of Congress. This argument takes on additional meaning when analyzed in light of the fact that the Congress has apparently abandoned its Constitutionally required responsibility to administer the financial affairs of the nation. It has not only abandoned it, but has irrevocably assigned it to an entity which it neither controls nor audits, which it neither monitors nor administers. Many feel that Congress has been negligent in following this course of action, and that Congress must reassume its constitutionally mandated duty of administering the money in this nation.

Relations with the Government

Because of the independence granted to the FED, many consider it a violation of the separation of powers provisions of the Constitution. It operates almost as a fourth branch of the U.S. Government, except that unlike the other three, it is free and independent of all of the checks and balances of the system. Based on these factors it is perhaps not so shocking that many call for the elimination of the FED and its money control and power. Many perhaps are correct in suspecting that the origins of the FED were nothing more than underhanded tactics of world financial powers having the ultimate purpose of destroying the financial integrity and power of the United States. The founding fathers rebelled against taxation without representation. Is it not plausible that manipulation of the money and our economy by control of credit in the United States is at least as powerful, if not more so, than taxation? Should not such power be subject to the voice of the people? And then there remains the unanswered question of just how the Congress could create an agency, a regulatory bureau, or an entity by any other name which you might care to classify the FED and then grant it powers which the Congress itself does not possess.

For example, the FED's Board of Governors has tenure for a much longer period of time than is given to any other elected official. The FED operates without having to answer to the Congress, and without being subject to audit. But certainly, the most impressive wrong wrought by Congress in the creation and continued allowance of the FED's existence is its immunity from the American people. We have no voice, no audit, no review, no power to control this creation of Congress. Perhaps the time is long overdue for a complete and exhaustive review of the FED's creation, its record, its purposes and those who actually pull its strings. It is most probable that we would find that the FED is being manipulated by powers beyond those of its Board of Governors.

The preceding analysis of the FED assumes the purpose of its creation was merely to provide for a more stable financial policy for the United States. There is another theory which suggests that its creation was in fact part of a massive money-power plot still ongoing today which has as its eventual outcome the collapse of the United States as a financial world power and the introduction of an international monetary system controlled by identified international bankers. To review this other side of the creation of the FED, we must first look to the history of its creation and the parties involved in its establishment.

Is the FED an Anti-American Secret Combination?

The heart of this growing second theory is that the FED was established to allow the world's most wealthy and influential money powers the ability to monopolize the American dollar.

In a clubhouse in a Georgia State park located on Jekyll Island, Georgia, is a private hunting club house and winter resort formerly owned by J.P. Morgan. On one of the doors to the rooms in this elaborate castle-like building stands a plaque declaring, "In this room, the Federal Reserve System was Created."

The plaque refers to an infamous, and at the time, secret meeting held by seven people in the year 1910. These seven people represented the worlds richest organizations and individuals. Together, it is estimated that the participants in this 1910 meeting represented one-quarter of all of the world's wealth. The result of that meeting was the establishment of the Federal Reserve System, a partnership between the United States Congress as the first party and the national and international money interests as the second party. Many of the participants in this then-secret meeting were competitors in the world of finance. The participants were:

- *Nelson Aldrich*, the Chairman of National Monetary Commission, whose duty it was to recommended to Congress any principles advisable to reform banking;
- *Abraham Andrew*, who was the Assistant Secretary of the United States Treasury;
- *Henry Davidson*, the Senior Partner of the J.P. Morgan Company;
- *Charles D. Norton*, President of J.P. Morgan's First National Bank of New York;
- *Benjamin Strong*, the head of J.P. Morgan's Banker's Trust Company, and who would later be named as the first chairman of the Federal Reserve Board;
- *Frank A. Vanderlip*, the President of National City Bank of New York, the most powerful bank then in existence, and who was also spokesman for William Rockefeller and for the international investment banking house of Kuhn, Loeb & Company; and

- *Paul M. Warburg*, partner in Kuhn, Loeb & Company, a representative of the Rothschild banking dynasty in England and France and brother to Max Warburg who was head of the Warburg banking consortium in Germany and the Netherlands.

Three important aspects of the United States financial setting for the meeting are very important. (1) Money was being shifted toward the West where many new banks were opening. In fact, a majority of deposits in United States domiciled banks were in other than the New York banks. The trend was for more banks and a continued shift of control away from the current money powers. (2) The economy, still based on the gold standard, was growing from internal profits rather than from debt. Profits were being used to expand because it was less costly than paying interest rates. Gold, because of its rarity, provided a too-limited source of allowing debt to operate as the medium of growth. (3) Banks were failing, which would cause the public to lose confidence in the banking system. The bank failures were the result of the individual bank's ability to lend more than it held in deposits, causing the potential for runs on the bank.

The simple answer to these problems was to create a Central Bank such as that housed in many European countries. However, the American people were against any type of a monopoly as anti-productive under our free enterprise system. Therefore, the participants agreed that their creation must not appear as an agreement among competitors. Accordingly, the men at Jekyll Island needed to come up with a plan which would stop the loss of control over the deposit money, eliminate the appeal of using profits rather than debt as the basis for business and industry growth, eliminate the reliance on gold or silver as the basis for issuing credit, and find a way to assure that the American people would accept the new concept.

The answer was the Federal Reserve System. This name is appropriately deceptive from the viewpoint that the activities of the organization mislead the American public.

The term "Federal" incorrectly implies that there is government control and monitoring as well as responsibility by government entities. In fact, the Federal Reserve System is exempt from government control, its officers are beyond voter reach, and the organization is in fact private, not public.

The term "Reserve" implies that there are reserves to back up and support the value of the notes issued by the Federal Reserve System. In fact, there are no reserves, never were, and never will be. The public has been mislead to believe that the federal reserve note has the same credibility as the silver certificate or the $20 gold piece.

The term "System" indicates that the banks in the West, South, North and East are all participants in the process and that the benefits are the same to all citizens. In fact, this may be the only truth associated with the name as the system is now in control of all financial transactions in the United States.

The parties at this meeting were competitors. One might wonder how you get competitors together to discuss a system which would eliminate the competition between them. The first requirement is that any such meeting must be kept secret. In the United States, a money monopoly would be illegal. Accordingly, the meeting had to be kept secret, as one of the purposes and desired outcomes of the meeting was to establish a plan whereby money could be monopolized. In later writings by one of the participants in the marathon meeting, Frank Vanderlip, the following appears:

> Despite my views about the value to society of greater publicity for the affairs of corporations, there was an occasion, near the close of 1910, when I was as secretive—indeed, as furtive—as any conspirator . . . I do not feel it is any exaggeration to speak of our secret expedition to Jekyll Island as the occasion of the actual conception of what eventually became the Federal Reserve System . . .
>
> We were told to leave our last names behind us. We were told, further, that we should avoid dining together on the night of our departure. We were instructed to come one at a time and as unobtrusively as possible to the railroad terminal on the New Jersey littoral of the Hudson, where Senator Aldrich's private car would be in readiness, attached to the rear end of a train for the south . . .
>
> Once aboard the private car we began to observe that taboo that had been fixed on last names. We addressed one another as Ben, Paul, Nelson, Abe—It is Abraham Piatt Andrew. Davison and I adopted even deeper disguises, abandoning our first names. On the theory that we were always right, he became Wilbur and I became Orville, after those two aviation pioneers, the Wright brothers . . .
>
> The servants and train crew may have known the identities of one or two of us, but they did not know all, and it was the names of all printed together that would have made our mysterious journey significant in Washington, in Wall Street, even in London. Discovery, we knew, simply must not happen, or else all our time and effort would be wasted. If it were to be exposed publicly that our particular group had got together and written a banking bill, that bill would have no chance whatever of passage by Congress.[3]

The meeting lasted for nine days, and at the end of that time, the party must have felt certain that their efforts would now be accepted by the Congress. Aldrich was chosen to be the spokesman for the new entity, and the bill was named after him. However, Aldrich's connections with United States and international money powers came to the light of Congress and the bill did not have a chance of passing with his name attached. Accordingly, by changing the name, moving some of the paragraphs around, but retaining the same objectives, the same bill was passed under a different name, the Federal Reserve Act of 1913. Originally, the bill contained many provisions not now included in the operative bill or the actions of the bill. For example, the FED was originally expressly prohibited from creating money from nothing. But that is what happens today. Since the inception of the bill, over one hundred amendments have occurred to it, with the vast majority of those amendments enhancing the ability of the FED to operate increasingly more independently of government influence and control.

The FED and the United States government established a sort of partnership which today allows the FED to control the money supply, manipulate the cost of money, tax the American people by creating inflation, control the growth of the economy and business by tightening credit, and in many other ways dictate principles of control adverse to a free economy, but beneficial for the private owners of the FED and for the government.

The benefit to the government of the FED system is that the Congress can go to the FED at any time and obtain money it does not have and to which it is not entitled. The money generates interest which is paid by the United States citizens. This in turn dilutes the value of the money held by American citizens as there is an increase in the supply and inflation is created. Inflation is not an increase in the price of goods, but rather a decrease in the buying power of the money held by Americans. In essence, then, the Congress benefited by establishment of a system whereby it could obtain access to unlimited funds without any apparent raising of taxes to the American people. Deficit spending facilitated by the FED made and continues to make its existence desirable for the government.

Finally, and most significantly, the FED benefits because it creates money from nothing, and then loans that money to banks who lend it to consumers who pay interest to their local bank which in turn pays interest to the Federal Reserve. It is an ingenious system, as it allows the FED to charge interest on nothing—paper it created without reserves.

The design of the Federal Reserve System accomplishes, today, all of the objectives of its founders who met back in 1910.

One might well comment, "But the system is working well. We have the greatest benefits and the highest standard of living the world has ever known. Should we not therefore accept it as good and not complain?"

It may be significant to note that factors indicate that times are getting rough. Counties and states declare bankruptcy because of fluctuations in the interest rate where a simple shift of a small portion of one percent costs institutional state and government investors billions of dollars because of leveraging and futures buying. Families often must have both spouses working to provide the same standard of living once produced by one working parent. Leisure time for families is shrinking. The American dream of a home is becoming less and less of an opportunity for today's married couples. A greater number of us are living below the poverty level. Bankruptcies have increased at alarming rates. Increasing percentages of Americans are retiring broke at the age of 65. Perhaps we are only appearing to live well as a result of debt. Perhaps a day of reckoning is coming. Perhaps it is even near at hand.

There is a steadily growing voice of educated people who are challenging the existence of the FED. This increasing opposition to the money monopoly is attempting to require the reformation of the FED, or preferably, its elimination. The outcome of the spending policies of the government, as facilitated by the FED, is inflation. This results in a lowering of the American standard of living, and perhaps eventually, a complete collapse of the financial house of cards erected by this monopoly. If this happens, we would perhaps as a nation be happy to consider, tolerate, or perhaps even embrace a world money system signaling farewell to United States sovereignty.

The reader is encouraged to look into this aspect of our system in greater detail. Much information is now available, previously kept for decades from the view of the general public. It is at least conceivable that the previous efforts to maintain secrecy have now been abandoned as the result of the belief by the manipulative forces behind the one-world movement that the opportunity for reversal of their objectives has passed.

Taxes

Generally speaking, taxation is the process of required contributions to a government entity. Tax is used as a means of supporting government spending for such purposes as public parks, highways, services and similar day-to-day benefits. It is also the means whereby a government is able to protect its citizens from outside forces which would destroy or attack the sovereignty of a nation. But taxes can also be used for other purposes such as equalizing the wealth, discouraging certain types of business or products, and otherwise forcing the citizenry of a nation to comply with the perceived good as determined by those in control at the time.

A government can only be effective in its effort to collect tax if its people are willing to comply with the taxation laws of the nation. When the taxing policies of a nation exceed the perceived benefit to the citizens, the stage is ripe for a revolution against the taxing authority. The revolution of this country from England is a classic example of a people who are not willing to be subject to unfair tax policies.

Principles of Taxation

Taxation in the United States has evolved into a complex three-level system. We are taxed at the Federal, State and local levels. Each level extracts different types of tax. Income tax can be withheld at the Federal, State and local levels. Sales tax benefits both the state and local levels. Real estate taxes are primarily for local use. Fuel taxes are levied by both the federal and state governments primarily for roads and related travel expenses. Special taxes often apply to goods considered by society to be harmful such as tobacco and alcohol.

Typically, a government is required to keep its expenditures within the amounts it is able to collect from taxes, and cannot operate a deficit budget. The exception is when a government, operating with fiat money, has the ability to create its own money. This is the case in the United States where the federal government is able to simply have more money printed to provide funds to meet its deficit-spending habits. State and local governments do not have this capability, and many argue that the federal government also lacks that ability under the Constitution except in time of war.

Taxes Should be Fair

Most believe that taxes must be inherently fair. How one defines fair is the subject of great debate. While many believe that fair means uniform or equal, others define it as being related to one's ability to pay. Still others define fair as that which exists when the taxes paid are proportional to the benefits received. It is not difficult to utilize the middle reason, ability to pay, as a good rational for the type of income tax we pay in the United States today. The tax is calculated such that those having the ability to pay are burdened with the task of providing the lion's share of the proceeds. Thus, to those who feel that a tax is only fair if it results in benefits proportional to the tax paid, the current system is grossly unfair. A similar conclusion is reached by those who feel that taxes should be borne at the same percentage of income for all. Each person is possessed of his own values and his values state whether or not he deems the currently used plan as fair. The Congress repeatedly struggles with the difficult decision of determining what is fair to the American public. It is studying methods, plans, and alternatives to the current unpopular system.

Tax Collection should be Easy

If a ruler, or a government, wants to be successful in the collection of taxes, the collection system needs to be easy and efficient. In the United States, we spend billions of dollars to sustain the IRS. Many suggest that this is not efficient and is the result of a system viewed as unfair. When otherwise honest people seek dishonest methods of altering the amount of tax they owe, it is a good indication that the system is fault ridden. This could certainly be the case in the United States where prominent citizens and even public officials are frequently charged with income tax evasion. Often, the IRS plays scare games by releasing stories about tax evasion and captured criminals about the same time people are beginning to think about having their taxes done (generally from January through April). A system which must operate by fear and through coercion lacks inherent fairness and efficiency. Fairness and efficiency are characteristics of which our tax system should be possessed.

Alternatives to Current Income Tax

In an effort to make taxes more fair, and with a realization that the current system is inherently unfair, the Congress has been struggling with alternatives approaches to produce tax income. The historical use of income as the base for tax collection has distinct unfairness as it is presently applied. The present system punishes incentive. The graduated scale punishes citizens in times of inflation. Thus, income may go up because of inflation, pushing the normal citizen into a higher bracket. It also causes Americans to lose actual buying power because spendable income does not keep pace with inflation. Finally, the higher income pushes the taxpayer into a higher tax bracket, causing him to pay a larger percentage or his income in taxes.

The Lord's system of paying ten percent as a tithe would seem to lend the most credence to a flat tax. However, the possibility of such a move by Congress seems impractical for at least one major reason. For the past two generations, Congress has used the tax system to control the American public, to stimulate areas of research and development, and to otherwise manipulate the economy and direction of this nation. To assume that Congress would give up this tremendous power of manipulative control without a significant struggle is not reasonable. Only a tax revolution spawned by numerous letters and a national movement could bring such a reformation to pass.

Taxes to Control the People

Ezra Taft Benson has observed,

> Even among free nations the observer will see the encroachment of government upon the lives of the citizenry by excessive taxation and regulation, all done under the guise that the people would not wilfully or charitably distribute their wealth, so the government must take it from them. One can further observe promises of security by the state, whereby men are taken care of from the womb to the tomb. Deception in high places, with the justification that the end justifies the means; atheism; agnosticism; immorality; and dishonesty appear to be the order of the day. The attendant results of such sin and usurpation of power lead

to a general distrust of government officials. Mankind therefore develops an insatiable, covetous spirit for more and more material wants, personal debt to satisfy this craving. This focus leads to the disintegration of the family unit. Today may well fulfill the times the Savior spoke of, times when "Iniquity shall abound, the love of many shall wax cold." (see Matthew 24:12)[4]

Many of the problems facing individuals today are the result of burdens placed on them by government.

Taxation has become a means whereby the government attempts to control business, regulate opportunity, administer punishment, destroy incentive, limit growth, prohibit prosperity, and then fund unrighteous ideas, concepts, principles and purposes. Very few of today's society would question the right of the government to tax income, tax business, tax real estate, tax food, tax fuels, tax commodities, tax inflation growth, and even tax the privilege of passing your previously taxed earnings to children. But many believe that taxation is out of control. The founding fathers would be appalled at the level of taxation in today's society. The "great society concept of this generation has produced a level of government power never before thought possible under our Constitution. The concept of taking forcibly from some and giving to others is rampant and destructive of the basic elements of freedom sought to be protected as rights under the Constitution.

When we first were introduced as a nation to the social security numbers, we were promised by the politicians that this number would never be used for identification, and that its sole purpose would be to provide for the benefits of retirement. However, today, a citizen cannot apply to open a bank account, borrow money, buy a home, buy a stock or mutual fund, or even be paid for services without utilizing his Social Security Number. That private, secret, nobody-will-ever-know number has become the nation-wide source of commerce in America. You cannot participate in business, employment, farming or any other private or public business or activity without reference to this number.

And recently, the burden has become worse. Now, even our little children, though not participants in the economy, must, by law, have their own Social Security number. Some consider this invasion far beyond anything considered conceivable by the founding fathers, or even by the veterans of World War II who witnessed Hitler's atrocities.

Income taxes were initially conceived as unconstitutional and some even today attempt to claim this basic right. However, history records that while it may have been unconstitutional to require a tax on income at the time of the establishment of the Constitution, today it has been ruled as constitutional, and citizens are legally bound to obey. However, at the time it was declared as constitutional and made an amendment to the Constitution, the Congressional Record discussions reveal that it was thought inconceivable that the tax could ever exceed three[3] percent. How far has the right to collect this tax progressed! Today, a citizen will pay all of the following taxes, plus hundreds of additional taxes hidden in the costs of goods and services:

Federal Income Tax	15% - 39.6%
State Income Tax	0.5% - 11.9%
Social Security Tax	7.5% - 15%
Disability and unemployment taxes	1.5% - 3%
Medicare tax	1% - 2%

Additionally some pay county and city income taxes. Then, if the taxpayer has anything left after direct taxation above, they pay some or all of the following taxes:

Sales Taxes	4% - 8%
Real Estate Taxes	0.5% - 4%
Fuel Taxes	47 cents per gallon
Business Property Taxes	0.5% - 1%

And finally, at death, if the person has been prudent and has anything left, the government taxes the privilege of passing accumulated assets to children. This tax, called the Unified Federal And Estate Gift Tax, taxes all of assets passed at death or during lifetime by gift at a rate beginning at 18% and going as high as 60%, with an overall maximum of 55%. While a Unified Credit eliminates tax on the first $600,000, any amounts in excess of that are taxed beginning at the 37% bracket. The tax is due in nine months and carries severe penalties and interest if not timely paid.

The author recently had a client whose father had died, leaving his second wife the right to the income during her life and also leaving this second wife the responsibility to properly arrange his affairs at his death. Unfortunately, when the second wife died and the property passed to the daughter, it came to light that the second wife had failed to put her husband's affairs in order. The tax, penalties and interest had to be paid. While the tax amounted to only $6,700, the penalties and interest amounted to a devastating $72,500! If we throw in the costs of probate, it cost the client over $80,000 to receive title to this $250,000 asset.

It is difficult for this author to conceive of a more unfair and unjust tax. After working all your life, and paying Federal income taxes, Social Security taxes, State income taxes, sales taxes, real estate taxes and a hundred hidden taxes, the government takes one final death-tax shot at your estate to prevent the family from building wealth.

President Benson's teachings about taxation are clear and unambiguous.

> I believe that every person who enjoys the protection of his life, liberty, and property should bear his fair share of the cost of government in providing that protection; that the elementary principles of justice set forth in the Constitution demand that all taxes imposed be uniform; and that each person's property or income be taxed at the same rate . . . .
>
> I consider it a violation of the Constitution for the federal government to levy taxes for the support of state or local government; that no state or local government can accept funds from the federal government and remain independent in performing its functions, nor can the citizens exercise their rights of self- government under such conditions.[5]

With this rampant taxation, the government seeks to actually control the prosperity of the nation. And not all who seek this control seek to control prosperity in an upward manner. Paul Volker, a member of the Trilateral Commission, the Council on Foreign Relations, and former Chairman of the Federal Reserve Board claims that the standard of living of the average American must decline. The only plausible explanation for this opinion is the desire of the money powers to break the financial back of these United States of America so we will submit to the one-world order. Excessive taxation as outlined in this section is one method used to bring about this back-breaking activity. This course of burdensome taxation penalizes incentive, discourages saving, and destroys individual freedom. Yet we tolerate it, despite all the negatives associated with excess taxation. The federal government uses taxes to control education, health care, welfare spending, the economy and practically every other aspect of our lives. It is indeed a great source of power citizens have abdicated from a local level to the federal level. For the most part, they have not done this of their own knowledgeable free choice, but simply by inactivity and failure to object to and oppose this local loss of government.

Taxes to Control the Pulpit

Notwithstanding the potential dangers referenced above whereby the government regulates and taxes citizens into a socialistic loss of freedoms, perhaps nowhere is the danger or presence of the adversary in this socialistic approach made more evident than when rules, laws and regulations are made applicable to religion. Utilizing the doctrine of separation between church and state, and the power to tax, evil-inspired men and federal legislation have conspired to almost totally silence criticism of politics from America's pulpits.

The stand of the church has always been to abide by the laws of the land in which it is established. Our twelfth Article of Faith states: "We believe in being subject to kings, presidents, rulers, and magistrates, in obeying, honoring, and sustaining the law." Acknowledging the Savior's comment that the Lord's "kingdom is not of this world:" (John 18:36), we wait patiently for the Lord's second advent when the law of the land and the law of the Lord will be one, the time when "out of Zion shall go forth the law, and the word of the Lord from Jerusalem." (Isaiah 2:3)

In this interim period, we remain subject to the laws of the land. It is true that those laws have evolved substantially from the days of the founding fathers. Particularly is this true in the present examination of the laws as they relate to taxation and religion. It was never the intent of the founding fathers to in any way limit the expression of religion. In fact, just the opposite was true. To insure that man's laws in this nation would not infringe on his ability to worship, the founding fathers established the right of all men to worship as they pleased. To codify the right and to insure that state religion as found in the European nations would not be reinstated in this new land, they established the First Amendment creating a separation between church and state, a part of our Bill of Rights.

However, utilizing that amendment as the basis of their stand, modern-day elements of government (including the Supreme Court and various legislators) have combined to not only separate church and state, but to legislate silence and eliminate criticism from the pulpit. Ezra Taft Benson stated,

> I support the doctrine of separation of church and state as traditionally interpreted to prohibit the establishment of an official national religion. But this does not mean that we should divorce government from any formal recognition of God. To do so strikes a potentially fatal blow at the concept of the divine origin of our rights, and unlocks the door for an easy entry of future tyranny. If Americans should ever come to believe that their rights and freedoms are instituted among men by politicians and bureaucrats, they will no longer carry the proud inheritance of their forefathers, but will grovel before their masters seeking favors and dispensations—a throwback to the feudal system of the Dark Ages.[6]

Today, separation of church and state has evolved to a status never envisioned nor intended by the founding fathers.

Under legislation not part of the Constitution, and to this author's perspective, in conflict with the Constitution, tax-free organizations may retain their charitable and tax- free status only so long as they agree that they will not conduct activities which influence politics. The IRS code provides a tax exemption for religious organizations under Section 501. However, the exemption is contingent on the organization's compliance with the following excerpt from Subchapter F of the code, to wit:

> Corporations . . . organized and operated exclusively for religious, charitable . . . or educational purposes . . . no substantial part of the activities of which is carrying on propaganda, or otherwise attempting to influence legislation . . . and which does not participate in or intervene in . . . any political campaign on behalf of any candidate for public office.[7]

Thus, the churches of this land, including the restored Church of Jesus Christ of Latter-day Saints, have been legislated into political silence.

Latter-day Saints could ill afford to be as generous with contributions as they now are if they could not deduct their contributions to the church from their taxable income. Nor could the church fare nearly so well as it does if all its assets and received contributions became subject to real estate taxes, income taxes and similar taxes.

Thus, the leaders of the church and in fact the church itself is unable to direct, influence, or otherwise instruct the members of this church with regard to specific political issues involving the decline or loss of freedom in this land. To do so would jeopardize the financial stability of the Kingdom. However, the limitation is as to the pulpit only. There is nothing which prohibits the members of the church from sounding the warning. The Elders and the Sisters of this Kingdom must consider raising the voice of warning as taught in the Book of Mormon, and must make it heard. The Church as an organization is unable to do so, being limited and bound by the legislative provisions of this land which have been implemented by the adversary in an attempt to silence the word of the Lord on these issues.

8

SECRET COMBINATIONS, COMMUNISM, AND THE CONSTITUTION OF THE UNITED STATES OF AMERICA

Perspectives on the Constitution

"We have no government armed with power capable of contending with human passions unbridled by morality and religion . . . Our Constitution was made only for a moral and religious people. It is wholly inadequate to the government of any other."[1] Thus spoke John Adams, the second President of the United States and one of the framers of the Constitution. It was truly the belief of the founding fathers that one of the purposes of the Constitution was to establish a government based on the morals, principles and concepts of Christianity.

This government of the United States does not possess adequate power to administer nor govern the people of this land unless this people are guided and controlled internally, in their own beings, by Christian morals and principles. The Constitution of the United States was written from the perspective that its people were guided by a higher law. That higher law was the Judeo-Christian standard found in the teachings of the Bible.

In the words of James Madison,

> We have staked the whole future of American civilization, not upon the power of government, far from it. We have staked the future of all of our political institutions upon the capacity of each of us to govern ourselves according to the Ten Commandments of God.[2]

Like John Adams, James Madison recognized the inability of a government to control the conscience of man. The moral fiber of a nation finds its roots in the basic beliefs and intents of its citizens. If they share a common source, a common foundation, and a common purpose, that fiber will bind together to assure that their government will not become oppressive, abusive or destructive of those common elements. When those common elements are founded in the principles taught by Christ, that fiber will bind to assure that the government will not become oppressive, abusive or destructive of the basic human liberties embodied in the language of the Founders, i.e., life, liberty, and the pursuit of happiness. But when the people of a nation do not share that basic fiber, then confusion, misdirection and abusive government can and will evolve.

Nephi made interesting comments about those who were brought to this land. He spoke of the condition of those among the kingdoms and nations of the earth prior to Columbus, stating that they were in captivity. Secret combinations were present in their midst.

> 2. And the angel said unto me: What beholdest thou? And I said: I behold many nations and kingdoms.
> 3. And he said unto me: These are the nations and kingdoms of the Gentiles.
> 4. And it came to pass that I saw among the nations of the Gentiles the formation of a great church.
> 5. And the angel said unto me: Behold the formation of a church which is most abominable above all other churches, which slayeth the saints of God, yea, and tortureth them and bindeth them down, and yoketh them with a yoke of iron, and bringeth them down into captivity.
> 6. And it came to pass that I beheld this great and abominable church; and I saw the devil that he was the founder of it. (1 Nephi 13:2-6)

Could there be any question that Satan would be the founder of such a church? In the pre-mortal existence, Satan's plan was to destroy the agency of man. He is still attempting that approach among the nations and kingdoms being shown to Nephi. Secret combinations bind the souls of men. Under their control, they have no freedom of conscience. They are bound by the chains of hell. They have no freedom of expression nor desire to seek truth. History students will affirm that this period of history evidenced a great yoke and burden on the people binding them to labor for the kings and rulers of the land. Indeed the captivity of which Nephi speaks must surely refer to economic captivity, political captivity, and religious captivity. Speaking of those in control of the Great and Abominable, the angel continues his instruction to Nephi; "And also for the praise of the world do they destroy the saints of God, and bring them down into captivity." (1 Nephi 13:9) History refers to some of those times as the Dark Ages. One can justifiably inquire just how Satan was able to obtain such a great power and influence over the hearts, minds, and souls of men, especially since the Savior of mankind had only recently made his debut and completed his mortal mission among the children of men.

As Nephi's vision continued, he saw Columbus and the Holy Ghost bringing him across the many waters to the promised land, " . . . and I beheld the Spirit of God, that it came down and wrought upon the man; and he went forth upon the many waters, even unto the seed of my brethren, who were in the promised land." (1 Nephi 13:12) Many other people followed Columbus to the promised land: "And it came to pass that I [Nephi] beheld the Spirit of God, that it wrought upon other Gentiles; and they went forth out of captivity, upon the many waters." (1 Nephi 13:13) Thus, like the dawn spreading across the darkness, a path was opened by a power beyond that of the prisoners. Those who sought truth and liberty were led by the Spirit of God to this land choice above all other lands.

And once here, they were blessed upon the land. Their faith was centered in Jesus Christ and in his gospel. They were a God-fearing, moral-bound people. And finally, when they could no longer tolerate the captivity of Europe, which attempted to rebind them and oppress them even across the many waters, they forged the Declaration of Independence. The following statement of John Quincy Adams is evidence of the attitude of the framers, drafters and signers of the Declaration of Independence.

> Is it not that, in the chain of human events, the birthday of the nation is indissolubly linked with the birthday of the Savior? That it forms a leading event in the progress of the gospel dispensation? Is it not that the Declaration of Independence first organized the social compact on the foundation of the Redeemer's mission upon the earth? That it laid the cornerstone of human government upon the precepts of Christianity?[3]

Despite the removal of such statements from today's texts and history books, the true historian cannot deny the belief, concept and intent of the original founding fathers. The belief of a need to base the laws of this nation on Christianity and the moral values attendant to that perspective is self-evident in their individual writings, in their lives, and in the documents they created. In the Declaration of Independence the Founding Fathers stated, in probably the most oft-quoted phrase of that document, "We hold these truths to be self-evident, that all men are created equal, that they are endowed by their Creator with certain unalienable rights, that among these are Life, Liberty, and the Pursuit of Happiness." The moral code established by the founding fathers declared that man was created and given absolute rights as a creation of God, rights of which no government, no law, and no system could arbitrarily deprive its people.

Patrick Henry stated, "It cannot be emphasized too strongly or too often that this great nation was founded, not by religionists, but by Christians; not on religion, but on the gospel of Jesus Christ."[4] And John Jay, who helped draft the Constitution and who was the first Chief Justice of the United States Supreme Court stated, "Providence has given our people the choice of their rulers, and it is the duty—as well as the privilege and interest—of our Christian Nation to select and prefer Christians for their rulers."[5]

It is almost as if John Jay had read the words of Mosiah in the Book of Mormon:

> 25. Therefore, choose you by the voice of this people, judges, that ye may be judged according to the laws which have been given you by our fathers, which are correct, and which were given them by the hand of the Lord.
> 26. Now it is not common that the voice of the people desireth anything contrary to that which is right; but it is common for the lesser part of the people to desire that which is not right; therefore this shall ye observe and make it your law—to do your business by the voice of the people. (Mosiah 29:25-26)

In talking about the circumstances surrounding the drafting and confirmation of the United States Constitution, James Madison stated,

> The real wonder is that so many difficulties should have been surmounted, and surmounted with a unanimity almost as unprecedented as it must have been unexpected. It is impossible for any man of candor to reflect on this circumstance without partaking of the astonishment. It is impossible for the man of pious reflection not to perceive in it a finger of that Almighty hand which has been so frequently and signally extended to our relief in the critical stages of the revolution.[6]

This nation, by the grace of God, prevailed above superior forces. It became a nation of the people, by the people, for the people. To assure the continuation of the purposes of this new experiment in government, the founding fathers created the Constitution. The Lord's words give us a better appreciation of this document and its purpose.

> 79. Therefore, it is not right that any man should be in bondage one to another.
> 80. And for this purpose have I established the Constitution of this land, by the hands of wise men whom I raised up unto this very purpose, and redeemed the land by the shedding of blood. (D & C 101:79, 80)

Latter-day Saints are blessed above all to have revealed knowledge of the divine intervention present in the establishment of the Constitution of this land.

In writing the Constitution, the founding fathers were attempting to accommodate two distinct theories of thought regarding the role of the new federal government.

The first theory was to preserve to the states greater power than was possessed by the federal government. This viewpoint included the concept that the federal government was a means of facilitating protection among the several states. The states had just defeated the world's greatest military power in a war they could not have won statistically. However, they were not impervious to attack from other world powers. By combining forces, they envisioned they could better protect the independence they had just fought to obtain. They also correctly believed that the new government could assist in promoting and facilitating commerce among the several states, assuring freedom of trade among the members of this new nation. This first viewpoint also envisioned that the federal government's role must be supreme in only limited areas and that the various states must retain their own ability for self government and control. Those who supported this first viewpoint resisted a growing federal government they viewed as having the potential to bring the states back into a subservient relationship with a centralized government. This was the position which they had just fought to eliminate.

The second position was indeed as polar to the first as the North Pole is to the South. The second ideology was that the federal government must be the central place of power and that it indeed was proper for the federal government to dictate policy in almost all matters. The rights of the several states, while important, must be viewed in light of what was best for the common good of all citizens. Thus, the rights of the states must be subjected to the power and authority of the larger and more powerful federal government.

The compromise was a system of representation whereby the voice of each state was equally heard in the senate, but the voice of the people of the nation as a whole would be also heard based on population in the House of Representatives. This enlightened solution provided comfort for those who believed that states rights must not be compromised by this new federal government, and also satisfied the arguments of those who felt that the federal government should have supreme power.

The great debate comprised today in the Federalist Papers contains the detailed arguments over the two polar positions.

It is conceivable that initially, both sides felt they had won their respective debate position. However, history has apparently evolved to favor the second position, as the tendency has been a growing and stronger federal government. Many powers once held by the states have been abdicated to the federal government.

The Constitution as a Changeable and Alterable Document

A faction of the United States Citizenry professes that the Constitution should not be changed. Relying on the theory that change erodes freedoms and threatens the rights of citizens, they argue that the document should remain static and unchanged. One Constitutional commentator states that this viewpoint "pickles" and does not "preserve" the Constitution.[7]

It was the intent of the founding fathers that the Constitution be flexible and alterable from its inception. This is evident from the amendment procedure established in the document itself. The founding fathers recognized that their document was not going to be perfect and with time would need to change to meet surrounding circumstances. The Bill of Rights consisting of the first ten amendments evidences that it was their intent that the document be subject to amendment and change. The First Amendment to the Constitution provided for the protection of our right to freely worship. Amendment II guarantees to all American citizens the right to keep and bear arms. Amendment IV protects against unlawful searches and seizures. Amendment VI guarantees a right to a speedy trial. Amendment X guarantees that state governments retain those powers not allocated by the Constitution to the United States government. Other amendments are equally impressive and necessary in their own context. Accordingly, change was envisioned and considered a necessary element of the document. Early changes to the Constitution enhanced the rights we hold as citizens.

The process for amendment was intentionally strict, but not impossible. Article V of the document requires that a proposed amendment must be approved by a two-thirds vote of the legislative bodies of the federal government, Congress and the Senate, and must thereafter be approved by a seventy-five percent majority of the state legislatures. The amendment process was made intentionally difficult as the founding fathers wanted to protect the basic principles established in the document they worked so long and hard to complete.

Having shown that the Constitution was designed to be a flexible document, can there be any real argument against changing the Constitution?

An Opposing View: The Constitution Must Not Change

Notwithstanding the foresight of the founding fathers allowing the Constitution to be changed, there is a valid argument professing that the Constitution should remain unchanged from at least one important perspective. While agreeing that the document was intentionally designed to be alterable, amendable and subject to change, these advocates declare that the Constitution must remain true in principle to the views and perspectives of the founding fathers. They believe the country should be run by the ideals professed by the Founding Fathers. Accordingly, and from their perspective, any act of Congress, the President or the Supreme Court which endangers, threatens or erodes the Constitutional principles espoused by the Founding Fathers should be opposed.

It is not uncommon for changes to spark great controversy in the hearts of the children of men. After the ascension of the Savior in Acts chapter 1, the apostles went out into the world to preach the gospel. Through revelation to Peter, they learned that it was necessary, and the will of the Lord, that their message be taken not only to the Jewish nation, but also to the Gentiles. This constituted a change of policy and procedure and was most certainly resisted by many holding to the previous principles of abstinence from contact with Gentiles. Later, many in the church felt that the newly converted Greeks and Gentiles must be circumcised pursuant to the Lord's covenant with Abraham. Bringing this controversy to the church presidency, and after adequate discussion, the decision was made under the influence of the Spirit that the Gentiles need not enter into circumcision, but rather the covenant of baptism and receipt of the Holy Ghost. The point of these two illustrations is that life is not static. Civilization is not static. The Church is not static, but rather as we mature in the gospel, as we increase in our spirituality, as we develop in our ability to bind Satan, we qualify for additional blessings and knowledge.

As surroundings change, as time progresses, as events occur, as economies mature, as citizens evolve, then needs arise. If we have a living prophet to guide us, we can know the Lord's will with regard to the changing circumstances.

Under the Constitution, we elect representatives whose duty it is to represent our views and support and sustain the Constitution. Under this republic form of government, the Constitution becomes the guiding principle. It is the supreme and ultimate source of law in the United States. The beauty of the republic form of government is that the bare majority cannot act by vote to eliminate rights of citizens under the Constitution. Accordingly, the majority vote is invalid if it violates the principles of the Constitution.

Under a republic, we instill power in our representatives to govern, protect and abide by the Constitution and to assure our continued freedom and rights. Knowing that the Constitution was originally established with the power to make changes, and also knowing that our freedoms thereunder must be protected, citizens must address the question of when changes to that document are good and when they are bad. Anytime change is possible, there is potential both for good use and for abuse.

The Church of Jesus Christ of Latter-day Saints, speaking of the Church as a whole and not as individual members, is viewed by the nation and the world as a conservative people. Many, if not most, of the members are acutely aware of the prophesies of Joseph Smith concerning the latter-day threats against the Constitution. More than any other class of citizens in this nation,

Latter-day Saints feel a concern about the stability, integrity and continued existence of that document.

Concerning the Constitution, Latter-day Saints have a much greater insight into its existence and purpose than most. The Lord has revealed much to the Church concerning the Constitution, nations and governments that is not known to the general public.

The Lord said, "Therefore, I, the Lord, justify you, and your brethren of my church, in befriending that law which is the Constitutional Law of the land." (D & C 98:6) But the Lord also continued with a warning: "And as pertaining to law of man, whatsoever is more or less than this, cometh of evil." (D & C 98:7) The Constitution as existing on August 6, 1833, (when the 98th Section was given) and on December 16, 1833, (when the 101st Section was given) was pronounced correct and acceptable to God and to his Church. The Lord continues,

> 8. I, the Lord God, make you free, therefore ye are free indeed; and the law also maketh you free.
>
> 9. Nevertheless, when the wicked rule the people mourn.
>
> 10. Wherefore, honest men and wise men should be sought for diligently, and good men and wise men ye should observe to uphold; otherwise whatsoever is less than these cometh of evil. (D & C 98:8-10)

In seeking these men, voters must not be slack nor passive. "We believe that governments were instituted of God for the benefit of man; and that he holds men accountable for their acts in relation to them, both in making laws and administering them, for the good and safety of society." (D & C 134:1) Saints have a divinely appointed individual and collective responsibility and duty to take positive and correct action toward government. Whenever God gives a blessing or knowledge, responsibility increases. To him who receives the greater light, to him is given the greater responsibility, and the greater condemnation if he sins against that light. (D & C 82:3) Few times in the history of the world have the children of Adam had the opportunity to live under a government inspired and directed by the hand of God. Under the divinely inspired provisions of the U.S. Constitution, citizens today share that opportunity.

The statement of the Church continues, "We believe that no government can exist in peace, except such laws are framed and held inviolate as will secure to each individual the free exercise of conscience, the right and control of property, and the protection of life." (D & C 134:2) Three distinct concepts are specified in this scripture which must be held sacred and upon which there must be no allowance for infringement. If a change or proposed change to the

Constitution endangers, limits, or threatens any of these three purposes, you can know for a certainty that it is not of God and must therefore be from the adversary. Herein lies the standard of the Latter-day Saints as to the characteristics and principles of the law they must uphold and sustain and not allow to change.

The laws of the land cannot produce peace unless those laws protect *free exercise of conscience*. Men are endowed with an inalienable right to believe as they choose. When any government or other entity attempts to eliminate that freedom of conscience, they are empowering the intents and purposes of Satan. To violate a man's right to believe in God, or even to deny God, is to violate the one of the three basic purposes of the Constitution. In the pre-mortal existence, Satan wanted to destroy the agency of man. He wanted to eliminate their ability to think and act and worship as they please.

> 3. Wherefore, because that Satan rebelled against me, and sought to destroy the agency of man, which I, the Lord God, had given him, and also, that I should give unto him mine own power; by the power of mine Only Begotten, I caused that he should be cast down;
> 4. And he became Satan, yea, even the devil, the father of all lies, to deceive and to blind men, and to lead them captive at his will, even as many as would not hearken unto my voice. (Moses 4:3-4)

Today, he may attempt the same objective through unfair, unjust, evil laws which remove the right and ability of men to worship God. Joseph Smith said in regard to this concept, "We claim the privilege of worshiping Almighty God according to the dictates of our own conscience, and allow all men the same privilege, let them worship how, where, or what they may." (*Articles of Faith*, 11)

Additionally, such unchangeable laws must provide that man has the right to *own and control property*. Men thrive when given a stewardship. Two men given identical parcels of land will generally administer that land with different results. A well-known radio commentator tells the story of a farmer who had a beautiful field, properly planted, watered and manicured, no weeds, no dry spots and no broken fences. A neighbor came by one day and admiringly said, "God has certainly blessed your farmland." To which the farmer replied, "Yes, he has. And I'm grateful. But you should have seen it when he had it all to himself."

Not speaking disrespectfully of the blessings of God, but recognizing that each person has different talents, different abilities and different weaknesses, and will yield different results, saints must acknowledge the individuality of which they are now possessed. This is a telestial existence, and just as one star differs from another star in glory, so individuals differ here. This does not imply that the one who produces more from his land is better than one who produces less. The purpose of the comparison to differing stars in the scripture verifies that individuals have the freedom to exercise control over their property pursuant to the gifts they have been given and that they will produce with different degrees of success.

The Constitution offers the same promise. If individuals have the opportunity to succeed, they must also have the opportunity to fail. When government takes away the right and control of property, when it attempts to protect individuals from failing, it is attempting to make everyone equal. Such is not now and never was God's plan. The framers of the Constitution understood well that men are not created with equal abilities, talents and gifts. However, men are entitled to be treated with equal opportunity under the law; equal opportunity to prosper from the labor of their hands and their minds; equal opportunity to express, increase and improve their God-given talents without unfair restrictions, impositions or interference of or by government; equal opportunity to pursue the valuable things of life; and equal protection under the law. These are requirements of a just government and promises found in the Constitution. Again, as Joseph Smith stated, "If there is anything virtuous, lovely, or of good report or praiseworthy, we seek after these things." (*Articles of Faith*, 13)

The third purpose of government which must not be violated is to provide us with *protection of life*. This protection aspect of government was well expressed by the intent of General Moroni in the Book of Mormon as written on the Title of Liberty: "In memory of our God, our religion, and freedom, and our peace, our wives, and our children—" (Alma 46:12), and later, "And thus he [General Moroni] was preparing to support their liberty, their lands, their wives, and their children, and their peace, and that they might live unto the Lord their God, and that they might maintain that which was called by their enemies the cause of Christians." (Alma 48:10)

This epitomizes the role of the government in protecting citizens, their liberties, rights, families, properties and religion. The Constitution was established to provide that protection and allow for the cause of the Christians, and more appropriately, the cause of Christ, to be promulgated from this bastion of freedom to the world.

Thus, the role of government must provide three basic protections. As Frederic Bastiat wrote in 1850;

> Each of us has a natural right from God to defend his person, his liberty, and his property. These are the three basic requirements of life and the preservation of

any one of them is completely dependent upon the preservation of the other two . . . if every person had the right to defend—even by force—his person, his liberty and his property, then it follows that a group of men have the right to organize and support a common force to protect these rights constantly . . .[8]

Indeed, the founding fathers drafted a document with a spirit familiar to the preceding quote and to that found in Doctrine and Covenants 134. Re-familiarize yourself with the Preamble of the Constitution:

> We, the people of the United States, in order to form a more perfect union, establish justice, insure domestic tranquility, provide for the common defense, promote the general welfare, and secure the blessings of liberty to ourselves and our posterity, do ordain and establish this Constitution for the United States of America.

There then follows seven articles establishing the three branches of government and assuring protection from abuse by separation of powers. The Constitution was later amended with Amendments I through X which are now known as the Bill of Rights. That these first ten amendment rights are to be considered as good and acceptable to the Lord can be implied from the statement of the Savior when he confirmed in 1833, some 50+ years after the amendments, that the Constitution (presumably as then existing with these amendments) was inspired by him and should be befriended by the Church. (D & C 101:80; 98:6)

Under the Constitution, this land became a land of freedom. It became a land wherein people could worship how, where and what they may. It became a land where free exercise of conscience, right and control of property, and protection of life would allow for and provide an environment wherein the gospel of Jesus Christ could be restored once again to the earth. All was ready. The land had been preserved from the knowledge of other peoples. The inhabitants had been brought to this land by the Spirit of the Lord, and had been blessed upon the land, and the law of the land, the Constitution, had been inspired by God according to foreordained missions of the founding fathers. The night of darkness and the silence of the heavens was about to burst forth with a new and bright light of hope, purpose and knowledge. A few short years yet remained for Joseph Smith to attain maturity adequate to conceive, accept and fulfill his divinely appointed mortal mission.

Federalism

History records that while freedom is generally won by some type of radical departure from the then-established norm (typically by revolution), the loss of freedom is most often an internal, slow, progressive, step-by-step erosion. The loss of freedom is generally never enough at any one time to trigger serious opposition. It is often couched in language of laws and drafted for purposes of some special interest group and to the detriment of liberty.

Reactions to loss of freedoms are often as that of the frog. Placed in hot water, the frog will immediately jump out. But placed in cool or warm water, where the temperature is gradually increased, the frog will stay put until cooked, never recognizing the increasing danger. We could examine many areas of lost freedom in this nation. But perhaps we can learn about the process by examining just one endangered area. The right to own and control property is perhaps the most basic right we enjoy under the Constitution. Certainly, from a scriptural point, it is one of the three reasons for which this government of the United States was established.

Today, the distinction between the polar positions of government ownership and private ownership of property has become clouded, diffused, and has perhaps even disappeared. There is little (if any) distinction between the philosophy which places the government in actual title ownership of business and property, and the system which places the government in control of the same through regulation and taxation. United States citizens today are in a situation where the right to own and control property is being eroded and threatened because of taxation and regulation. This most basic of Constitutional rights is indeed threatened.

In the tradition of the founding fathers, the right to own and control property is basic to the American way of life and if this right is ever abrogated or lost to the government, the very foundations upon which this nation stands and the system by which it operates will crumble into oblivion.

A major threat to this basic right is Socialism. Socialism is defined as a political and economic theory of social organization based on collective or governmental ownership and democratic management of the essential means for the production and distribution of goods. George Bernard Shaw, a successful advocate of socialism, considered that socialism reduced to its simplest legal and practical expression means the complete discarding of the institution of private property by transforming it into public property and dividing the resulting income and produce equally and indiscriminately among the entire population.

The elimination of private property rights is one of the greatest threats to the ability of man to comply with the opportunities guaranteed by the Constitution and the founding fathers. It is an infringement upon the principle of free agency for which the pre-mortal war in Heaven was fought. Socialism is a doctrine and movement aiming at collective organization of the community in the interest of the masses of the people by means of the common ownership and collective control of the means of production and exchange.

While Socialism is often portrayed as a doctrine and philosophy distinct from other forms of forced government ownership, the similarities suggest that in fact they are the same. For example, the distinction between Communism and Socialism, as represented by various socialist and labor parties of Europe and the New world, is one of tactics and strategy rather than of objective.

Communism is indeed only Socialism pursued by revolutionary means and making its revolutionary method a cannon faith. Communists, like other socialists, (1) believe in the collective control and ownership of private property including the vital means of production and (2) seek to achieve through state action the coordinated control of the economic forces of society. Early in the development of the socialistic concepts, two broadly different approaches for institution of socialist objectives were developed.

German Socialism came about as a result of a split from Communism in 1875 when the German Democratic party set forth its intent to obtain winning power by taking over control of the state's political power rather than by overthrowing it. In effect, the German Socialist Party determined to attempt to obtain control and to institute the objectives of socialism by political means rather than by revolution, as proposed by Communism. This peaceful transition of power was much more acceptable to the educated and those who would benefit from this transition than was the former method of revolution.

Several years later, (in the 1880s) a small group of intellectual and influential activists in England established the Fabian Society. The term *Fabian Socialism* was named after a Roman general who desired to avoid armed conflict. This Roman leader would simply locate his army near the entrance of a city as an intimidation. Small battles would occur in which the Romans were always victorious. The city, not desiring an extended siege, and knowing their forces were inferior, eventually negotiated with the army allowing a peaceful settlement, surrender and concessions acceptable to Roman rule while retaining much internal influence by the captive city. Thus, Rome won many battles without loss of a single life. Today, Fabian Socialism works in much the same way, patiently, slowly, but always steadily eroding freedoms.

This movement has had a major influence on the development of modern socialism. Thus, Fabianism stands for the evolutionary conception of socialism, endeavoring by progressive reforms and the nationalization of industries to turn the existing state into a welfare state. The brilliance of the Fabian Society movement is that it aimed at permeating and penetrating the existing parties with socialistic ideas rather than by creating a new party. The Fabian

Society movement appealed to the public not as revolutionaries, but as reformers seeking only peaceful transformation of the system, not revolutionary overthrow of the government or existing ideas. They proposed an evolution of thought, rather than a discarding of founding principles. But we must remember that all forms of Socialism advocate:

> That private ownership of property and the vital means of production be abolished and that all such property pass under some form of coordinated public control.
>
> That the power of the state be used to achieve their aims.
>
> And that with a change in the control of industry, will go a change in the motives which operate in the industrial system i.e., without the "evil" of private property, a man's greed will be controlled by government and all will share in a mutually acceptable utopian society where all are equal and all receive equal benefits—without regard to contribution of time, effort or skill.

Under this system, the idler will receive the same benefits and rewards as the worker, incentive is destroyed, and work ethic becomes eroded. The nature of man decays to a condition of reliance rather than self-attainment, self-sustainment and self-worth.

In the United States, Fabian Socialism is converting the Constitutional government based on self-worth and work-reward incentive to a welfare state. The nation has adopted much of Socialism. Specifically, much of the fruits of citizen labor is diverted to governmental control. Individuals, businesses and even state governments have abdicated and surrendered control of much of their local rights and powers to the federal government. People have adopted the use of the power of the federal government to control and distribute the fruits of individual labors and industry. This transfer of power is not by accident nor chance, but is the result of a planned, contrived and well-executed progressive program of deceit and misrepresentation designed to deprive the American citizen of the constitutional right to own and control property.

In the 1964 Congressional Record, page 6142, under Remarks of the President to a group of senior citizens leaders, on March 24 of that year, the President of the United States is quoted as saying: "We're going to take all the money we think is unnecessarily being spent and take it from the haves and give it to the have nots." This then is the real objective and purpose of Socialism; *to take*. To take private property, to take the fruits of labor, to take the rights of the forefathers, to take the right to pass the result of labors to children, to take incentive and reward, to take free agency; in effect, to take the right to own and control property.

In pondering this transfer of power from the individual to the state, one must consider the probable conclusion that the ultimate result is in fact a condition of slavery. Citizens become enslaved to a government which controls all of the means of production and sustainment in our borders, and then grants to the citizens that which it deems them to need to sustain life and whatever standard of living the government shall determine.

The purposes of Socialism are advanced greatly by the current system of taxation. Indeed, the Fabian Socialist condition expressed above finds its most successful implementation in the form of taxes.

The courts of this land have labored diligently to safeguard the right to private ownership and control of property. The cases of law show a consistent effort and policy of the courts to guarantee the right of an individual to possess, manage, and control his or her property, and to keep that right uninfringed by others who would unjustly take it away. Sir William Blackstone wrote, "So great moreover is the regard of the law for private property, that it will not authorize the least violation of it; no, not even for the general good of the whole community."[9]

Truly, the right to own and control property is a right the founding fathers considered inalienable. The right to own and control property was included in the Constitution not as an afterthought, but as an integral part of the very fabric of that great document.

This desire of man's to own his home, his business, his goods and his other properties is good. It is basic to man's desire to improve and enhance both for himself and for others. Utopian and communitarian schemes that eliminate property rights are not only unworkable, they also deny to man his inherent desire to improve his station. They are therefore, contrary to the pursuit of happiness.

Without property rights, man's incentive is lost and progress is stifled. Without property rights, there would be no sanctity in our workplace, our churches or our homes. There would be no incentive, no motive, no benefit, no purpose, no liberty and no pursuit of happiness. Indeed, all would be slaves of the one-world movement if people surrendered their rights, properties, and liberties.

Much may have already been lost. Citizens complain of over-taxation and they are burdened with what many consider excessive rules and regulations. The law making bodies of this land, in an apparent effort to justify their very existence, continue to pass laws which are becoming more and more abusive and limiting to freedoms and liberties. Citizens must act unitedly to preserve this most important right, that of being able to own and control property.

Communism

Direct attack against the Constitution did not constitute Satan's entire portfolio. To blind, deceive and captivate those in other parts of the world, Satan employed the on- going work of the secret combinations. Through instruments responsive to his teachings, Satan influenced the creation of an organization with teachings and philosophies in direct opposition to the teachings of Christ. He structured this organization for the purpose of binding the souls of men. This organization spawned a new political order and found its most successful exposure through a document titled *The Communist Manifesto*. Written by Karl Marx and Frederick Engles, this document is currently professed to be the most widely read political document ever to have been written by man.

It is worthy of noting that the timing and coming forth of this document corresponds to the era wherein the Book of Mormon was published and when the Constitution was written. *The Communist Manifesto* has had great effect upon the children of Adam, and literally billions have been and are currently held captive by those who have adopted, advocated, professed and espoused its tenants. Despite the recent crumbling of the iron curtain, hundreds of millions of people are still captivated by its tentacles. The document is straightforward concerning its purpose. By its own internal summary, it is to convince mankind:

- to abolish religion, conventional morality and the family;
- to abolish private ownership of property;
- to impose a heavy graduated income tax;
- to abolish all rights of inheritance,
- to establish government-controlled banking;
- to control communication and transportation; and
- to provide for free public school education for all children.

As a United States public, we have accepted many of these concepts as permissible, acceptable and even desirable in our United States society. Others still strike a great deal of abhorrence, disdain and even anger.

A summary of Communism and its objectives might include a paragraph such as this:

> The Communist Manifesto advocates that greed is the source of the world's ills. As people have a desire for more and more power and wealth, they use their influence to take advantage of others around them and increase their prosperity at the expense of the underprivileged. Accordingly, if the incentive for greed can be removed, people will lose their greed and become more sociable and more interested in the overall success of everyone. Greed can be removed by transferring ownership and control of the elements which create greed to an unselfish and overseeing government which is above the corruptible curse of greed. The ele-

ments identified which create greed are private ownership and control of land, industry and money. If you can therefore eliminate private ownership of property and industry and control the money, you can remove greed from the system and allow all men and women to live relatively equal lifestyles and have relatively equal benefits from the system. Greed will not exist because all will have access to their needs and the system will not provide for nor allow one person to attain a standard of living nor possessions in excess of another. Accordingly, greed is eliminated, peace is established and harmony can result. The accomplishment of these objectives is the overriding objective of all true Communists and to attain that goal, it is permissible to engage in any conduct or endeavor which will progress you, your family, your associates, and your government toward those purposes. The overriding principle in accomplishing these objectives is that *the end justifies the means*. Religion threatens this concept since religion teaches morals and enhances the conscience of man. Religious morality stands in the way of the communist principle by teaching that the end does not justify the means, and that man is answerable to a source higher than that of the government. Additionally, religion teaches of a divine being on whom man must rely to attain a better life and a more meaningful life in the hereafter. Communism teaches that there is no God because that authority would call into question the authority of the government. The family is also a threat to the continued existence of any such system as parents can indoctrinate their children against the Communist principles relying instead on the traditions and beliefs of their fathers. Accordingly, religion and families must be eliminated, turning the responsibility for teaching and training new minds to the government which can teach proper perspectives of life and purpose.

The preceding summary paragraph is a great oversimplification of the communist objective, and one which the author readily admits is very subjectively written. Yet, it is included herein for the purpose of helping the reader to identify with and understand the perspective from which this section has been written.

Not all of the individually professed objectives of Communism are all bad. For instance, the concept that all will have their needs satisfied ties in closely with the experiences found in the Book of Mormon:

> 26. And when the priests left their labor to impart the word of God unto the people, the people also left their labors to hear the word of God. And when the priest had imparted unto them the word of God they all returned again diligently unto their labors; and the priest, not esteeming himself above his hearers, for the preacher was no better than the hearer, neither was the teacher any better than the learner; and thus they were all equal, and they did all labor, every man according to his strength.

27. And they did impart of their substance, every man according to that which he had, to the poor, and the needy, and the sick, and the afflicted; and they did not wear costly apparel, yet they were neat and comely.

28. And thus they did establish the affairs of the church; and thus they began to have continual peace . . .

30. And . . . they did not send away any who were naked, or that were hungry, or that were athirst, or that were sick, or that had not been nourished; and they did not set their hearts upon riches; therefore they were liberal to all, both old and young, both bond and free, both male and female, whether out of the church or in the church, having no respect to persons as to those who stood in need.

31. And thus they did prosper and become far more wealthy than those who did not belong to their church. (Alma 1:26-28; 30, 31)

And again, "They had all things common among them; therefore there were not rich and poor, bond and free, but they were all made free, and partakers of the heavenly gift." (4 Nephi 1:3)

While Communism seeks this utopian existence, it does so by force rather than by free choice. Accordingly, in the words of David O. McKay, "The position of the Church on the subject of Communism has never changed. We consider it the greatest satanical threat to peace, prosperity, and the spread of God's work among men that exists on the face of the earth."[10]

It might be argued that the recent apparent failure of the economic policies behind the iron curtain are an indication that Communism no longer threatens us and is no longer to be an item with which church members should be concerned. However, before throwing caution to the wind, observers should consider the following additional two possibilities.

First, the dropping of the iron curtain may be a signal that the communist government believes that the socialism practiced by the Western powers has advanced to a degree that the two systems (Socialism and Communism) are significantly compatible. In the words of Senator Strom Thurmond,

> There can be no question but that some, even in high places in our Government are not aware of the interrelation between communism and socialism, and incidentally, socialism is nothing more or less than the welfare state . . .
>
> Not only is the welfare state no defense against communism, but there is a serious question as to whether, in practical effect, the welfare state is even an alternative to communism. Both, in essence, are founded on the identical theories of state socialism and are equally antagonistic to the concept of private property. Under communism all property is vested in the state; under the welfare state, the outward vestiges of title to property remain in the individual, but all meaningful attributes of property are exercised by the state through regulation, control, and taxation. Whatever differences might exist are differences in form, rather than substance. The basic premise of both communism and welfare statism is that

individual responsibility and initiative are unreliable for accomplishment of the goal for society which both profess, and their goal is conceived solely in terms of materialistic values. Welfare statism must, therefore, be equated with communism in its mistrust of individual liberty and reliance on state control.[11]

It is at least possible that the rampant socialist state of Europe, the advance of socialism, regulation, and the welfare state in the United States resulting from the excessive legislation and taxation now prevalent, has caused the distinction between the economic system of communism and the socialism we have experienced here to become indistinguishable from a practical standpoint. It is possible that United States citizens continue to experience relative good welfare in this nation (compared to the rest of the world) not because of the righteousness of our living, but rather because of the character of this land, still the land choice above all other lands.

During a recent Presidential administration, it is reported that we created over fourteen thousand pages of new legislation. This does not include the thousands of pages of rules and regulations established each year by agencies and state governments. It is proposed by this author that this proliferation of legislation and taxation is comparable to coercion and control.

The second alternative would propose the possibility that the lowering of the iron curtain is a move, by those who administer Satan's work on the earth through secret combinations, to receive billions of dollars of welfare and other aid from the western worlds. Under no other circumstances would the free enterprise system be willing to divest itself of billions of dollars to catch up the communist world to the economic status of the rest of the world. It may well be good for American business to invest in the system of the post-communist era. But they should at least be cautious.

The People vs. The System

It is, perhaps, not so significant to the Church why the iron curtain fell. It may well be that it fell as the result of God's promise that he would destroy the secret works of darkness. "Wherefore, for this cause, that my covenants may be fulfilled which I have made unto the children of men, that I will do unto them while they are in the flesh, I must needs destroy the secret works of darkness, and of murders, and of abominations." (2 Nephi 10:15) We can remember watching in awe and almost disbelief as the iron curtain fell. Prior to its fall, many considered how difficult the path would be to preach the gospel behind the iron curtain. Many thought that surely a third world war would have to be waged for the purpose of freeing those nations and allowing the missionaries to teach the believers in those countries. But, in what can only be viewed as a miracle, the curtain dropped without a shot. The missionaries were allowed to enter, and the gospel is now being preached to millions who have waited silently and patiently for their opportunity to again walk in the light of the Father and the Son. It is exciting to see this opportunity and to be witnesses of this miracle of the last days come to pass.

Notwithstanding our joy over the ability to preach the gospel to the eastern bloc of nations, we must still await the opportunity to preach to those yet in political bondage behind the bamboo curtain. Many exciting latter-day stories tell of the time when there will be stakes and temples in China. It is a time of great anticipation and hope, a time of watching and observing. It seems possible that the bamboo curtain will fall with the same amount of wonder and amazement as attended the falling of the iron curtain. One can only speculate at what method the Lord will use to allow the gospel to be preached to the one billion plus residents of China. But this much we do know, that eventually, missionaries will be able to follow the Lord's admonition to preach the gospel to all nations, tongues and peoples.

As an interesting note, it might be observed that Ezra Taft Benson, as an ordained President and prophet of the church, did not dwell on the Communist threat. Perhaps he already knew the plan of the Lord for opening these nations, and perhaps they do not now hold the same threat to the church that they did in the past. This is the benefit of having a living prophet. A living prophet can guide us along lines we must presently follow. A living prophet can help us to understand conflicts, problems and options which may not have previously existed in the history of man. Perhaps other secret combinations or Gadianton Societies now pose greater threats to the saints of God. In fact, it is a noticeable change that the teachings, sermons and writings of President Ezra Taft Benson, as President, Prophet, Seer and Revelator, emphasized three areas: (1) proper use of the Book of Mormon by church members, (2) elimination of pride as a Church and as a people, and (3) proper preparation for the future, including food storage.

In another sense, as a High Priest group leader recently stated, "Perhaps the Prophet's admonition to the church members to read, study and share the Book of Mormon was the most powerful political statement the Prophet could ever make."[12]

Notwithstanding the foregoing, individuals still have the eternal responsibility to support and sustain eternal principles of righteousness as pertaining to the government of this land and the Constitution which assures those rights.

Communism was designed by Satan to counter the Lord's work of the latter days, and was intended to retain captive those souls subject to its political and military might. Increased knowledge will assist in the objective to distinguish between the dangers of this type of a society and the principles espoused by the founding fathers and the prophets of the Book of Mormon.

9

SECRET COMBINATIONS AND ONE-WORLD GOVERNMENT

One-World Government

Near the center of the war against the secret combinations, stands the battle for sovereignty of the United States. Today, some government leaders at the highest levels are actively and publicly advocating participation in a one-world government. Though they have taken a sacred oath to uphold the laws of this land and its Constitution, once in office, some have worked openly, some subversively, to undermine and destroy it. Perhaps some are even unaware of the agenda which is evidently being orchestrated.

Leaders of this nation, from both major political parties, have professed the great benefits of a one-world government, a one-world judicial system, a one-world military body, and a one-world financial system. Recent population studies show that the United States has only seven percent of the world's population. Why would a nation such as ours entertain subjecting the government, the judicial system, the military, and financial security to the rule and control of a one-world government?

Some justify this action as the only way to create and preserve world peace. Others propose that as the only surviving super power in today's world, we no longer need to maintain our military strength and should thus participate in a one-world government to uplift other nations and peoples. Some see it as a way to establish global economic stability and thus avoid financial disasters which often plague smaller nations. Still others desire to become a part of a system which provides basic human needs for all of earth's inhabitants, thus avoiding the deadly results of famines and other natural disasters which have become so prevalent in some parts of the world.

Some envision the patriotic American as the enemy. World court justice Phillip C. Jessup says, "'National sovereignty is the root of all evil."[1] Former senator J. William Fullbright claimed that national sovereignty is akin to "international anarchy."[2] A former presidential advisor asserted that it is "an American interest to see an end to nationhood as it has been historically defined."[3]

While some view the benefits of a one-world government as superior to the current system in the United States, many Americans oppose this invasion upon sovereignty and express disagreement with the proposition. But most Americans have not taken a stance on the issues involved. Though there have been pockets of people who oppose the loss of American sovereignty, most have evidenced no expression of concern or even recognition of the issue being faced. While it is possible to argue that this silence from mainstream America is the result of unbelief or apathy, the author believes it to be nothing more than ignorance—a simple lack of understanding of what is taking place. This lack of understanding results from the fact that the movement against the sovereignty of this land is facilitated by secret combinations which desire to keep their agenda secret.

One of the last great hurtles for the one-world government advocates to overcome is the Constitution of the United States of America. It has been and continues to be the great beacon of freedom for all peoples of the world. It signals to the people of this nation and to the world the definition of those inalienable rights which must never be surrendered. These rights were purchased with patriots' blood. Those who truly desire to invoke divine intervention for the welfare of this land will defend, struggle and even die to provide future generations with the continuation of these inalienable rights.

Almost fifty years ago, advocates of one-world government made this statement:

> There is no indication that American public opinion . . . would approve the establishment of a super state, or permit American membership in it. In other words, time—a long time—will be needed before world government is politically feasible . . . [this] time element might seemingly be shortened so far as American opinion is concerned, by an active propaganda campaign in this country.[4]

Since that report, we have witnessed such propaganda campaigns on not only a national, but also a world-wide basis. The attack against the sovereignty of the United States of America, nationalism, patriotism, and the Constitution, has many major fronts. Space allows for a brief summary of only some of these efforts. Much is available to support the arguments stated herein, and common sense will speak to the reader of the truths of these matters. The concepts herein identified as propaganda efforts to create world unity and destroy nationalism and sovereignty in the United States are (1) international finance, (2) environment protection, (3) population control, (4) education of youth, (5) control of civil unrest, and (6) religion.

International Finance

The argument for global economy rests on the premise that inflation, deflation, recession and depression of a nation's economy is, at least in significant part, a reflection of its relationship with other nations. As one nation suffers setbacks caused by crop failure, industry collapse, political unrest or similar disharmony, that nation's monetary system becomes prey to those who would take advantage of or otherwise unduly profit from the misfortune of a neighbor.

A global economy could eliminate, or at least minimize, the great distinctions now found between the major nations of the world and those identified as third-world powers. The tendency would be to equalize the living standards of all peoples. Thus, the economy of major world powers would be lowered and the economy of developing nations would be enhanced through funding of the International Monetary Fund.

The above outlined approach has, to date, been very successful. It has not been a quick or sudden advancement of these concepts. Rather, it has been a deliberate, calculated, slow and methodical exercise through decades of time. It began in 1913 with the Federal Reserve Act and has steadily propelled us to today's financial status.

Our legislators exhibit only a verbal commitment to halt deficit spending, talking only about lowering the deficit spending in coming years with the future objective of eventually arriving at a balanced budget. There are apparently none who want to address the reduction or elimination of the national debt. And each year, we continue to get into greater and greater debt.

This debt has the capability of eventually resulting in the financial collapse of the nation. Those orchestrating the move toward one-world government realize that as long as the United States is solvent and financially strong, there would be no incentive, no basis, and no reasonable cause sufficient tc motivate citizens to surrender sovereignty. But, if the citizens of the nation were to be faced with the option of governmental bankruptcy or participation in a one-world financial system, they would, perhaps, elect to have the international financial market buy them out. This could be accomplished by the international money concept replacing the United States currency with a new one-world government currency. This would also result in free trade among nations providing for a leveling of the standard of living all over the world. Significant recent steps toward this objective include such things as NAFTA, GATT, the European Common Market, and the new face of the former iron curtain.

Some may doubt that this collapse could come, but recently available statistics indicate that we could be on the edge of financial disaster. More than half of the work force in the United States is now directly or indirectly supported by the government. That means that less than half of the work force is in the private sector, paying taxes which support those on the government payroll. Interest on the national debt consumes over one-half of the individual income tax paid by citizens.

Many feel there is little hope that the baby boomers will find anything left in the Social Security system when it comes time for them to retire. Despite many serious studies concerning this futuristic problem, the government continues to ignore it, stating that the money is there or a solution will appear, when in fact there is no apparent solution and the money has been loaned to the government and spent. It is conceivable that the American public and the world will lose confidence in the ability of this government to pay the interest or redeem the bonds it has issued. We have seen bankruptcy of county governments (Orange County, California, one of the richest counties in the nation). At the point in time when confidence lapses, if it does, and the United States becomes unable to raise funds via sale of new bonds, the only course available to the Treasury will be to have the FED purchase the bonds it prints and pump needed money into the system. Inflation for the American public and debt payable to the owners of the FED will result. The money needed to pay off the outstanding interest and debt will be generated with additional debt. The concept is similar to the idea of you going to the bank when unable to make the mortgage payment and asking the bank to extend a new loan to pay the service fee on the existing loan. While politicians in the capital have been able to arrange this type of dealing in the past, it has all been based upon the confidence level of the citizens of this nation and the international investors. If that confidence level deteriorates, it could lead to this nation becoming indebted to and controlled by international financial powers.

It may be of interest to the reader to note that by the end of 1997, over 71% of the currently issued short-term bonds will become due. If they cannot be replaced in the private market because of a lack of confidence from the American Public and the world, the FED must step in to purchase the new bonds. That action could conceivably result in the collapse of this nation's pattern of borrowing from Peter to pay Paul.

Meanwhile, the national debt continues to rise. Debt is anticipated to be approximately seven trillion dollars by the end of the century. The amount of tax citizens will then have to pay to service just the interest on the debt is staggering. Consider your plight if taxes were to double in the next decade. This national debt is like having a great second mortgage on the right of citizens to live in this land. Today's recipients of government handout programs and excessive spending habits are bankrupting tomorrow's work force.

Citizens would not accept submission to the international powers without first being brought into desperate conditions and financial bondage by the Federal Reserve System. Signs indicate that we may be close to this bondage. Some sound the alarm by declaring that the crisis is now beyond a brewing point. Some say it has been warming up at an increasing rate over the last two decades, and is now near the boiling point.

Environment Concerns

Please do not prejudge this area of concern. Most people support worthwhile and prudent use of the world's reserves and resources. Like most who read this section, the author appreciates the beauty of the nation and world. Most support reasonable efforts to use those resources wisely and prudently.

However, many of the scientific allegations currently being placed before the American public simply cannot be supported by facts. Some of the environmentalist elite would have us believe that we are on the verge of extinction because we have treated the environment unkindly. There are numerous factually-supported materials to show convincingly that often, the media hype about the dangers posed to environment are exaggerated beyond reasonableness. Why would this be the case?

Let's explore just one potential reason. Some nations ignore the warnings of the environmentalists and rather continue in a path felt justified by their needs, heritage, history and government. They ignore the demands of other countries to submit to the pleas and persuasions of the environmentalists. Accordingly, in the view of those supporting an international system of law, those countries need to be brought into line with current thought for the good of the world.

But how can that infringement of national sovereignty be accomplished? Nations risk the bad will of the entire world if they force their will on a smaller, less powerful nation. This is especially so if the smaller nation's plight is found to be worthy of international sympathy. The only way to accomplish the targeted outcome of having a non-conformist nation submit to the environmentalist is to establish international enforcement.

This argument, simple though it may be, has been widely and strongly accepted and endorsed by many in internationally influential positions. This argument indirectly argues against United States' sovereignty and advances the concept of one-world government. What better argument for the existence of an international enforcement agency is there than for the purpose of requiring all nations to submit to the demands of a unified world for the purpose of saving the world?

While the concept contains definite appeal to anyone interested in preserving the natural beauty and resources of this world, one should at least entertain the possibility that an environmental alarm may be a propaganda campaign for the purpose of uniting the educated and influential peoples of advanced nations into using international force to make sovereign nations comply with international standards and laws at the loss of their sovereignty. This effort could result in forced compliance if necessary.

Thus, while some environmental questions and concerns are legitimate and need to be supported for the benefit of man, others may be scare tactics. Some may be designed with the objective to have all agree on the need to establish a stronger United Nations and eliminate or reduce the sovereignty of nations. The argument for international control of environmental issues for the purpose of saving the world could sound the demise of the capitalist system which made this nation great.

Accordingly, no environmental issue should be accepted blindly or without examination of both sides of the question. When all of the facts are understood, the investigator will be in a better position to judge. Many perhaps will find that there is indeed an underlying and hidden agenda in many of the calls for world control of the environment.

Population Control

The author remembers vividly those instances in the seventies and early eighties when with more than two children, he often felt chastised by actual voice, snickers and unfriendly stares from those in grocery lines, buses, and restaurants. The propaganda experts had told their story convincingly. Millions were converted to the school of thought that we must have zero growth in population.

This dangerous and unprecedented involvement in the family life of Americans came as the result of studies projecting that the world would be populated beyond its capacity to feed by the year 2000 if the population growth did not stop or even decline. To allow for their story to produce results, rights were given to our population which allowed for the married or unmarried person to stop population growth at the individual level. Through contraception and abortion, the advocates of no-growth population publicized their story to the world. Prevention of conception or elimination of the fetus became ways to control the human population.

One-world government advocates continue to utilize this world population scare the same way they use their environmental tactics. No super power nation has the right to interfere with internal affairs of another nation. Personal issues such as population control, contraception, abortion, and other growth-inhibiting actions must be left to the control of individual nations. Population measures which seem to many in the United States to be barbaric are regularly practiced in some nations.

One-world government is presented as the only plausible and reasonable method available to solve the over-population crisis of the world, which they assert surely can't feed itself. An international population growth prohibition enforced by a one-world government could control the rate of growth or perhaps even orchestrate a population decrease.

But the earth is full, and food supplies are far from exhausted. We still pay farmers for not raising crops. America is still able to produce more food than the world can consume, and with advancement of science, it is possible to provide the world's future needs. There is room and food enough.

Youth Education

Control of the education of youth is perhaps the surest, fastest and most certain method available to convince a society of the benefits the governing body bestows upon its constituents.

Education can allow each person in the world to understand his neighbor. In the proposed one-world society, all would live friendly with one another. Gone would be the barriers of nationality, the burdens of language differences, and the inequality of some citizens not receiving educational benefits elsewhere available to the others.

The language barrier, which in the past has hampered communications among members of different nations, will be overcome, allowing reasonable minds to come to agreements. Even today, software programs are being developed which will almost immediately translate communications from one language into another allowing instant communication via satellite between common citizens of different nations and tongues.

Today many text books, teachers, and other education tools and personnel advocate humanism as the only way to better society. This theory advocates that we are by nature good and it is only one's environment, family, surroundings, teachings, friends, or other external stimuli which make man bad. Accordingly, if we can some way educate man as to his "real" nature, and awaken him to what made him bad, he will become naturally good. All tendencies in his nature to do bad will be replaced, and we will thus have an uplifted and naturally good society.

The scripture states that men are bad because of the fall of Adam. The prophets teach that men are not made bad by their environment, family, teachers, television, movies or other external agents. That those factors may have an effect for good or evil cannot be denied, but you do not change the nature of the man by placing him in a new home, giving him free education or the opportunity to have a job. This approach has failed for generations in the United States. Its main result has been the creation of multi-generation welfare recipients who find it almost impossible to break out of the free lunch offered by the over-generous spending congresses found at both national and state levels. The only way to change a man is to change his heart. The most effective way to change his heart is to bring to him the gospel of Christ and allow the Spirit to work its soul-changing process. Then the man will change his own circumstances and all will work for his good and benefit.

But even in the face of devastating failure, both in this country and behind the iron curtain, the one-world advocates continue to admonish the benefits and projected changes which they proclaim this type of system can bring. This nation may be asked in the near future to respond to the betterment of all mankind with a surrender of personal educational goals, objectives and opportunities. Parents may be asked to participate in the new educational horizons which promise unlimited educational benefits to all. These benefits will become available to all through the information highway, education, and similar opportunities which can be monitored, manipulated and controlled.

Some say that in the one-world system, there will be no private education, no parental involvement in a child's education, and no individual student dedication capable of overcoming the decisions of an educational agency designed to maximize each individual's benefit to society.

Control of Civil Unrest

Many nations of the world are unable to control their internal affairs. Others struggle with friction from other nations. In the past, these nations have been used as pawns between the super powers. One-world proponents explain how beneficial it would be if other nations did not fight over these pawns, but instead some unified world power had authority and military might to simply move in at the admonition of its administrators and establish peace. This can be further and even more effectively accomplished if the countries over which control is sought can be relatively free from internal military might. National or even international gun possession laws could establish the inability of arguing factions to generate adequate firepower to mount an offensive. Accordingly, there can be no form of meaningful resistance to the military might of the United Nations Army.

Recent events including Desert Storm, Bosnia, and similar civil crises around the world highlight the platform of significant elected officials who appear to support world order and United Nations military involvement in these world affairs. The potential effect of these applications to the United Nations forces is to grant that body significant and unparalleled power and influence in world affairs. Recent administrations have supported a buildup of military strength in the U.N. They have sought and attained the blessing and leadership of the U.N. This has allowed the U.S. to take a supportive, but back-seat, subsidiary role in many of today's international affairs. This nation provides military might, money and knowledge, but submits its forces to the direction and control of the United Nations command. The lack of direct involvement by U.S. troops appeals to many Americans, but the concept has the potential to backfire on citizens.

If the United States first financially funds the U.N., then provides military personnel, and finally submits military command to the control or direction of the United Nations, it is possible that through these commitments, this nation will have lost its sovereignty. This slow movement toward international control by a world government will be accomplished only with great cost in money, liberties, and self determination to United States citizens. Once United States military power and control has been assigned to others, or has been destroyed by debt, budget cuts, military cuts, unilateral and bi- lateral weapons disarmament, then this nation will be no longer sovereign.

The danger is that the transfer of power comes gradually, slowly and without fanfare. To do otherwise would alert even the passive American citizen. Once the freedoms are lost, it may be that they can only be regained by bloodshed.

Religion

America was founded as a new land with a new promise—a land where the captivity of the European nations could be unshackled. It is a land where the religious demands of unrighteous rulers could be bound and where a man could believe in his God according to the dictates of his own conscience. Freedom of religion was promised for all who inhabit this land.

Yet, there has developed in the sacred halls of Congress and the Chambers of the Supreme Court somewhat of a dichotomy . Each day in Congress, proceedings begin with prayer, but that same body failed to resist, and thus supported a ban on school prayer. Above the bar of the Supreme Court is engraved the Ten Commandments, but that same court prohibited the teaching of those moral principles by schools. These seemingly contradictory positions are allegedly supported by the "separation of state and religion" concept embraced by the founding fathers. In an effort to construe the separation as broadly as possible, some have expanded the concept from its original intent and scope to encompass all participation or involvement between government and religion. This view of the separation clause supports the intents and views of those who propose a one-world government.

The beliefs, teachings and standards of organized religion can confound the purposes, designs and actions of the one-world advocates. Religion discredits the image of the one-world government by teaching that the end does not justify the means. Religion further proposes that there is a higher law than that of man. For these reasons, some propose that the broadening of the separation clause has been one long, steady movement to remove religion from the educational platform, from the schools, from the government, from the children, and eventually from the family. It is the contention of one-world advocates that religion is one of the sources of great conflict in the world. They teach that much of the disharmony between and among mankind can be eliminated if religion ceases to be a protected right. They teach that believing in the foolish traditions of fathers is closed mindedness and promotes disharmony among mankind.

The one-world advocates apparently believe that the Constitution which allows preservation of religious traditions must be altered. Their philosophy states that foolish beliefs taught by organized religions can motivate men toward fictitious purposes. These purposes include looking toward a source higher than man for direction and life- hereafter promises. Accordingly, perhaps more than any other factor, organized religions teach concepts, beliefs, traditions and promises for which men are willing to fight and die. This level of commitment is destructive to the one-world objectives of peace and harmony. History records adequately that men have been motivated by religion through the ages for both good and evil, and that many wars of the past have been the result of religious belief and tradition. To end this threat to peace, advocates propose that religion must be destroyed or be brought into subjection and compliance with the powers of government. In this manner, the one-world advocates also project the danger of allowing parents any educational involvement in the lives of their children. We have witnessed the beginning of this effort in the educational arena where individual rights to worship who, where or what we may have become limited. The eventual end as proposed in their stated intents is to remove parental rights to teach children religion.

The United Soviet Socialist Republic is a prime example of this effort. In countries under prior Communist rule, and in China today, parents are not determinative as to the religious beliefs or educational pursuits of their children. This nation may be only a few steps from conditions similar to this. Among other things, this nation has already signed a United Nations charter for the rights of the children which severely hampers and limits the rights of parents with regard to religious, political, educational and social preferences with regard to their children.

But to many, the intent of the founding fathers is clear and obvious. Many believe that this nation was founded on the principles of Judeo-Christian law. Many propose that this nation was formed on a moral basis consistent with the philosophy taught in the ten commandments. Many teach that this system of government and free enterprise is not capable of functioning properly in a nation where morality is not taught and honored.

Summary

There are definitely many and more diverse methods being utilized by the advocates of this one-world status of peace and harmony. The ones explored herein are simply examples of methods used and are in no way comprehensive. Citizens must become knowledgeable and conversational about the threats to national sovereignty. It would be desirable for each to be able to succinctly and plainly state his position on issues and then be able to justify that position with facts or figures of substantiation. President Ezra Taft Benson observed,

> Many well-intentioned people are now convinced that we are living in a period of history which makes it both possible and necessary to abandon our national sovereignty, to merge our nation militarily, economically, and politically with other nations, and to form, at last, a world government which supposedly would put an end to war. We are told that this is merely doing between nations what we did so successfully with our thirteen colonies. This plea for world federalism is based on the idea that the mere act of joining separate political units together into a larger federal entity will somehow prevent those units from waging war with each other. The success of our own federal system is most often cited as proof that this theory is valid. But such an evaluation is a shallow one.[5]

One-World Banking

Money is defined as cash, checks, bills of exchange, banknotes, numbers in a checking account, or any unit of measurement used for exchange. Banks serve as essential dispensing units in the money exchange process. Thomas Jefferson understood the power of banks:

> I sincerely believe that banking establishments are more dangerous than standing armies; and that the principle of spending money to be paid by posterity, under the name of funding, is but swindling futurity on a large scale[6]

Money has been controlled by banks for several centuries. The first formal bank was established in England as the Bank of England, in 1694, by William Paterson. The Bank of England was a private corporation devised as a scheme to assist the King of England in raising gold to finance a war with France. Paterson convinced the King that he could provide the king all the gold he would need if the king would authorize him to issue bank notes. Paterson was given authority from the crown to print this paper money. He next offered to the English public a return of 4% on their gold in exchange for his printed bank notes. The gold he received was then loaned to the crown at 8%. The 4% notes given in exchange for gold were used as legal exchange and the Bank of England promised to redeem the notes upon demand by returning the gold. However, the gold was loaned to the king and used to finance the war. Far more notes existed than there were reserves in the bank. Accordingly, when too many people became insecure in the bank's future and requested a return of their gold, the king allowed Paterson to suspend gold redemption payments.

As a result of this experiment, France, Germany and other European powers duplicated the system for their own purposes. In the late 1700s and early 1800s, Meyer Armschel Rothschild and his five sons obtained monetary control of much of Europe by duplicating the methods and concepts of Paterson in Frankfort, Vienna, London, Naples, and Paris.

Shortly after their success in the European nations, these same banking powers attempted to institute a privately controlled central bank in the newly formed United States of America. But early fathers of this nation were not deceived by this attempt at monetary monopoly. Andrew Jackson is credited with insight into their hidden intents. President Jackson twice caused revocation of national bank charters, persuading the American public that the financial interests in this nation should be controlled by citizens of this nation and not by foreign powers or interests. To a delegation of bank supporters, he is quoted as saying:

> The bold effort the present bank has made to control the government, the distress it had wantonly produced . . . are but premonitions of the fate that awaits the American People should they be deluded into a perpetuation of this institution or the establishment of another like it . . . You are a den of vipers. I intend to rout you out. And by the Eternal God, I will rout you out. If the people only understood the rank injustice of our money banking system, there would be a revolution by morning![7]

The bank, identified as the Bank of the United States, was operated by Nicholas Biddle, a wealthy citizen from the East. The bank's stock was owned by Biddle and foreign investors. Jackson's attack on this concept was so persuasive with the American public that the attempt to again establish a central bank was not completely successful until the early Twentieth Century.

While the attitude of the average citizen toward a privately owned central bank did not change, the Federal Reserve Act passed in 1913 established just that. In his expose, *The Creature from Jekyll Island*, the author, G. Edward Griffin, reveals and documents the passing of the Federal Reserve Act as a deliberate and intentional act by a delinquent congress, a sympathetic president and a plan masterminded and developed by national and international money powers. The bill was first presented under the name of the congressman sponsoring it, Nelson W. Aldrich, as the Aldrich Bill. When the body of Congress discovered the contacts Mr. Aldrich had with international money powers, the bill was immediately killed.

However, the second presentation of the bill, this time called the Federal Reserve Act and introduced by a different sponsor, resulted in a positive vote. Some perceive that those who orchestrated the passing of this bill had unfavorable intentions to obtain monopoly-like control of the money supply in the United States. Their concerns became somewhat justified when, in the late 20s and early 30s, the Federal Reserve Banks of the United States did the same thing done by Paterson and the Rothschilds in Europe. They suspended certificate redemption. Gold payments were officially suspended in 1933 and silver redemption was suspended in 1968. Today, it is no longer possible in the United States of America to convert paper money to gold or silver.

The Constitution requires that no governmental entity ". . . make anything but gold and silver coin as tender in payment of debts;" (Section 10). This section of the Constitution has never been repealed or amended. Accordingly, many would conclude that the federal reserve notes currently used as legal tender in the United States are in violation of the Constitution.

Joseph Smith expressed his view on how banking should proceed in the United States. His opinion which was based on public control through the power to elect bank officials, was,

> Let Congress show their wisdom by granting a national bank, with branches in each state . . . where the capital stock shall be held by the nation for the Central Bank, and by the states . . . for the branches; and whose officers and directors shall be elected . . . The net gain of the Central bank shall be applied to the national revenue.[8]

This would truly allow for the people to control the banking operations in a free market. Instead, we have the Federal Reserve Banks. Many make the mistake of assuming that the FED is owned, managed, controlled and operated by the government. Considering the name, this is an understandable mistake—

one purposely perpetrated by the advocates of the system. However, nothing is farther from the truth. The Federal Reserve Banks consist of twelve member banks who collectively comprise the organization. Much secrecy surrounds the ownership of these twelve member banks as they are controlled by private interests. These banks each have authority to issue Federal Reserve Notes pursuant to the direction of the Federal Reserve Board. The Board determines the rate of interest the borrowing banks will be charged.

Some may look at the scientific advancements and historically high standard of living produced during the last eight decades and argue that the FED has been responsible for great success in the United States. They might further argue, "If this has been the system since 1913, and it has produced the greatest standard of living in the history of the earth, what is wrong with the system?

But perhaps the problem is not reflected by the ability of the citizens of the United States to produce a high standard of living. It seems just as reasonable, or perhaps even more reasonable, that the inhabitants of this land prosper because it is the land choice above all other lands. To attribute the growth to the FED would appear to be unsubstantiated. More likely, American ingenuity and work ethic coupled with blessings of the Lord have been the source of our success, not the FED.

The problems evidenced by the nation's current economic difficulties result from irresponsible actions of elected representatives who have spent trillions of dollars which the people have not authorized them to spend.

The funds to finance deficit spending are raised by the United States through the sale of bonds. But if the American public and/or the world governments who buy those bonds suddenly lose confidence in the government's ability to pay the interest on the notes or the intrinsic value of the bonds, America could face financial disaster of unparalleled proportions.

Abraham Lincoln warned about the power of those who control money:

> The money power preys upon the nation in times of peace and conspires against it in times of adversity. It is more despotic than monarchy, more insolent than autocracy, more selfish than bureaucracy. I see in the near future a crisis approaching that unnerves me and causes me to tremble for the safety of my country. Corporations have been enthroned, an era of corruption in high places will follow, and the money power of the country will endeavor to prolong its reign by working upon the prejudices of the people until the wealth is aggregated in a few hands and the republic is destroyed.[9]

And lastly, consider the words of Thomas Jefferson. "A private central bank issuing the public currency is a greater menace to the liberties of the people than a standing army."[10] And on another occasion, he advised, "We must not let our rulers load us with perpetual debt."[11]

Right to Bear Arms

Today, the issue concerning the individual citizens' right to own and bear arms is hotly contested. Spurred on by recent events such as the nation experienced in Texas, Idaho, New York, Oklahoma, and Montana, combined with a rampant increase in violent crime involving guns, the debate will not soon subside.

At the heart of the issue is the Second Amendment to the Constitution, a part of the Bill of Rights, which reads simply, "A well regulated militia being necessary to the security of a free state, the right of the people to keep and bear arms, shall not be infringed."[12]

Those professing implementation of ever-more-strict gun control legislation use the wording of the amendment to support their position. Advocates of gun control point out that when the Second Amendment was adopted, people held their own guns because there was no organized state army. They rationalize that the phrase well regulated militia removes the entire amendment from a personal perspective and right and instead relates it to a relationship between the federal government and the state governments. They often point out that today we have state national guard units which replace the need for state militia. Accordingly, since the national guard units have their own guns and munitions, there is no need for the citizens to have guns. The states are adequately protected and armed.

Additionally, gun control advocates illustrate the fact that times have changed and so have constitutional rights. Therefore even if the right, as intended by the founding fathers, was to apply the Second Amendment at a personal level rather than to protect state rights, that need no longer exists. The reason the need does not exist today, they state, is because the world has changed. To illustrate their point, they often refer to the change in the President's declaration of war powers. While the Constitution requires the President to obtain the approval of Congress to declare war, that approach is not practicable today as foreign missiles could totally destroy the United States before a meeting could be called. Today the president, by acting individually in his office, can declare war and commit the armed services without congress approval.

Using this theory of logic, gun control advocates are able to argue that times have changed and the states no longer need to raise militia as they might have had to do when the nation was created. In the 18th century, the governments had no weapon arsenals and when called to duty, each citizen was expected to bring his own gun. Today, the governments, both federal and state, have capability to provide the citizens with guns via the National Guard units, and therefore, there is no need to have individuals with weapons. In fact, H. Richard Uviller, professor of law at Columbia University is quoted as stating, "Without a state militia, armed by members own weapons, the entire substance of the Second Amendment has become obsolete."[13]

However, the argument most frequently used by gun-control advocates is the need to control guns which are being used with increased frequency to commit violent crimes in the United States. Believing that gun control will stem the tide of violent crime, they push for more and more stringent control. Speared on by the emotional appeals of the Brady Bill debate, advocates appeal to the public, stating that with more strict controls citizens will be safer in their homes, at their jobs, and in the streets and neighborhoods.

Of particular interest to the gun-control advocates is the rapidly increasing gun use and crime among juveniles. Quoting accounts of increased gun use by those under the age of 18, advocates press to remove guns from the private sector. A step in that direction is found in the new restrictions guarding gun purchasing and qualifying time limits. These limits may discourage someone from committing a crime while in the heat of anger, by providing a mandatory cooling off period before purchase of a gun is possible.

Finally, the advocates of gun control attack the right of para-military organizations to form, train and function. In the words of one advocate, "[The Second Amendment] was not intended to give a group of weekend warriors in California, Michigan or anywhere else the right to decide for themselves when it would be OK to take up arms against a duly elected federal government."[14]

The argument may be an over-reaction to the tragedies of this decade. Responding to the Oklahoma terrorist bombing, gun-control advocates have moved swiftly and surely to micro-analyze citizens of the United States who oppose the status quo of government. Acts of barbarism as performed in Oklahoma give government almost carte blanche authority to exploit the situation to the detriment of the rights of innocent citizens. The theory proposed is that for the protection of the masses, the individual Constitutional rights must fall. Thus anyone speaking against current American main-stream policy may run the risk of FBI checks, IRS investigations, Secret Service analysis, and/or CIA review. To some, these may be considered invasions of privacy. The tendency of these types of actions may act to silence and eliminate opposition and move the government toward greater and increased control.

Accordingly, the other side of the Second Amendment argument is that the intent of the founding fathers was to guarantee that *individuals* have a right to keep and bear arms and that that right should not be infringed. To explore this perspective, we need to analyze the setting in which the amendment was framed. The several states of this continent as individual governments united in their opposition to British taxation had just won their independence. That war had been waged by the collective formation of individual state militia, each composed of citizens using their personally owned guns. Without those guns, the Revolution could not have taken place. The ownership of a gun meant that citizens could obtain food, resist evil doers, defend against raids, and join in the mutual defense of their homes, their families and their rights of worship (in many aspects similar to Captain Moroni's people in the last chapters of Alma).

The Second Amendment was originally written by James Madison. His original version of the amendment read as follows: "The right of the people to keep and bear arms shall not be infringed; a well armed and well regulated militia being the best security of a free country: but no person religiously scrupulous of bearing arms shall be compelled to render military service in person." On September 25, 1789, a combined Senate and House committee submitted the final version of the Amendment.

To proponents of this second argument, it seems important to note the basis on which Madison first proposed this concept as a part of The Bill of Rights. All states were requested to submit suggestions. New Hampshire, Maryland, Virginia, New York, and Massachusetts all submitted proposals advocating the individual right to bear arms. But Pennsylvania's proposal was perhaps the most specific stating, "The people have a right to bear arms for the defense of themselves and their own state, or the United States, or for the purpose of killing game; and no law shall be passed for disarming the people." The foregoing sets the scene for the creation of the final draft of the amendment, perhaps pointing to the intent that the founding fathers were seeking to protect a personal, individual right with the drafts which preceded the final concept.

For some, the most convincing argument that the Second Amendment extends to the individual and not just the state can be found in the words themselves. Both the initial proposed version and the final version used the key words, *the right of the people*. Those same words were used in the First Amendment guaranteeing the freedom of religion. Advocates of individual rights to possess arms argue that it is not consistent with the language to argue that "the right of the people" phrase in the First Amendment referred only to the state governments. Additionally, the phrase is found in the fourth Amendment wherein the right of the people to be secure against unreasonable searches and seizures is protected. Could the gun control advocates argue that the phrase refers only to state papers, buildings and employees? The phrase, they argue, being used three times in the Bill of Rights, clearly indicates that the rights being addressed therein are rights guaranteed to the individual people, not the state governments.

In arguing in favor of individual rights to bear arms, one commentator stated, "It might be difficult using that argument to persuade the citizens of South Central Los Angeles, many of whom preserved their lives and property only at the point of their own guns after being abandoned by the police."[15]

To many, it seems clear that the United States Congress, fresh from winning independence and freedom because the citizens possessed guns, intended to preserve that right to future generations at an individual level. Proponents of the adverse view feel that even if that was the initial purpose, that concept has evolved out of existence.

Both sides in this debate mix their arguments with substantial emotional fervor and appeal. It appears that the issue will not soon be settled. In the interim, the current position holds that the individual still does retain the right to bear arms. Future legislation will determine to what degree this right will continue.

10

SECRET COMBINATIONS AND THE COMMITMENT OF THE LATTER-DAY SAINT

It is a challenging time to be here in mortality. Many events, great and terrible, sweet and wonderful, plain and dramatic, simple and devastating are occurring all around us. Yet these last days are a time of danger for the Lord's people. He has warned, "Behold, the enemy is combined. And now I show unto you a mystery, a thing which is had in secret chambers, to bring to pass even your destruction in process of time, and ye knew it not." (D & C 38:12-13)

Because Satan and his hosts often work in secret, many do not recognize the methods he employs to obtain his ultimate designs or purposes. Secret combinations will continue to attempt to destroy the Kingdom of God. All the powers of hell and evil will combine against the kingdom and its members. The objective of the adversary has been and will be to destroy "in process of time" that which the Lord has restored. The unfortunate indication of the scripture is that many will not know of the adversary's work or progress.

Yet, protection is available. Many can come to know if they will seek to protect themselves and others from these combined enemies.

The Book of Mormon is replete with information and knowledge about how the saints can know. Alma, speaking to his son Helaman, quoted the Lord:

> 23. I will prepare unto my servant Gazelem, a stone, which shall shine forth in darkness unto light, that I may discover unto my people who serve me, that I may discover unto them the works of their brethren, yea, their secret works, their works of darkness, and their wickedness and abominations . . .
> 25. I will bring forth out of darkness unto light all their secret works and their abominations; . . . and I will bring to light all their secrets and abominations, *unto every nation that shall hereafter possess the land.* (Alma 37:23, 25)

What a wonderful blessing it would be if each Latter-day Saint who so desired, and who was striving to live the gospel, could receive such a stone! This stone could show forth those who are actively seeking to overthrow the principles of liberty in this nation, those who were unknowingly participating in that effort, and the acts, plans and methods being used to destroy our political and spiritual liberties. With this knowledge, Latter-day Saints could shine forth their light to the condemnation of those fighting against righteousness.

But perhaps we would error in this wish. Perhaps we would be falling short by looking beyond the mark. Perhaps we already have the stone and do not recognize it. Perhaps the Lord has given us a stone just like Gazelem and we just have not yet identified it. Perhaps the stone today is each person's copy of the Book of Mormon.

The Book of Mormon contains teachings, warnings, advice, counsel and guidance from prophets speaking to today's citizens. Each Latter-day Saint should become familiar with the teachings of the Book of Mormon and latter-day prophets, that they may say, "I fought the good fight. I was not totally deceived. I was not fully asleep. I was not complacent. And though my efforts may be small and even meaningless in the eternal perspective—and though my actions may go totally unnoticed by my countrymen and my fellow saints, and though I may win the battle against secret combinations and evil only in my own soul—yet, I will fight. I will oppose the evil of this day. And I will win."

Acquiring that frame of mind requires preparations.

Increased Knowledge of God's Plan

Alma, recognizing the most powerful instrument available to man, realized that in his efforts to save souls he needed to use the gospel of Jesus Christ.

> And now, as the preaching of the word had a great tendency to lead the people to do that which was just—yea, it had had more powerful effect upon the minds of the people than the sword, or anything else, which had happened unto them—therefore Alma thought it was expedient that they should try the virtue of the word of God. (Alma 31:5)

This same power was used by the Lamanites when Gadianton Robbers were found in their land:

> 1. And it came to pass that when the sixty and second year of the reign of the judges had ended, all these things had happened and the Lamanites had become, the more part of them, a righteous people, insomuch that their righteousness did exceed that of the Nephites, because of their firmness and their steadiness in the faith. . . .
>
> 18. And now behold, these murders and plunderers were a band who had been formed by Kishkumen and Gadianton. And now it had come to pass that there were many, even among the Nephites, of Gadianton's band. But behold, they were more numerous among the more wicked part of the Lamanites. And they were called Gadianton's robbers and murderers. . . .

Secret Combinations and the Commitment of the Latter-day Saint 165

> 20. And now it came to pass that when the Lamanites found that there were robbers among them they were exceedingly sorrowful; and they did use every means in their power to destroy them off the face of the earth. . . .
>
> 37. And it came to pass that the Lamanites did hunt the band of robbers of Gadianton; and they did preach the work of God among the more wicked part of them, insomuch that this band of robbers was utterly destroyed from among the Lamanites. (Helaman 6:1, 18, 20, 37)

The Lamanites totally destroyed the Gadiantons not with the sword, nor with a great legal system, nor with government spending, nor with mandates; not with sociologists or psychologists or criminologists nor lawyers nor judges; but with the word of God.

In these last days, the Lord has commanded the saints that they should take his word to the ends of the earth. He has not said they should arm themselves with weapons of destruction to fight the enemy within our borders. He has not instructed saints to rise up in rebellion against the injustice of government and evil men as they have conspired to lessen freedoms and to economically and politically enslave the peoples of this nation and the world. Rather, he has told us that we have been warned and we must warn our neighbors.

And so the church sends tens of thousands of missionaries into the world each year with the message of hope and the salvation of Jesus Christ. And members increase in understanding of the principles of the Gospel of Jesus Christ. No better defense could exist.

Increase Individual Knowledge and Understanding of Secret Combinations

Along with an effort to understand the gospel of Jesus Christ, the saints have been advised by the Book of Mormon prophets to understand the workings of the Gadianton Societies.

> And this [The Book of Mormon] cometh unto you, O ye Gentiles, that ye may know the decrees of God—that ye may repent, and not continue in your inequities until the fullness come, that ye may not bring down the fullness of the wrath of God upon you as the inhabitants of the land have hitherto done. (Ether 2:11, see also Ether 8:23-24)

Saints do not need, nor should they desire to know, the secret oaths and covenants utilized by secret combinations. However, by understanding their methods and manners of operations, they will know how to recognize when combinations are operative. By coming to know their methods, Latter-day Saints will become able to discern these organizations. The best and most basic source for coming to understand the secret combinations is to read and study the Book of Mormon.

In addition to the words of council, advice, and warning in the Book of Mormon, there are other books which contain much information on the Gadianton societies of this day and age. The adversary has spent generations of time conceiving, designing, and building these organizations. His objective is to mount a great battle against the Kingdom, just prior to the return of Christ. That time is now or fast approaching. It would be well for Latter-day Saints to be continually learning about freedom, dangers, and how to counteract those dangers.

Informed Family Members

Modern scripture contains the Lord's instruction that "I have commanded you to bring up your children in light and truth." (D & C 93:40) Every parent bears the burden of teaching his or her children the principles of light and truth, the Gospel of Jesus Christ, the Plan of the Everlasting God, the fall of Adam, and the redemption and atonement of the Savior. And parents must teach their children light and truth as it is applied to principles of political freedom.

While confined in Liberty Jail, Joseph Smith received some of the most moving and heartfelt revelations of these last days. In the 123rd Section, Joseph explains that the chains of hell can be passed on from one generation to the next. Speaking of those who persecuted the Church and its members, the prophet stated;

> 7. It is an imperative duty that we owe to God, to angels, with whom we shall be brought to stand, and also to ourselves, to our wives and children, who have been made to bow down with grief, sorrow, and care, under the most damning hand of murder, tyranny, and oppression, supported and urged on and upheld by the influence of that spirit which hath so strongly riveted the creeds of the fathers, who have inherited lies, upon the hearts of the children, and filled the world with confusion, and has been growing stronger and stronger, and is now the very mainspring of all corruption, and the whole earth groans under the weight of its iniquity.
>
> 8. It is an iron yoke, it is a strong band; they are the very handcuffs, and chains, and shackles, and fetters of hell. (D & C 123:7-8)

The evil spirit of which the prophet speaks is still upon the earth. The influence of this evil spirit is still strongly riveted in the minds and behaviors of peoples such that they can pass their evil creeds to their own children from generation to generation. The prophet continues in words which are as valid and important today as they were on the day they were first written.

> 11. And also it is an imperative duty that we owe to all the rising generation, and to all the pure in heart—

12. For there are many yet on the earth among all sects, parties, and denominations, who are blinded by the subtle craftiness of men, whereby they lie in wait to deceive, and who are only kept from the truth because they know not where to find it— (D & C 123:11-12)

This duty of which the prophet speaks is owed to the rising generation (children) as well as to the balance of the good men and women of the earth. The prophet then continues,

Therefore, that we should waste and wear out our lives in bringing to light all the hidden things of darkness, wherein we know them; and they are truly manifest from heaven— (D & C 123:13)

The saints must not hesitate to teach their children of the things of light. Neither must they delay nor refrain from teaching them to be aware of the things of darkness, the secret combinations and Gadianton societies. Joseph continues,

14. These should then be attended to with great earnestness.
15. Let no man count them as small things; for there is much which lieth in futurity, pertaining to the saints, which depends upon these things. (D & C 123:14-15)

The things of the future depend upon the teaching of our children of the good and the bad, of things of light, and of the things of darkness. These are not small things. This is not a small duty, nor one which can be sidestepped nor abandoned to the Church, to the schools, or to the government. It is a personal duty parents owe to their children, and each Church member owes to mankind.

President Benson has not been silent on what saints should do:

We have not been using the Book of Mormon as we should. Our homes are not as strong unless we are using it to bring our children to Christ. Our families may be corrupted by worldly trends and teachings unless we know how to use the book to expose and combat the falsehoods in socialism, organic evolution, rationalism, humanism, and so forth. Our missionaries are not as effective unless they are "hissing forth" with it. Social, ethical, cultural, or educational converts will not survive under the heat of the day unless their taproots go down to the fullness of the gospel which the Book of Mormon contains. Our church classes are not as spirit-filled unless we hold it up as a standard. And our nation will continue to degenerate unless we read and heed the words of the God of this land, Jesus Christ, and quit building up and upholding the secret combinations which the Book of Mormon tells us proved the downfall of both previous American civilizations.[1]

And again,

> We must protect this base of operations [America] from every threat—from sin, from unrighteousness, from immorality, from desecration of the Sabbath Day, from lawlessness, from parental and juvenile delinquency. We must protect it from dirty movies, from filthy advertising, from salacious and suggestive television programs, magazines and books.
>
> We must protect this base from idleness, subsidies, doles, and soft government paternalism which weakens initiative, discourages industry, destroys character, and demoralizes the people.[2]

These concepts cannot be adequately learned at school, in church or by osmosis. It must be an active part of the teachings from father to son, mother to daughter, grandparent to grandchild.

Be Involved in the Freedom Process

President Kimball stated,

> The sad part of it is that a lot of us take our civil rights for granted. We were born in a free country. We think freedom could never end. But it could. It is ending in many countries. We could lose it too.
>
> The only way we can keep our freedom is to work at it. Not some of us. All of us. Not some of the time, but all of the time.
>
> So if you value your citizenship and want to keep it for yourself and your children and their children, give it your faith, your belief, and give it your active support in civic affairs.[3]

To allow members of the Church to take a more active role in their citizenship responsibilities, the Church has created the block plan with the intent of decreasing the number of Church meetings a member must attend. One of the hopes has been that those in the Church would thereafter have more time and take more opportunity to become involved in civic affairs.

Where local civic decisions are being made, it is important for saints to make their voices heard. Ways they may participate would include actions such as writing more letters, making more phone calls, and simply becoming more involved.

Perhaps too many are silent on issues which are of local importance. Just as the family is the foundation organization of The Church of Jesus Christ of Latter-day Saints, it also serves as the political foundation of this nation. From the family, the foundation grows to support neighborhoods, cities, counties, states, and finally the nation. If the saints are not involved as families, if they do not teach their children the consequences and warnings from the Book of Mormon, if they do not take local government seriously and influence local policy, how can they possibly hope to influence national policies and national government? Generally, local politicians are more responsive to local voices than are the national powers. Accordingly, the saints can often bring to pass much good, change and progress at the local level. The local government must set the tone for national issues.

Become a Zion People

In preparing for the future, the saints are admonished by the Savior to "prepare every needful thing." (D & C 88:119) We have not yet endured the devastation to be wrought by secret combinations. We have not yet seen the fullness of the wrath of the great and abominable. We have not yet experienced all the hail and wind and mighty storm Satan will bring to bear against the Kingdom.

Speaking of the last days, Bruce R. McConkie states:

> Despite medical advances, people are to suffer from diseases, plagues, and pestilences of undreamed proportions in the last days. Men's hearts shall fail them. (Luke 21:26.) New and unheard of diseases will attack the human system. After the times of the Gentiles comes in there shall be an overflowing scourge, and "a desolating sickness shall cover the land." (D & C 45:31.) Also: "I the Lord God will send forth flies upon the face of the earth, which shall take hold of the inhabitants thereof, and shall eat their flesh, and shall cause maggots to come in upon them; And their tongues shall be stayed that they shall not utter against me; and their flesh shall fall from off their bones, and their eyes from their sockets." (D & C 29:18-19.) The plagues and pestilences of the past will be as nothing compared to what is yet to be as the great winding up scene approaches.[4]

During this time before the coming of the Son of Man to rule in righteousness, the secret combinations and Gadianton societies of the last days will apparently be in their hour of greatest power. Speaking of the power of the adversary in this time period, the Revelator stated:

> 12. And he exerciseth all the power of the first beast before him, and causeth the earth and them which dwell therein to worship the first beast, whose deadly wound was healed.
>
> 13. And he doeth great wonders, so that he maketh fire come down form heaven on the earth in the sight of men.
>
> 14. And deceiveth them that dwell on the earth by the means of those miracles which he had power to do in the sight of the beast; saying to them that dwell on the earth, that they should make an image to the beast, which had the wound by a sword, and did live.
>
> 15. And he had power to give life unto the image of the beast, that the image of the beast should both speak, and cause that as many as would not worship the image of the beast should be killed. (Revelation 13:12-15)

Many times in the Book of Mormon, the believers were threatened with death if they refused to deny the gospel of Jesus Christ.

Only one time in my life have I seen hate of this degree. But to see it is to know and realize that it could come again to pass. My experience came in an unexpected manner as I was working my way through BYU, by selling furniture at a department store. I was working with a non-citizen of the United States who had come to this land from the middle east. In a casual discussion, I ventured into world affairs and brought up the conflicts of the Middle East and the difficulty between the PLO and the Israelites. To my dismay, the entire demeanor of this individual instantly transformed. His eyes darkened, his attitude became channeled, and he spoke with conviction I have seldom seen in this life. His determination was, that given the opportunity, he would kill without hesitation any person who was a member of a certain organization he named. The mere mention of this organization had the ability to generate intensely true and pure hatred in this person's soul. It was indeed one of the most sobering events of my life. I saw a normal, intelligent and likable person change right before my eyes into a person possessed. He was one who could take the life of another human being without even so much as a second thought, simply because the other person was a member of a certain organization.

Just as the secret combinations and Gadianton societies of the Book of Mormon used hate and anger to stir up the people and to gain control over them, those same tactics can and probably will be used by Satan in these last days to stir up persecution and great opposition toward members of The Church of Jesus Christ of Latter-day Saints.

In recording his revelation, John continues: "And he causeth all, both small and great, rich and poor, free and bond, to receive a mark in their right hand, or in their foreheads: And that no man might buy or sell, save he that had the mark, or the name of the beast, or the number of his name." (Revelation 13:16-17) Later, John reports what would happen to those who accept the mark of the Beast.

> 9. If any man worship the beast and his image, and receive his mark in his forehead, or in his hand,
>
> 10. The same shall drink of the wine of the wrath of God, which is poured out without mixture into the cup of his indignation; and he shall be tormented with fire and brimstone in the presence of the holy angels, and in the presence of the Lamb:
>
> 11. And the smoke of their torment ascendeth up for ever and ever: and they have no rest day nor night, who worship the beast and his image, and whosoever receiveth the mark of his name. (Revelation 14:9-11)

Members of the Church will not accept the mark of the beast. Accordingly, the indication of the Revelator is that the saints will not be allowed to participate in the commerce of the earth. As outcasts, rebels, separationists and enemies of the adversary, they will find themselves condemned by the system.

Additionally, and apparently at the same time as the great control exercised by the adversary as discussed above, angels will be sent forth to try the souls of men. One angel will destroy all green grass and a third of the trees; a second angel will destroy a third of the sea and the life in the sea. A third angel will cause one-third of the waters of the earth to become unfit for human consumption. The fourth angel will darken the sun and the moon and the stars, and a fifth angel will cause great anguish to mankind. The sixth angel will cause the eventual destruction of one-third of men. (Revelation 8 & 9) We have previously examined the statement by prior prophets indicating that some angels have already been loosed upon the earth and the trials, pestilence, plagues, famines, and difficulties of the last days are now upon us. They will continue to increase in severity and consequence.

However, amid all this projected evil, difficulty and persecution, there is a great promise and hope. Initially, the hope appears from the promise made in the Book of Mormon that "the righteous need not fear. (1 Nephi 22:17) While this does not promise that the saints will be spared from all persecution, it does evidence that their burdens may be lightened. They are told that "If ye are prepared ye shall not fear. (D & C 38:30) Why is this so, and why do we need not fear? In Revelation, John speaks of priesthood blessings which will be given to 144,000 high priests. It will be given to them so that they shall not be hurt by the elements nor by the angels nor their plagues and pestilences of the last days. Is it not probable that this protection is a direct priesthood blessing, and is it not further probable that those who receive this blessing will thereafter bless those who seek refuge from the storm with that same blessing? Additional protection is prophesied. Elder McConkie observed,

> For the time soon cometh that the fulness of the wrath of God shall be poured out upon all the children of men; for he will not suffer that the wicked shall destroy the righteous." Israel are the righteous among mankind; they are the ones who worship the true God; they believe the true gospel, belong to the true church, and seek to walk in paths of truth and righteousness. The wicked are those whose whole hearts are not centered on their Creator, upon the God who made heaven and earth and the seas and the fountains of waters. "Wherefore, he will preserve the righteous by his power—Israel shall come off triumphant—even if it so be that the fulness of his wrath must come, and the righteous be preserved, even unto the destruction of their enemies by fire. Wherefore, the righteous [Israel!]

need not fear; for thus saith the prophet, they shall be saved, even if it so be as by fire. . . . For behold, the righteous shall not perish; for the time surely must come that all they who fight against Zion shall be cut off." Worldly people always have been and always will be the ones who oppose the church, who persecute the saints, who fight against Zion.[5]

To prepare for this blessing, this protected state, the saints must become a Zion people. In the Doctrine and Covenants, the Lord speaks of the blessings of the Saints who gather together in Zion. "And the gathering together upon the land of Zion, and upon her stakes, may be for a defense, and for a refuge from the storm, and from wrath when it shall be poured out without mixture upon the whole earth. (D & C 115:6) The saints of Zion can be protected from the storms of Satan.

One purpose for the protection of the Saints in the latter days is to prepare a people ready to receive the Lord at his second coming to take us through the refiner's fire. As a Church, Latter-day Saints are aware of the fact that during the Millennium, Satan will be bound for a thousand years.

Nephi stated what it means to bind Satan and how it is accomplished:

> And because of the righteousness of his people, Satan has no power; wherefore, he cannot be loosed for the space of many years; for he hath no power over the hearts of the people, for they dwell in righteousness, and the Holy One of Israel reigneth. (1Nephi 22:26)

Satan is bound by a people's righteousness. Commission of sin gives Satan control over body, mind and actions. When one binds Satan, he does it because he no longer responds to the devil's temptations. He becomes as the people of King Benjamin who said, "The Spirit of the Lord Omnipotent, . . . has wrought a mighty change in us, or in our hearts, that we have no more disposition to do evil, but to do good continually." (Mosiah 5:2) He becomes as the people taught by Alma and Amulek of whom it was stated, "Now they, after being sanctified by the Holy Ghost, having their garments made white, being pure and spotless before God, could not look upon sin save it were with abhorrence," (Alma 13:12) To achieve this state of heart and mind, one must become spiritually begotten of Christ. Each must be worthy of having someone say, "Ye shall be called the children of Christ, his sons, and his daughters; for behold, this day he hath spiritually begotten you; for ye say that your hearts are changed through faith on his name; therefore, ye are born of him and have become his sons and his daughters." (Mosiah 5:7)

It may well be folly and foolish to assume that saints will suddenly have a change of heart and disposition just because the Savior returns. Men's hearts will not necessarily change just because he returns. A person will not suddenly become righteous and full of power sufficient to bind Satan just because the Savior comes. Therefore, each should seek to become capable of binding Satan prior to the Lord's return. Each should prepare his or her heart and mind by being born again, by being repulsed by sin, by becoming a Zion saint. Each must acquire the ability to say to Satan in words binding upon him, "Satan, get thee hence." Once we attain that capability, we will be prepared as a Zion people. Satan will be bound and the times of refreshing shall be fully present and in our midst.

The Lord will not tolerate a modern Sodom and Gomorrah. It is probable that freedom still exists because saints still pray for freedom. As individuals and as a people, Church members still petition the Heavens for intervention in their lives, in the lives of leaders, and in the destiny of this nation. Indeed, many are not unlike the Nephites in their petitions.

> 22. Yea, and I say unto you that if it were not for the prayers of the righteous, who are now in the land, that ye would even now be visited with utter destruction; yet it would not be by flood, as were the people in the days of Noah, but it would be by famine, and by pestilence, and the sword.
>
> 23. But it is by the prayers of the righteous that ye are spared. (Alma 10:22-23)

Follow the Prophet

Often because of increased learning, increased wealth, sin or priestcraft, people fall into a state of mind contrary to that needed to humbly follow the living prophet. It is easy to follow dead prophets whose words cried repentance to their generation and whose teachings can be rationalized and pointed away from today. It is difficult to rationalize a living prophet who testifies of our sins and weaknesses.

The saints are promised that the living prophet will not lead them astray. Said Elder Theodore M. Burton,

> A seer then is one who may see God, who may talk with God, who may receive personal instruction from God. Our prophet is a seer and a revelator. I do not know who originally taught the doctrine. I was told once that it was taught by President Heber J. Grant, but I was taught this doctrine by Elder Marion G. Romney, who told me that the Lord will never let his prophet the seer, lead his people astray. Men in all ranks on this earth and in the Church have fallen from grace, but the Lord will never permit the great prophet, our seer, and revelator, to fall or to lead the people astray. Before this could happen God must of necessity remove that man from the earth. [6]

Elder Harold B. Lee taught,

> Yes, we believe in a living prophet, seer, and revelator, and I bear you my solemn witness that we have a living prophet, seer, and revelator. We are not dependent only upon the revelations given in the past as contained in our standard works—as wonderful as they are—but we have a mouthpiece to whom God does reveal and is revealing His mind and will. God will never permit him to lead us astray. As has been said, God would remove him out of his place if he should attempt to do it. You have no concern. Let the management and government of God, then, be with the Lord. Do not try to find fault with the management and affairs that pertain to Him alone and by revelation through His prophet—His living prophet, His seer, and His revelator.[7]

And Ezra Taft Benson said,

> Christ has provided us the gift of a prophet. Of all mortal men, we should keep our eyes most firmly fixed on the captain—the prophet, seer, and revelator, and President of The Church of Jesus Christ of Latter-day Saints. This is the man who stands closest to the fountain of living waters (Jeremiah 2:13; 1 Nephi 11:25). There are some heavenly instructions for us that we can only receive through the prophet. A good way to measure your standing with the Lord is to see how you feel about, and act upon, the inspired words of his earthly representative, the prophet-president. The inspired words of the President are not to be trifled with. All men are entitled to inspiration, and various men are entitled to revelation for their particular assignment. But only one man stands as the Lord's spokesman to the Church and the world, and he is the President of the Church. The words of all other men should be weighed against his inspired words. Though his prophet is mortal, God will not let him lead His Church astray.[8]

A Word of Caution

In our battle for freedom, President Kimball made a plea for us to remember—a sacred word of caution:

> Please avoid, even by implication, involving the church in political issues. It is so easy, if we are not careful, to project our personal preferences as the position of the church on an issue.[9]

Only the prophets speak for the Church, and only they have the right and duty to speak forth the word of God unto the members of the Church and the peoples of the world. Therefore, in this effort and battle against the secret combinations and Gadianton societies, we must be cautious to walk a line parallel to the teachings of the prophets and yet not represent our personal actions as including the Church or any of the brethren in leadership in the kingdom.

If in this text I have in any way violated that sacred duty, I hereby revoke that implication and state emphatically that the ideas and concepts as abridged, compiled and commented on herein are a reflection of my views of the issues. They do not necessarily represent the Church nor the prophets' views on the issues.

It is not our calling in the gospel in these latter-days to rise up in individual or group rebellion. We must observe the law of God on this matter.

Rather, the saints are to proclaim peace. How great the need for a living prophet! Latter day saints cannot rise up in open rebellion against the loss of our freedoms and go to active war unless the living prophet sends them to battle. The living prophets have spoken on this matter. President Kimball stated;

> Remember that the gospel of Jesus Christ is NOT compatible with radicalism, or Communism or any other of the "isms". There could be those among you who would profess to be your saviors. They could enslave you with their force or their so-called doctrines. If some of their leaders have motives that are selfish or questionable, you should have nothing to do with them. Perhaps some would even excite you to riot. Beware of them. Keep your feet on the ground and your head in the air.[10]

This counsel contains great wisdom. Hate and anger are tools Satan uses to enslave his servants in sin. Thus, while the church condemns evil actions, yet members are not admonished by leaders to violate the law.

It is possible for those who become involved to become one-minded about the cause for which they labor, blocking out other elements of life. They can become obsessed. In the words of President Kimball, they can envision themselves as a *savior* to the cause for which they labor. Their obsession can too often lead to illegal action and even the grossest of crimes, even murder, as we have seen several times in the last few years. How important it is to have an ear which listens and a heart which understands the counsel of the Lord's anointed.

Summary

And so, the Latter-day Saints strive to become a Zion people, to teach their children, and to prepare their hearts for the future. The word of God is taught, and the Spirit of the Lord bears witness of the truthfulness of the teachings. People are asked to be still and listen and feel the power of God.

Notwithstanding the word of caution, saints must nevertheless be ready. Compared with what will be asked of the saints tomorrow, the Lord's requests today are very simple. The saints must sanctify themselves and their families. They must study the teachings of the prophets to determine how to protect themselves and their families. They must come first to personal understanding and then share that light and understanding with their families and loved ones.

In assisting the Lord to bring about his purposes, the saints must be careful not to expect somebody else to do all the work. After describing the great and powerful dominions held by the great and abominable, and the few dominions of the saints, and after declaring that the great and abominable would seek to destroy those who belong to the church of the Lamb of God, Nephi states: "I, Nephi, beheld the power of the Lamb of God, that it descended upon the covenant people of the Lord, who were scattered upon all the face of the earth; and they were armed with righteousness and with the power of God in great glory. (1 Nephi 14:14)

The effort must be that of every worthy Latter-day Saint. It must be the work of parents, children, neighbors, and brothers and sisters in the Church. The Lord will assist us in these battles and will grant us the power of God in great glory, not personal glory, but glory in his work. The battle is ours. While we will have divine intervention as his power descends upon us, yet we must even now resist the advances, concepts, philosophies, principles and practices of the adversary. It is our fight!

Many great battles still face the saints of the Most High. Many of these battles for the saints will not be battles of guns and knives, of death and carnage, of maimed and wounded. Rather, they will be battles of righteousness versus evil. They will be battles fought in the hearts and homes of the citizens of this world and of this nation, and, most importantly, within the hearts, families, and homes of members of this Church. For members of the Church, it would be difficult to conceive of more weeping, mourning, or lamentation than that suffered for a loved one who has chosen the evil part.

The prophets of this day have warned us, again and again, that parents must strengthen their families. They must teach principles of righteousness. Fathers must teach sons and daughters and grandchildren. Saints must build a recognition of the sovereignty of the family.

The individual and family preparation must be financial, spiritual, and temporal. Families might well consider the building of family alliances and storehouses. Members may be relying too much on the welfare system of the Church and placing thereon too great of a financial burden. Saints should seek assistance from the family before approaching the Church. In many stakes, fast offerings must increase to meet increased needs.

Once saints have prepared families, they must prepare priesthood quorums. There must be a unity of faith and purpose. Brothers and sisters must be strengthened within quorums. Only when saints are able to create unity and purpose within priesthood quorums will they be able to withstand the adversary. In cannot be done if some are pursuing, as the first order of business, their personal monetary pursuits and goals.

To therefore summarize what we can and must do as American Citizens and as members of The Church of Jesus Christ of Latter-day Saints, let us again turn to the writings of Ezra Taft Benson:

> How then can we best befriend the Constitution in this critical hour and secure the blessing of liberty and ensure the protection and guidance of our Father in Heaven.
>
> First and foremost, we must be righteous . . .
>
> Second, we must learn the principles of the Constitution in the tradition of the Founding Fathers . . .
>
> Third, we must become involved in civic affairs to see that we are properly represented . . .
>
> Fourth, we must make our influence felt by our vote, our letters, our teaching, and our advice.[11]

This is our land. It is a land of opportunity; a blessed land; a land under siege of the influence and power of Satan; a land of our forefathers and a land of our posterity. This is a land at a crossroad in its history; a land burdened almost to an unbearable strain with regulation, legislation, and sin; a land in which each must make critical decisions; a land we must return to its divine heritage. For if we do not, then God will. And if God does it, wo be unto the inhabitants of this land for he will do it with fire and brimstone, with pestilence and famine, with earthquake and with death and judgment to reward mankind for their evil deeds. When he does it, the secret combinations and Gadianton societies will be destroyed. And we will not be found guiltless who have been warned, have witnessed the collapse of freedom, have participated in its fall, tolerated its demise or just stood idly by and watched it crumble. Wo unto those who find themselves in these categories.

May each of us be strong and work diligently and with dedication toward preservation of righteousness, freedom, and Christianity. May we each enter the battle to oppose the advancement of the purposes of Satan and to withstand his struggle against us, our families, and The Church of Jesus Christ of Latter-day Saints. May we be found even as Moroni, and may it be said of us, "If all men [and women] had been, and were, and ever would be, like unto . . . [you], behold, the very powers of hell would have been shaken forever. (Alma 48:17)

END NOTES

CHAPTER 1
1. Ezra Taft Benson, *Teachings of Ezra Taft Benson*, Salt Lake City, Utah: Bookcraft, 1988, p. 619.
2. Bankhead, Reid E. and Pearson, Glenn L., *Building Faith With the Book of Mormon*, Provo, Utah: The Joseph Foundation, 1992, p. 115.
3. Clark, J. Rueben, *Conference Report*, The Church of Jesus Christ of Latter-day Saints, Salt Lake City, Utah: Printed by Deseret Press, April, 1944, p. 166.

CHAPTER 4
1. Neal A. Maxwell, *Notwithstanding My Weakness*, Salt Lake City, Utah: Deseret Book Company, 1981, pp. 95-96.
2. *Los Angeles Times*, Orange County Edition, Orange County Section, October 11, 1993, p. 1.
3. Don Feder, *Boston Herald*, August 19, 1993.
4. Roe vs. Wade, 410 U.S. 113,93 S.Ct. 705, 35 1.3d.2d 147 1973.
5. Monagie, Katie, "How We Got Here," *MS Magazine*, May/June, 1995, p. 17.
6. Hedges, Stephen J., Bowermaster, David, and Headden, Susan, "Abortion: Who's Behind the Violence?", *U.S. News and World Report*, November 14, 1994, p. 50.
7. *Ibid*, p. 55.
8. Simmons, Judy Dothard, "On the Front Line," *MS Magazine*, May/June, 1995, p. 17.
9. John Sanko, "400 Protest Tribute to Abortion Doctor," *Rocky Mountain News*, February 8, 1995, p. 4.
10. Benson, Ezra Taft, *The Red Carpet*, Salt Lake City, Utah: Bookcraft, 1962, pp. 238-239.
11. Kimball, Spencer W., *Teachings of Spencer W. Kimball*, edited by Edward L. Kimball, Salt Lake City, Utah: Bookcraft, 1982, pp. 188-189, 274.
12. Benson, Ezra Taft, *Teachings of Ezra Taft Benson*, Salt Lake City, Utah: Bookcraft, 1988, pp. 295-296.
13. Kimball, Spencer W., *Teachings of Spencer W. Kimball*, edited by Edward L. Kimball, Salt Lake City, Utah: Bookcraft, 1982, p. 269.

END NOTES 179

14. J. Reuben Clark, *Relief Society Magazine*, The Church of Jesus Christ of Latter-day Saints, Salt Lake City, Utah: Deseret Press, December, 1952, p. 793.
15. Ezra Taft Benson, *Improvement Era*, The Church of Jesus Christ of Latter-day Saints, Salt Lake City, Utah: December 1949, p. 803. See also *Conference Report*, October 1949, p. 194.
16. Alvin R. Dyer, *Conference Report*, April, 1969, p. 54.
17. Ezra Taft Benson, "Do Not Despair," *Ensign*, Salt Lake City, Utah: The Church of Jesus Christ of Latter-day Saints, October, 1986.
18. Kimball, Spencer W., *The Miracle of Forgiveness*, Salt Lake City, Utah: Bookcraft, 1969, pp. 225, 227-228.
19. McConkie, Bruce R., *Doctrinal New Testament Commentary*, Vol. 3, Salt Lake City, Utah: Bookcraft, 1973, p. 563.
20. Benson, Ezra Taft, BYU Ten-Stake Fireside, Provo, Utah, 7 May 1972, as quoted in *Teachings of Ezra Taft Benson*, Salt Lake City, Utah: Bookcraft, 1988, p. 326.
21. Kimball, Spencer W., *The Miracle of Forgiveness*, Salt Lake City, Utah: Bookcraft, 1969, p. 231.
22. Hinkley, Gordon B., *Improvement Era*, Salt Lake City, Utah: The Church of Jesus Christ of Latter-day Saints, December, 1970, p. 72.
23. Woodruff, Wilford, *Young Woman's Journal*, Salt Lake City, Utah: The Church of Jesus Christ of Latter-day Saints, August 1894, pp. 512-513.
24. Smith, Joseph Fielding, *Signs of the Times*, Salt Lake City, Utah: Deseret News Press, 1952, pp. 11-12.
25. Fine, Jason, "Seeking Evil," *The California Lawyer* (a periodical published by the *Daily Journal*, San Francisco, California), July, 1994, pp. 50-53.
26. *Ibid*, p. 53.
27. Bennett, William J., *The Index of Leading Cultural Indicators*, Empower America and The Heritage Foundation, Vol. 1, 1993, p. i.
28. *Ibid*, p. 2.
29. *Ibid*, p. 4.
30. *Ibid*, p. 5.
31. *Ibid*, pp. 8-10.
32. *Ibid*, p. i.

CHAPTER 5

1. Marx, Karl, "The Communist Manifesto," with Introduction by William P. Fall, *American Opinion*, Appleton, Wisconsin, 1974, p. 22.

2. Clinton, Hillary Rodham, Commencement Address, George Washington University, May 8, 1994.
3. Kimball, Spencer W., *Teachings of Spencer W. Kimball*, edited by Edward L. Kimball, Salt Lake City, Utah: Bookcraft, 1982, p. 340.
4. John J. Vandenberg, *Conference Report*, The Church of Jesus Christ of Latter-day Saints, April 1965, p. 49.
5. "Announcer," *Conference Report*, The Church of Jesus Christ of Latter-day Saints, October, 1954, p. 90.
6. Benson, Ezra Taft, *Teachings of Ezra Taft Benson*, Salt Lake City, Utah: Bookcraft, 1988, p. 446, containing a partial quote from *Holy Bible*, King James Version, The Church of Jesus Christ of Latter-day Saints, Salt Lake City, Utah, 1987, Ephesians 4:26, footnote a, *Joseph Smith Translation*.
7. Shapiro, Joseph and Schrof, Joannie, "Honor Thy Children," *U.S. News and World Report*, February 27, 1995, p. 39.
8. *Ibid*, p. 42.
9. *Ibid*, p. 39.
10. Bennett, William J., *The Index of Leading Cultural Indicators*, Empower America & The Heritage Foundation, Vol. 1, 1993, p. ii.
11. *Ibid*, p. iv.
12. Kurtz, Paul and Wilson, Edwin H., *Humanist Manifesto I & II*, edited by Paul Kurtz, Buffalo, New York: Promethus Books, 1973, Introduction to *Humanist Manifest II*.

CHAPTER 6

1. Colson, Charles, *Imprimis*, Hillsdale College, Hillsdale, Michigan, Vol. 22, No. 4, April, 1993.
2. *Ibid*.
3. *Ibid*.
4. *Ibid*.
5. *Ibid*.
6. *Ibid*.
7. Stormer, John A., *None Dare Call it Conspiracy, 25 Years Later*, Florissant, Missouri: Liberty Bell Press, 1990, p. 25.
8. Denton, Jerry, *When Hell was in Season*, Traditional Press, 1982, p. 183.
9. David Barton, *America, To Pray or Not to Pray*, Aledo, Texas: Wall Builder Press, 1988, p. iv.
10. Jacob Waserman, *Columbus, Don Quixote of the Seas*, Translated by Eric Sutter, Little Brown & Company, 1930, as quoted by Mark E. Petersen, *The Great Prologue*, Salt Lake City, Utah: Deseret Book, 1975, p. 26.

END NOTES 181

11. Smith, Joseph, *History of the Church*, Vol. III, copyright by George Albert Smith, for The Church of Jesus Christ of Latter-day Saints, introduction and notes by B. H. Roberts, Salt Lake City, Utah: Deseret Book, 1948, p. 175.
12. Smith, Joseph, *History of the Church*, Vol. IV, copyright by George Albert Smith for The Church of Jesus Christ of Latter-day Saints, introduction and notes by B.H. Roberts, Salt Lake City, Utah: Deseret Book, 1949, p. 80.
13. Mills, James, *The Underground Empire*, New York: Dell Publishing Co., Inc., 1987, pp. 32, 35.
14. Walinsky, Adam, "The Crisis of Public Order," *The Atlantic Monthly*, July 1995, p. 40.
15. *Ibid*, p. 44.
16. *Ibid*, p. 53.
17. Benson, Ezra Taft, "The Task Before Us," Logan, Utah: American Dairy Science Association, 26 June 1979.
18. Benson, Ezra Taft, *Teachings of Ezra Taft Benson*, Salt Lake City, Utah: Bookcraft, 1988, p. 325.
19. Ward, Admiral Chester, U.S.N., (ret), [a twenty year member of the CFR], *Kissinger on the Couch*, New Rochelle, New York: Arlington House, 1975, pp. 146, 149-50.
20. Helms, Senator Jesse, [R-NC], *Congressional Record*, December 15, 1987, p. S18148.
21. McManus, John E., *Financial Terrorism*, John Birch Society, Appleton, Wisconsin, 1985, p. 38.
22. Goldwater, Senator Barry, *With no Apologies*, New York, New York: William Morrow & Co., 1979, pp. 284-285.
23. Robertson, Pat, *The New World Order*, Word Publishers, p. 102.

CHAPTER 7
1. *U.S. Constitution*, Article 1, Section 8.
2. Jaffee, Dwight M., *Money*, Encarta Multimedia Encyclopedia, Microsoft, 1973.
3. Vanderlip, Frank A., "From Farm Boy to Financier," *The Saturday Evening Post*, February 9, 1933, as quoted by G. Edward Griffin, "The Creature From Jekyll Island," *American Opinion*, Appleton, Wisconsin, 1995, p. 11.
4. Benson, Ezra Taft, *This Nation Shall Endure*, Salt Lake City, Utah: Deseret Book, 1977, p. 8.

5. Benson, Ezra Taft, *Teachings of Ezra Taft Benson*, Salt Lake City, Utah: Bookcraft, 1988, pp. 618-619.
6. Benson, Ezra Taft, "Freedom is our Heritage," LDS Business and Profesional Men's Association, Glendale, California, November 10, 1970.
7. *Internal Revenue Code*, Subchapter F.

CHAPTER 8
1. Adams, John, *The Works of John Adams*, Vol. 14, Compiled by Charles Francis Adams, Boston: Little & Brown, 1854, p. 229.
2. Stone vs. Grahm, 449 U.S. 39 at 42.
3. Adams, John Quincy, an oration delivered before the inhabitants of Newburyport on the 61st anniversary of the Declaration of Independence, 4 July 1837, Newburyport Publisher, Charles Whipple, 1837, p. 5.
4. Dawson, Steve C., *God's Providence in American History*, Rancho Cordova, California: Steve C. Dawson, 1988, p. I:5.
5. Jay, John, 1794-1826, (October 12, 1816) *Correspondence and Public Papers of John Jay, Vol IV*, Compiled and edited by Henry P. Johnson, Reprinted by Burt Franklin, New York, 1970, p. 393.
6. Madison, James, *The Federalist Papers*, Letter 37, New York, New York: North American Library of World Literature, 1961, p. 230.
7. Davis, Richard, "Preserving or Pickling the Constitution," *Brigham Young Magazine*, Provo, Utah: Brigham Young Press, May, 1995, p. 33.
8. Frederick Bastiat, *The Law*, Translated by Dean Russell, Irvington-On-The-Hudson, New York, New York: The Foundation for Economic Education, Inc., 1977, p. 6.
9. Sir William Blackstone, *Commentaries on the Law*, 9th Edition, Vol. 1, London, England, 1765, p. 139.
10. McKay, David O., *Conference Report*, Salt Lake City, Utah: The Church of Jesus Christ of Latter-day Saints, April 9, 1966, p. 109.
11. Thurmond, Senator Strom, *Congressional Record*, 26 July 1961, as footnoted in *Prophets, Principles and National Survival*, Jerrald L. Newquist, Salt Lake City, Utah: Publishers Press, 1967, p. 331.
12. Quoting Sam Meeks, High Priest Group Leader, Orange 2nd Ward, Orange California Stake, November, 1993.

CHAPTER 9
1. Jessup, Phillip C., *International Problems of Governing Mankind*, Claremont, California: Claremont College, 1947, p. 2.
2. Fullbright, Senator William J., *Old Myths and New Realities*, New York, New York: Random House, 1964, p. 87.

3. Rostow, Walt Whitman, *The United States in the World Arena*, New York, New York: Harper and Brothers, 1960, p. 549.
4. Dulles, Allen W. and Beatrice Pitney Lamb, *The United Nations* (Booklet), Headline Series, No. 59, New York, New York: The Foreign Policy Association, September-October, 1946, pp. 44, 86; Quoted by Alan Stang, *The Actor, the True Story of John Foster Dulles, Secretary of State, 1953-1959*, Appleton, Wisconsin: Western Islands, 1968, pp. 127, 180.
5. Benson, Ezra Taft, *An Enemy Hath Done This*, Salt Lake City, Utah: Parliament Publishers, 1969, pp. 156-157.
6. Cleon Skousen, *The Real Thomas Jefferson*, Washington, D.C.: National Center for Constitutional Studies, 1983, p. 356.
7. Jackson, Andrew, *Andrew Jackson*, compiled by Herman J. Viola, New York, New York: Chelseu House, 1986, p. 86.
8. Smith, Joseph, *History of the Church, Vol. VI*, The Church of Jesus Christ of Latter-day Saints, introduction and notes by B.H. Roberts, Salt Lake City, Utah: Deseret Book, 1948, p. 206.
9. Lincoln, Abraham, in a letter to Wiliam F. Elkins, 21 Nov. 1864, Archer H. Shaw, Ed., *The Lincoln Encyclopedia: The Spoken and Written words of A. Lincoln*, New York, New York: MacMillan Co., 1950, p. 40.
10. Jefferson, Thomas, *Writings of Thomas Jefferson, Vol X*, New York, New York: G.P. Putnam & Sons, 1899, p. 31.
11. Jefferson, Thomas, *The Basic Writings of Thomas Jefferson*, New York, New York: Willey Book Company, 1944, p. 749.
12. *U.S. Constitution*, Bill of Rights, Amendment 2.
13. Uviller, H. Richard, "Opinion," *California Bar Journal* published by the California State Bar, Sacramento, California, August 1995.
14. Tartarian, Roger, "Opinion," *California Bar Journal* published by the California State Bar, Sacramento, California, August 1995.
15. Wright, Randy, "Opinion," *California Bar Journal*, published by the Califronia State Bar, Sacramento, California, August 1995.

CHAPTER 10

1. Benson, Ezra Taft, *A Witness and A Warning*, Salt Lake City, Utah: Deseret Book Company, 1988.
2. Benson, Ezra Taft, *Title of Liberty*, Salt Lake City, Utah: Deseret Book Company, 1964, p. 90.
3. Kimball, Spencer W., *Teachings of Spencer W. Kimball*, edited by Edward L. Kimball, Salt Lake City, Utah: Bookcraft, 1982, p. 405.
4. McConkie, Bruce R., *Mormon Doctrine*, 2nd Editon, Salt Lake City, Utah: Bookcraft, p. 725.

5. McConkie, Bruce R., *A New Witness for the Articles of Faith*, Salt Lake City, Utah: Deseret Book Company, 1985, p. 563.
6. Burton, Theodore M., *Conference Report*, Salt Lake City, Utah: The Church of Jesus Christ of Latter-day Saints, October 1961, p. 122.
7. Lee, Harold B., *Stand Ye in Holy Places*, Salt Lake City, Utah: Deseret Book Company, 1974, p. 164.
8. Benson, Ezra Taft, *Teachings of Ezra Taft Benson*, Salt Lake City, Utah: Bookcraft, 1988, p. 140.
9. Kimball, Spencer W., *Teachings of Spencer W. Kimball*, edited by Edward L. Kimball, Salt Lake City, Utah: Bookcraft, 1982, p. 406.
10. *Ibid,* p. 408.
11. Benson, Ezra Taft, *Teachings of Ezra Taft Benson*, Salt Lake City, Utah: Bookcraft, 1988, pp. 621-622.

INDEX

A

Abomination(s)   25, 32, 34, 46, 70, 78-79, 84, 143, 163
Abortion(s)   2, 36, 41-47, 50, 60, 65, 74, 92, 150, 151
Abraham   80-82, 113, 115, 131, 158
Abuse   2, 36, 53, 59, 68, 70, 71, 74, 75, 131, 135
Abusive   70, 125, 126, 139
Adams, John   77, 125
Adams, John Quincy   127
Adversary   24, 31, 40, 50, 53, 84, 122, 124, 133, 163, 166, 169, 171, 176, 177
Agency   2, 10, 14, 19, 26, 34, 40, 56, 57, 92, 112, 126, 133, 136, 138, 149, 152
AIDS   37, 38, 74
Alcohol   54, 71, 74, 75, 118
Amalickiah   29, 30
Amendment   42, 116, 121, 123, 130, 135, 159-161
America   2, 3, 10, 11, 44, 50, 59, 60, 74, 76, 77, 85, 86, 93, 95, 99, 100, 120, 122, 125, 135, 146, 151, 153, 156-158
Anger   1, 31-34, 89, 92, 140, 160, 170, 175
Arms   3, 12, 32, 45, 93, 130, 159-162
Atonement   2, 166

B

Bank   105, 106, 108-111, 113, 114, 116, 120, 148, 156-158
Benson, Ezra Taft   9, 46, 48, 49, 51, 52, 119, 123, 144, 155, 174, 177
Bible   74, 82, 83, 90, 125
Bill of Rights   123, 130, 135, 159, 161, 162
Blood (Bloodshed)   11-13, 22, 38, 45, 59, 69, 77, 85-87, 93, 128, 146, 153
Boggs, Lilburn W.   85
Book of Mormon   1, 11-13, 16, 25-27, 29, 31, 32, 34, 36, 67, 76, 79, 82, 83, 89-92, 97, 124, 128, 134, 140, 141, 144, 163-168, 170
Bound   1, 12, 13, 15, 18, 27, 36, 41, 53, 76, 77, 121, 124, 126, 127, 153, 172, 173

C

Cain   15, 16, 22, 24, 25, 27, 28, 58
Captive (Captivity)   11, 14-15, 25, 76-77, 84, 126, 133, 137, 140, 144, 153
Chains   11, 14, 15, 76, 95, 103, 126, 166
Checks   112, 155, 160
Child   2, 19, 32, 34, 36, 38, 42, 44, 47, 48, 62, 65, 66, 68-70, 75, 152
Choice   2, 42-44, 75-79, 89, 91, 122, 127, 142, 143, 158
Christ   1, 10-14, 18, 21, 22, 24, 29, 32, 40, 47, 48, 51, 58, 63-65, 70, 77-83, 86-90, 124,125, 127, 131, 134, 135, 140, 152, 164-168, 170, 172, 174, 175, 177
Clark, J. Rueben   12
Columbus   76, 126, 127
Commerce   62, 94, 105, 120, 129, 171
Communism   3, 125, 137, 140-144, 175
Condemnation   85, 86, 132, 164
Condoms   37, 69, 74
Constitution   3, 9-13, 30, 39-42, 84-86, 93, 99-100, 102, 105, 112, 118, 120-125, 127-136, 139, 140, 144-146, 154, 157, 159, 177
Control   2, 3, 9, 12-14, 19, 21, 26, 27, 30-34, 37-39, 54, 56-60, 68, 71, 88, 90, 92, 94, 95, 98, 101, 102, 106, 108, 109, 111, 112, 114-117, 119, 120, 122, 125, 126, 129, 132-143, 145, 146, 150-153, 156-160, 162, 170-172
Council   37, 95, 100-102, 122, 166
Court   33, 41, 43, 44, 46, 47, 69, 71, 74, 86, 92, 93, 123, 127, 130, 145, 153
Creationism   73, 74
Crime   2, 54, 60, 69, 74, 80, 85, 88, 91, 93-95, 97, 159, 160

D

Death   11, 16, 22, 28, 44, 67, 90, 98, 104, 121, 122, 170, 176, 177
Deceit   14-15, 17, 23, 26, 29, 34, 53, 58, 62-63, 80, 100, 133, 138, 140, 156, 154, 167
Democracy   99
Desert Storm   21, 152
Destruction   2, 13, 14, 25, 33-35, 40, 55, 63, 64, 78, 79, 84, 87, 104, 108, 163, 165, 171, 173
Division   2, 43, 78, 82, 83
DJs   40, 50
Drugs   52, 53, 74, 92, 94, 97

E

Economic (Economy)   42, 65, 66, 69, 76, 94, 100, 101, 106, 108-114, 116, 119, 120, 122, 126, 136, 137, 142, 143, 145, 147, 158
Education   2, 3, 19, 20, 36, 37, 39, 48-50, 56, 57, 60-62, 71-73, 91, 94, 103, 122, 140, 146, 151, 152
Enemy   9, 21, 32, 33, 100, 145, 163, 165
Environment   39, 52, 56, 57, 66, 69, 72, 91, 135, 146, 149-151
Ephraim   76, 78
Ethics   20-22, 71, 72
Everlasting Covenant   87

F

Fabian   137-139
Fair promises   1, 28, 29, 33, 89, 92
Faith   12, 18, 21, 26, 42, 64, 70, 72, 73, 77, 78, 80, 81, 83, 86, 123, 127, 133, 134, 137, 164, 168, 172, 176
FBI   43, 60, 94, 160
FED   2, 106, 109-113, 116, 117, 148, 157, 158
Federalism   3, 135, 155
Financial   9, 13, 42, 43, 52, 64, 65, 85, 94, 101, 108-110, 112-115, 117, 122, 124, 145, 147-149, 156, 158, 176
Flattery   1, 22, 29, 30, 33, 34, 91, 92
Food storage   144
Foolish   1, 18, 23, 32, 76, 154, 172
Foreordained   11, 13, 65, 135
Foundation   9, 21, 30, 57, 63, 77, 100, 125, 127, 168
Founding Fathers   9-11, 13, 21, 40, 71, 99, 105, 111, 112, 120, 123, 125, 127, 128, 130, 135, 136, 139, 144, 153, 155, 160, 161, 177
Framers   125, 127, 134
Franklin, Benjamin   77
Free   10, 11, 19, 39, 40, 42, 50, 57, 76, 77, 95, 106, 111, 112, 114, 116, 119, 122, 123, 132, 133, 135, 136, 138, 140, 142, 143, 147, 152, 155, 157, 159, 161, 168, 170
Freedom   9-11, 19, 26, 39, 58, 76, 77, 79, 86, 120, 122, 124, 126, 129, 131, 133-136, 146, 153, 161, 162, 166, 168, 173, 174, 177

G

Gadianton   9, 25-27, 32, 34, 87, 96, 144, 164-167, 169, 170, 174, 177
Gain   1, 15, 16, 22-24, 26, 28, 29, 31, 33, 34, 52, 65, 79, 90, 95, 157, 170
Gang(s)   2, 33, 89, 92-93, 95-97
Gentiles   13, 34, 76, 79, 81, 83, 84, 88-90, 126, 127, 131, 165, 169
Gold   94, 105-110, 114, 156, 157
Goldwater, Barry   101
Great and Abominable   34, 53, 126, 176

H

Hate   1, 31-34, 51, 89, 92, 170, 175
Heart(s)   9-11, 17, 22-23, 27, 28-31, 33, 45, 51, 54, 70, 79, 80, 82-84, 86-88, 92-93, 100, 113, 126, 131, 142, 152, 159, 166, 169, 171-172, 173, 175-176
Henry, Patrick   127
Hell   11, 14, 15, 34, 74, 103, 126, 163, 166, 177
Holy Ghost   23, 30, 76, 80, 81, 126, 131, 172

I

International   3, 9, 94, 100, 101, 106-108, 110, 113, 115, 145-153, 157
Iron Curtain   140, 142-144, 147, 152
IRS   91, 92, 118, 119, 123, 160
Isaac   81, 82
Isaiah   123
Israel   9, 55, 75, 81, 82, 87-89, 108, 171, 172

J

Jacob   20-22, 70, 81, 82, 88
Jared   27-29, 75-77
Jay, John   127-128
Jefferson, Thomas   77, 158
Jew, Jewish   10, 42, 46, 84, 90, 131
Joseph   1, 55, 56, 75-77, 85, 86, 131, 133-135, 157, 166, 167
Judeo-Christian   125, 155
Judge(s)   26, 27, 29, 84-85, 95, 128, 150, 164, 165
Justice   11, 33, 41, 52, 69, 79, 85, 97, 98, 122, 127, 135, 145

K

King Benjamin   172

L

Lamb of God   84, 176
Land   2, 9-13, 21, 25, 26, 29, 30, 32, 34, 39, 40, 46, 52, 57, 59, 74-80, 84-86, 88-90, 92- 94, 123-128, 132-135, 139, 141, 143-146, 149, 153, 158, 163-165, 167, 169, 170, 172, 173, 177
Latter Days   55, 56, 90, 175
Law   10, 22, 29, 33, 40, 42, 43, 45, 46, 57, 77, 78, 84, 89, 91, 98, 99, 120, 123, 125, 127, 128, 131-135, 139, 149, 154, 155, 160, 161, 175
Lee, Harold B.   174
Lehi   76
Liberty   10-13, 21, 30, 86, 122, 126, 127, 134-136, 139, 143, 163, 166, 177
Light   24, 34, 36, 44, 70, 75, 76, 78, 112, 115, 121, 129, 132, 135, 144, 163, 164, 166, 167, 175
Livingston, Roger   77
Love   10, 32-34, 45, 51, 53, 58, 66, 69, 71, 72, 103, 120

M

Madison, James   125, 128, 161
Mafia   94, 95
Manasseh   76, 78
Maxwell, Neal A.   36
McKay, David O   142
Money   2, 21, 22, 24, 29, 37, 40, 51, 52, 54, 92, 94, 97, 98, 103-118, 120, 122, 138, 141, 147, 148, 153, 155-158
Morality   35, 36, 49, 75, 125, 140, 141, 155
Morals   20, 21, 39, 49, 52, 66, 71, 93, 97, 125, 141
Mormon   1, 11-13, 16, 17, 25-27, 29, 31, 32, 34, 36, 39, 51, 67, 76, 79, 82, 83, 89-92, 97, 124, 128, 134, 140, 141, 144, 163-168, 170, 171
Moroni   11-13, 25, 51, 80, 134, 177
Moses   15-17, 22, 24, 29, 58, 75, 82, 133
Mosiah   128, 172
Murders   25, 26, 33, 34, 59, 79, 80, 93, 97, 143, 164

N

National Debt   104, 147, 148
National Sovereignty   145, 149, 155
Nehor   22, 24, 29

O

One World   3, 9, 72, 101, 102, 109, 117, 122, 139, 145-147, 149-152, 154, 155
Organized Crime   2, 94, 95

P

Peace   21, 26, 33, 51, 55, 57, 84, 87-89, 93, 132-134, 141, 142, 145, 152, 154, 155, 158, 175
Petersen, Mark E.   9, 76
Pilgrims   76, 77
Politicians   2, 13, 33, 72, 95, 98-101, 120, 123, 148, 169
Politics   9, 92, 95, 122, 123
Population Control   3, 146, 150, 151
Pre-mortal   17, 29, 58, 126, 136
Pride   21, 23, 29, 30, 62, 63, 65, 69, 79, 80, 83, 88, 144
Priestcraft   24, 63, 79, 80, 83, 173
Propaganda   50, 124, 146, 150
Property   9, 12, 13, 39, 43, 74, 100, 121, 122, 132-142, 162
Prosper   20, 21, 75, 134, 142, 158
Protection   2, 39, 55, 78, 87, 88, 92, 94, 122, 128, 130, 132, 134, 135, 146, 160, 163, 171, 172, 177

R

Rationalize   14, 21, 45, 57, 64, 159, 173
Religion   3, 12, 39, 58, 72, 76, 79, 86, 90, 103, 122, 123, 125, 127, 134, 140, 141, 146, 153, 154, 161
Repent   13, 34, 54, 79, 86-89, 95, 165, 173
Republic   99, 100, 131, 154, 158
Revolution   35, 36, 38, 50, 61, 117, 119, 128, 135, 137, 156, 161

S

Satan   1, 2, 11, 13-17, 19, 22, 23, 25, 26, 29, 31-33, 35, 53-56, 58-60, 62-65, 68, 91, 92, 126, 131, 133, 140, 143, 144, 163, 169, 170, 172, 173, 175, 177

Savior   10, 11, 31, 32, 39, 45, 63, 68, 69, 75, 80-82, 87, 90, 120, 126, 127, 131, 135, 166, 169, 172, 173, 175

Secret   1-3, 9, 13-19, 21, 22, 24-31, 33-35, 62, 65, 68, 74, 79, 85, 87, 89, 91, 92, 94-96, 98, 103, 108, 113, 115, 120, 125, 126, 133, 140, 143-146, 160, 163-165, 167, 169, 170, 174, 177

Sex   2, 36-38, 40, 41, 46-50, 52, 61, 73, 74

Sexual   2, 33, 35, 36, 38, 46-48, 50, 53, 61, 70, 75

Sherman, Roger   77

Silver   105-108, 110, 114, 157

Sin   11, 12, 16, 22, 23, 29, 35, 36, 38, 40, 46, 47, 49, 54, 58, 65, 68, 79, 88, 119, 168, 172, 173, 175, 177

Socialism   57, 136-139, 142, 143, 167

Sovereignty   9, 13, 101, 102, 117, 145-147, 149, 150, 153, 155, 176

Stakes   78, 79, 144, 172, 176

States   2, 3, 10-13, 20, 21, 37-39, 41, 42, 44, 48, 55, 57, 60, 61, 68, 74, 77, 78, 82, 85, 86, 89-91, 93, 94, 97, 99-101, 103-110, 112-119, 122, 123, 125, 127-131, 135-138, 140, 143, 145-149, 151-154, 156-162, 168-170, 176

Supreme Court   41, 71, 74, 92, 123, 127, 130, 153

T

Tax   3, 41, 92, 116-123, 140, 148

Taxation   3, 57, 71, 77, 112, 117-123, 136, 139, 142, 143, 161

Taxed, Taxes   3, 57, 42, 65, 104, 116-118, 120-122, 139, 148

Trilateral Commission   100

Truth   10, 14, 15, 17-21, 24, 33, 38, 41, 47, 66, 71, 81, 83, 86, 91, 115, 126, 127, 158, 166, 167, 171

U

U.S.   10, 37, 91, 101, 102, 104, 105, 107-112, 132, 153

United Nations   100, 101, 152-154

United States   2, 3, 10, 11, 13, 21, 37-39, 41, 42, 48, 55, 57, 60, 61, 74, 77, 85, 86, 89-91, 93, 94, 97, 99-101, 103-110, 112-118, 122, 125, 127-131, 135, 136, 138, 140, 143, 145-149, 151-153, 156-162, 170

V

Vex, Vexation   85, 94
Violent Crime   60, 74, 80, 97, 159, 160
Vision   18, 63, 81, 126

W

War   10, 12, 13, 29, 31, 44, 46, 62, 77, 85, 87, 90, 97, 104, 105, 107, 108, 118, 120, 128, 136, 143, 145, 155, 156, 159, 161, 175
Wicked   26-29, 31, 34, 80, 83, 85-87, 132, 164, 165, 171
Wisdom   20, 35, 41, 48, 54-57, 71, 76, 79, 83, 86, 157, 175
Word of Wisdom   35, 54-56
World Order   101, 122, 153

Z

Zion   3, 24, 34, 51, 66, 78, 84, 88, 89, 123, 169, 172, 173, 175